Return to Casablanca

Return to Casablanca

JEWS, MUSLIMS, AND AN ISRAELI ANTHROPOLOGIST

André Levy

The University of Chicago Press CHICAGO & LONDON

ANDRÉ LEVY is a senior lecturer at Ben-Gurion University of the Negev in Beersheba, Israel. He is coeditor of *Homelands and Diasporas: Holy Lands and Other Places*.

The University of Chicago Press, Chicago 60637
The University of Chicago Press, Ltd., London

Printed in the United States of America

24 23 22 21 20 19 18 17 16 15   1 2 3 4 5

ISBN-13: 978-0-226-29241-0 (cloth)
ISBN-13: 978-0-226-29255-7 (paper)
ISBN-13: 978-0-226-29269-4 (e-book)
DOI: 10.7208/chicago/9780226292694.001.0001

Library of Congress Cataloging-in-Publication Data
Levy, André, author.
Return to Casablanca : Jews, Muslims, and an Israeli anthropologist / André Levy.
pages cm
Includes bibliographical references and index.
ISBN 978-0-226-29241-0 (cloth : alkaline paper) — ISBN 978-0-226-29255-7 (paperback : alkaline paper) — ISBN 978-0-226-29269-4 1. Ethnology—Morocco—Casablanca. 2. Jews—Morocco—Casablanca. 3. Jewish diaspora. I. Title
DT329.C3L48 2015
305.892'4064—dc23
2015006382

♾ This paper meets the requirements of ANSI/NISO Z39.48–1992 (Permanence of Paper).

For my parents.
In memory of my father, who unfortunately never traveled back.
In memory of my mother, who fortunately did.

CONTENTS

ACKNOWLEDGMENTS

So many people who bettered the content, shape, and logic of this book should be thanked! Unfortunately, I can't thank them all by name. This is particularly true with regard to the people in Morocco and Israel who opened their doors and hearts. I'll have to be satisfied, unfortunately, with only those who can be mentioned by name. As is customary in anthropological writing, and following the requests of many, the names and other identity markers of people appearing in this book have been camouflaged. I hope that the erasure of identity will not obscure my deep and sincere feeling of gratitude to them.

I would like to thank Harvey Goldberg and Yoram Bilu, my teachers in the deepest sense of the term. Michael Herzfeld, Susan Miller, and Larry (Lawrence) Rosen inspired me in different stations of my life.

Morocco, as a field of research, was practically neglected by English-writing anthropologists after the 1980s. Less as an anthropologist, and more as a native Moroccan, I saw that this writing was missing. Therefore, it was exciting to meet scholars of a younger generation who returned to this intriguing country. With one of them particularly, Aomar Boum, I keep up a constant exchange of ideas about Jewish-Muslim relationships in Morocco. I believe that I speak in the name of both of us when I say that these intimate relationships, with their fluctuations, are a source of comfort and hope for a better future in the Middle East.

Michal Baharav-Uzrad and Noa Leuchter read the manuscript in its initial form and wisely offered ideas to improve the text.

Last, but not least, I feel immensely indebted to my love, Ricky. She is the source of my thoughts and ideas.

INTRODUCTION

My most primal memories, those deeply ingrained in me from the first years of my childhood, are connected with movement: movement between Morocco and Israel. One particular sensory memory is branded onto my body. It is the memory of being jolted around in a taxicab, our bodies bouncing as the cab passed over the train tracks on its way to the dock in Casablanca. We were heading for the ship that would begin our journey to Israel. My second memory is a visual one; my father held my hand tightly as we walked on the ship's deck. He was afraid I might let go of his hand and slip on the wet surface. There were so many wonderful sights and I was curious to see them. A ship passed us in the distance; the people walking on the deck seemed like dolls able to walk on their own. The open horizons of the ocean mocked the perception of a child of five. Years later I still searched for those magical automatic dolls that knew how to walk on their own and wave goodbye with their hands.

The jolt of separation from Morocco at age five undermined the certainty of its memory. All that was left, adamant in their steadfastness, were the memories of leaving. Since that time, I repeatedly longed to return and strove to restore the memories from before our emigration; I attempted this through family stories or gatherings with relatives who left after us and who, unlike us, immigrated (later on) to France. When I was a youth, these relatives seemed to have a higher level of authenticity than my parents to anything connected to life in Morocco. They stayed behind, and they didn't have any of the bitterness that came with post-factum reflections about the decision to immigrate to Israel, which, I was then convinced glorified my parents' memories of a place that for decades there was no possibility that we could return to. I also tried returning to Morocco by way of reflecting on my childhood in an Ashdod neighborhood which was mostly "Moroccan": Morocco in Israel. When it turned possible, I sought to meet it again through journeys and went on voyages that were a mixture of nostalgia and the study of roots made by travelers like me, who were bound to Morocco. I am unable to claim that I succeeded. The intimacy which I crave is found again and again to be unattainable. Not that there is anything in Morocco's "essence" that is particularly unique; nonetheless, Morocco, to my regret, remains as elusive as ever.

This book comprises a retrospective view of an anthropological study over the course of around thirty years, a view that attempts in different ways if not to remove this bothersome obstacle then at least to decipher it. Moving between times and sailing between spaces, the book travels between Morocco and Israel; it turns toward the nineteenth century and returns back to the twenty-first century. Instead of separating times and places, the movement of the writing binds them together. Notions such as "Morocco," "Israel," "past," "present," and so forth aren't complete, fixed categories that stand on their own or are independent of each other. From within this deliberately loose framework of times and spaces the reader is invited to wander amidst my life experiences, experiences that are personal but not idiosyncratic. In the personal vignettes one may find no small amount of a generic story.

The book is engaged in constant movement, in a sort of *flânerie*, and as such it is not a conclusion of my work, but a reference point, a moment, in the continuous inquisitive wanderings in which one may stop and reflect back. This continuous motion is not completely cut off from the place it left, and upon arriving at another, new place it does not emphatically demand total assimilation such that the past is denied, even if parts of it had been forgotten and had sunk into the depths of oblivion. The hint of nostalgia that crops up from between and within different sentences is the glue that synthesizes times and places which might otherwise seem separate and clearly disconnected. The nostalgia leaves its mark on the logical consecutive structure of an individual's life events that otherwise might seem out of place; it unites fragments of memories which seem scattered, engraved in the milestones spread in scattered spaces. Thus, the continuous movement in the book from one place and time to another comes together as one story, even if only for the moment of surrender to the nostalgia within these pages.

The lenses through which I look at this journey and decipher it are anthropological. In my eyes, anthropology, more than any other discipline in the social sciences, aspires to be present in life itself, in order to make sense of it and to give it meaning. It attempts to understand human action from an immediate closeness of which there is no comparison in social sciences. The anthropology that I favor seeks cultural intimacy and includes anthropology into the fabric of the lives of the people it seeks to understand. Its analysis is not cold and distant; it is involved and committed. This closeness is meant to turn the anthropologist's insights into a shared asset between him and the people he attempted to understand during his field research and even afterward in the years after he left.[1] Therefore, the recognition of these shared insights must be explicit and noticeable within the text and not only in the acknowledgments at the beginning of the book, as is the standard in ethnographies. Recognition and gratitude must appear again and again in the body of the text, but this recognition must not allow for the evasion of responsibility for what is said (or for what is written). Indeed, the responsibility for this book is entirely my own.

*

The Introduction to this book is devoted to a discussion on issues related to what is called in anthropology, in a somewhat loose language, "fieldwork-at-home." The chapter focuses on research that I conducted in Casablanca. My primary research in Morocco, intended for my doctoral thesis, took place over a fourteen-month period, beginning the second half of July 1990. I had been to Morocco before, for graduate studies and for defined periods of times, more than I can count or specify, before I returned to do research there. At times I went as a researcher and at times as a tour guide; frequently I combined the two. Chapter 1 therefore deals with basic methodological questions arising from my choice of research field, the Jewish community in Casablanca, the city where I was born and where I spent the first years of my childhood. My work is a type of fieldwork "at-home" not only because of the biographical fact that up until the age of five I lived there but also, perhaps mainly, because the Jews of Morocco occupied my thoughts daily from the time that I left, and in research over the years. The choice of this arena raises expected issues and begs predictable questions about conducting research "at-home." For me these issues are complex and complicated because my migration from Morocco as a child does not sit easily with the questions about research work at-home. To what extent could Morocco be "home" for me? This book will demonstrate that precisely because of migration, national borders that seem to indicate and define a home become fluid and interchangeable. Therefore the commonplace issue of conducting "participant observation" (the type of research employed by anthropologists) at-home becomes deceptive.

If chapter 1 relates to a point near the end of the story I recount, then chapter 2 touches on a time that heralds the beginning of the end: the beginning of the end of the life of a significant Jewish community in Morocco. Specifically, the chapter focuses on a single historical figure in Morocco, a man of the Jewish Enlightenment movement at the end of the nineteenth century, when European countries became major political players and interfered with the fabric of life in Morocco in an increasingly aggressive manner. This man, Yitzhak Ben Yais Halevi, was a writer for *Hatzfira*, a Hebrew-language paper published in central Europe. Contrary to popular opinion in Israel, the series of Ben Yais Halevi articles in *Hatzfira* demonstrates that the horizons of Jewish residents of Morocco exceeded far beyond their country. His articles reveal even more, and through them one may understand some of the burning questions affecting the lives of the Essawira Jewish community (also known as Mogador). But mostly one may concern oneself with the situation and the complex position of the Jews in the face of the impending colonialism. As the second chapter presents the Jewish community leading toward its demographic peak, when Jews numbered about a quarter of a million people, chapter 3 comes to describe the demographic aspects of its twilight, of its being less than four thousand Jews. It recounts the institutional and social changes that took place within the Moroccan Jewish community following its massive migration, while particularly analyzing these changes in Casablanca. In contrast to typical migration studies, which follow the immigrants' story in their country of destination, this chapter examines the process that takes place in the personal and community life of those who chose to remain behind. A pivotal notion is introduced here: "contraction." This notion, or rather concept, concisely depicts the way in which Jews deal with the endless ramifications of their demographic dwindling. In order to better understand the dynamic and its repercussions, chapter 4 presents the way in which Jews cope with their diminution; it analyzes their recruitment of imaginary spatial divisions of spheres in order to obtain better control over interactions with Muslims. It demonstrates how Jews move within and without their spaces in Casablanca. Chapter 5 focuses in even greater detail on one space, offering a microscopic analysis of the interaction between Jews and Muslims in a unique sphere: a beach in Casablanca. The activity in which both groups are involved is exceptional as well: card games. Its uniqueness stems from its being a recreational site that is mutual to Jews and Muslims. The ethnography depicts in great detail the means of survival employed in such a "frivolous," yet highly competitive, activity employed by an insignificant minority within a vast majority. Chapter 6 turns one's attention from the relationship between Jews and Muslims in Casablanca and in the surrounding environment to the "outside" relationships; that is, those within social-political categories beyond Moroccan borders. My distinction between "inside" and "outside" is for rhetorical purposes alone; for I am discussing notions that overlap the concepts "close" and "far." These notions stem from formal definitions of citizenship ("Moroccan," "Israeli," or "French"); however, in the Moroccan Jew's experiences I am discussing categories that are somewhat blurred. More specifically, this chapter critically examines the model of relationships that allegedly exist between Morocco as a "diaspora" and Israel as a "homeland." Chapter 7 continues addressing issues related to our present times but also to the ways in which the past is conceived. It presents the relationship between the homeland and the diaspora from the perspective of Jews born in Morocco who live in Israel. This chapter examines the complexity of the interwoven process of a "search for roots" in Morocco. It primarily examines the essential paradox that arises from a journey home into diaspora and between the present-day Israeli identity and the past Jewish one.

CHAPTER 1

An Anthropological Journey to My Birthplace

"This book is an outgrowth of my ongoing interest in Morocco."
or possibly:
"This book is an outgrowth of my ongoing interest in anthropology."

While I was trying to define the basic idea of this book, the above pronouncements were some thoughts I jotted down for myself, but there they remain, as indecisive doodles. Readers may be wondering at this time if this book is properly prepared and edited, complete with a linear and continuous argument, as befits a serious scholarly work. Well, to be honest, no, this book presents no such argument; it does not need to. This is a book about a journey, and travelers have no interest in behaving like tourists who travel on the beaten path; travelers strive to walk on unfamiliar roads, which curve and fork into many different directions. This book is about a Moroccan journey. It is about an anthropological voyage. This book is about my explorations.

At the time the journey took place, it was fraught with unpredictable twists and turns. As I look back, it seems (how unsurprising!) to have, like any story of a journey, not only parallel paths but also twisted ones, some going toward "Morocco" and others directed to "anthropology." Yet, it also makes claim to a clear shape, content, and direction, and in retrospect it seems to have possessed a solid logic entirely its own. It is similar in this way to the twists of the arabesque: at any point in the journey, at any time or place, it seemed to turn and twist without following any logic or order. However, from a distance, one may see a clear geometric and symmetrical pattern. This journey ended up being so logical and structured that it seemed (how depressing!) that there could not have been any other path to begin with. In retrospect, it seems that though there may be freedom of choice, everything is preordained. Like so many other travelers, I realized retrospectively that I was a tourist.

For this reason, and in order to make things clear to the readers from the beginning, I will start from the end. I will begin from the point where one may see a recurring pattern from a distance: a retrospective reflection of both time and space. From the point where the beginning and end of time and space connect, but possibly don't, where they converge after having been separated. I will start from my anthropological journey to my place of birth, to Morocco, the place where things are meant to become clear, the place of the beginning and the place of the end. This journey was an initiation of sorts for me; it took place more than two decades ago, in the summer of 1990, and transformed me from being a student into being an anthropologist. In those days, many thought my plan to do fieldwork for my doctoral research in Morocco was unrealistic, not to mention dangerously foolish. Officially, I worded the research objective (wording that hid more than it revealed) as the desire to understand the way Jews in Casablanca live, with the clear undisputed awareness that they, as a collective community at least, are approaching their end. Following a period in which they numbered a quarter of a million people, their numbers had diminished to three thousand or so. They are demising demographically and they are aware of this.

My plan was seen as unrealistic, in part, because at the time there were no formal diplomatic relations between Morocco and Israel. Morocco was (and still remains) a member of the Arab League, and the Moroccan king—as the Amir al-Mouaminin ("Commander of the Faithful"), a title he awarded himself by virtue of his alleged lineage from the prophet himself—headed the Al-Quds Committee, a committee charged with safeguarding the interests of the Muslim nation in Al-Qouds/Jerusalem.[2] Despite these formal positions, Morocco's foreign policy and its then head, King Hassan II, were, for a variety of complex reasons, in practice almost neutral to things concerning the Israeli-Palestinian conflict.[3] One of the public expressions of this somewhat aloof policy was revealed in a statement the king made in an exclusive interview that he granted the state television channel in Israel (the only channel at the time). In addition to the irregular and highly exceptional conception of the idea of consenting to an interview on Israeli national television, which constituted a true breaking of taboos, the contents of the interview were in themselves surprising. In the interview, the king invited natives of Morocco to return home. Despite a rather wide dispersion of Moroccan-born Muslims throughout the world, he directed his words to Jews living in Israel. Formally, this statement was based on the concept of Moroccan nationalism, which combines the central principle of citizenship by virtue of kinsmanship ("Blood Rights," or *Jus sanguinis*) with the secondary principle of staying within the territory ("Rights of Soil," or *Jus soli*). In practice very few Israelis returned to settle for good or even for a long period of time in Morocco. However, this statement paved the way for organized travel arrangements for Moroccan-born Israelis to their birthplace.

These trips had been the focus of my graduate studies (master's program) some years earlier. Beyond my intellectual curiosity (to understand issues concerning the Mizrahi identity in Israel), I chose to conduct this study specifically because I desired to see this place that I had heard so many stories about as a child: most of which, I embarrassingly admit, I did not believe. I joined one of the first organized tours to Morocco and asked my mother and older sister to join me. They responded with great enthusiasm. I thought that the idea behind the invitation was clever; since the trip was for a short period of time it would be necessary to win the trust of our fellow passengers quickly. From my failed attempts to interview some of them before the trip, I knew that because of the semi-legitimate feelings surrounding the trips to Morocco, I would find it difficult to achieve cooperation quickly (the trip was to last only three weeks). I could not wait for a long-term confidence-building process. I thought that the fact that my mother was with me would help to break the ice quickly. I wanted my sister to come for two reasons: first, to serve as another pair of eyes and ears and to help in the research. The second and main reason was that she would serve as a buffer between my mother and me when I would need to meet the demands of my research. My mother quickly located childhood friends, and my fears proved childish.

Integrated as part of the trip's itinerary were ten free days. During this time, my mother, sister, and I went to Casablanca to look for the house we used to live in, prior to my family's immigration to Israel. I knew the house was on rue de Longwy, a street with mostly private homes of middle-class families, petit bourgeois.[4] During those days, few Jews lived there; the majority were the *colons*, or the French settlers' (colonialist) families, and one Italian family. I hoped that the encounter with the house I lived in as a young child would arouse dormant memories. After all, most of my time at that age was spent at home. I wasn't convinced of the reliability of those dim memories that I had. I suspected that I didn't really remember characters such as Monsieur Block (a Frenchman converted to Judaism, who would probably be called "Bloch" in Israel), the tall, overweight neighbor who scared us children. I feared that my memory of him, like other memories of sight, color, and taste, was more a fabrication that was built later than it was a memory from that time and place. I was consumed with doubt lest those evenings with family members telling stories and reminiscing about life in Casablanca had become lodged in my mind and now functioned as my own memories. The lower-class neighborhood where I grew up in Israel (later incorporated in "Project Renewal"), which was mostly made up of Moroccan immigrants, also reconstructed through language, holiday celebrations, customs, and games a Moroccan past. Like any act of reconstruction, it was a commentary of the present on that past. Indeed, this reconstruction intensified the differences between the different neighborhood residents—the "chelohim" (Amazighs speaking tachelhit) from the high Atlas Mountains as opposed to the city dwellers—among whom there were often disagreements. I remembered stopping by with my father on Shabbat and holidays at the synagogue, which was only a few steps away from our house. My father was not meticulous about keeping the commandments, and in fact, only after we immigrated to Israel did he begin following the religious rules more strictly. As part of this change, he began to frequent the synagogue on Friday evenings, Shabbat, and holidays. In Morocco, he used to work on Saturdays. On one of these occasions, I think it was during the month of the Tishre festivals, the cantor of the synagogue opened services with a speech where he stressed that all those coming to pray must remember that this was a "Sephardi" synagogue, that is to say, a synagogue of "deportees" who arrived in Morocco following the Alhambra Decree. My father was offended and decided then and there to leave the synagogue and join the synagogue belonging to the people of Meknes. This while sharing his dissatisfaction that there was no "Marrakechi" (of his hometown, Marrakech) synagogue within reasonable walking distance. The encounter in Israel between different groups of Moroccan immigrants sharpened the differences between them, some of which were taken seriously and some with humor. Occurrences such as this event in the synagogue became for me a part of the Moroccan reality, of Morocco in Israel. This to such an extent that I had suspicions that my memories of walking as a child from my house to the playground in the center of Casablanca, of going to Vivoli, the ice cream parlor at the end of the street, were tinted by stories and events of my childhood in Ashdod. These memories were, furthermore, affected by pictures taken by my grandfather, who was a talented amateur photographer. Through his pictures, photographed with an 8 mm movie camera, he brought the images I imagined from the neighborhood in Morocco to life even stronger.

The visit to Morocco, as a roots travel meant to arouse dormant memories and confirm existing ones ended in bitter disappointment. Our home was destroyed and in its place stood a commercial bank. My mother, in her bitter disappointment, let out a cry in Maghrebi Arabic of "Allah have mercy, our house," as if saying that our house had died. This disappointment was not unique to us; it was the lot of the majority of travelers to Morocco. Perhaps, and not surprisingly, one of the outcomes of the journey to find roots in Morocco was the increasing feeling that things about the past remained unresolved, a bothersome nuisance, a project waiting to be completed. There were many who hoped that these same missions would be resolved in the next trip (be it the second, third, or even fifth). There were those who hoped that next time they would find the burial place of their father or mother; there were those who hoped that in the next trip "they would bring back to Israel the lost sister they left in Morocco who married an Arab"; those who wanted to restore the remaining fragments of the grandfather's grave; or those who wanted to find their old house or the neighbor who lived next door. Part of the disappointment relates, of course, to the illusiveness of the "home" toward which they yearned to return. Often both the concrete and metaphorical home exists in more than one place. Thus, as soon as you reach it you find that it is already somewhere else; upon arriving at one "home" you disturbingly discover that this just inundates you with memories of and glorifies the other that is left behind.

Following this journey-research trip, which examined the social and cultural meanings of Israelis' journey to their roots in Morocco, one of my supervisors, Harvey Goldberg, titled me "*Hajj* André." In his style of doing things, this crowning had multilayered meanings. I will risk interpreting his words and state that except for the obvious fact that he imagined a trip to a Muslim country would be interspersed with Jewish and Muslim holy sites, a pilgrimage in fact, he apparently wanted to indicate that I was essentially conducting my own professional pilgrimage (an anthropological rite of passage, if you wish). I assume he also wanted to congratulate me on my private-collective pilgrimage as a native of Morocco. My journey to my roots in Morocco planted within me the desire to designate Morocco as the research site (my "field," as anthropologists call it) for my doctoral studies. As mentioned above, almost anyone I told of my intention to conduct extended fieldwork in Morocco expressed the fear that I was going on an unnecessary escapade. One of the few who stood out in their optimism was Clifford Geertz, who himself conducted research in the city of Sefrou, Morocco. During his visit to Israel he encouraged me to go without asking too many questions or without asking permission from the Moroccan authorities to carry out research. "If you ask permission, you will run into bureaucratic obstinacy," he said. However, unlike him, the majority were pessimistic. Some were especially dramatic: "What if war breaks out?!" I was asked defiantly. (To my complete surprise this speculation proved correct.

I left for Morocco in early July 1990, and a few days later (on August 2, 1990) Iraq invaded Kuwait. On January 7, 1991, the Allied countries opened a war against Iraq.) Most of my interlocutors were a bit more correct minded and asked: "What if they don't allow you to enter Morocco?" Fortunately, this possibility did not materialize.

At the time though, the second possibility seemed to be the more realistic one. In spite of the absence of diplomatic relations between the two countries, winding paths that would allow visits to Morocco did exist, though their legitimacy was not always evident to the participants. The most common point of entry to Morocco was by means of the Moroccan consulate in Malaga, Spain. Travelers were required to deposit their Israeli passport, and in return they received a *laissez passer* (transit visa), a document that would accompany the visitor throughout the entire period of their visit. The document was a plain piece of paper bearing a photo of the document holder, in which the Spanish authorities were requested to assist in passage to Morocco. In addition, the document declared that the original nationality of the document holder was Moroccan, while the "Current Nationality" section usually remained blank, apparently to avoid mentioning the name of Israel on an official document of the Moroccan kingdom. For reasons incomprehensible to me, in this section my current nationality was written as Moroccan.

The choice of the Moroccan bureaucracy to grant a document such as this one was not coincidental. A transit visa is a document issued by a government requesting from other countries that they permit passage into their country, while being assured that the visa holder will return to the country that issued the visa and won't stay in the transit country.[5] In this way, the Moroccan kingdom declared that I, like any other traveler from Israel to Morocco, was defined as a returning subject and not as a visiting tourist. This declaration was consistent with the Moroccan interest at the time not to declare to the world, and especially to the Arab world, that Israelis were welcome tourists in Morocco. Because I entered Morocco with this document as opposed to a tourist visa, my stay there was not limited in time. As a researcher this was a significant advantage for me, because I didn't have to justify that the length of my stay in Morocco was for fieldwork; after all I was Moroccan. This enabled a period of research time of fourteen consecutive months in Casablanca.

Because this document was not widely familiar, many people were bewildered by the transit visa, and there were many misunderstandings when I needed it to serve as an ID card: such that when I wanted to convert US dollars to Dirham, the local currency, senior officials at the bank branch were required to intervene in order to allow me to do so. However, the greatest difficulty that this document raised for me was that of finding an apartment. Landlords had difficulty understanding the legal status of the document and feared getting into trouble with the authorities. They were afraid mainly because they knew, although I did not volunteer this information, that I was from Israel. For this and other reasons that I won't go into here, involving how Jews relate to Muslims in Morocco, Jews that I met in Casablanca recommended that I contact only Jewish real estate agents.

After spending a day or two at a modest hotel conveniently close to the center of Jewish institutions in Casablanca, I began my search for an apartment to rent. At first, I acted in accordance with the advice I had gotten and approached only Jewish agents. There were not many, and each of them disappointed me. It was evident that they lacked enthusiasm to help; maybe this was due to bitter experiences with Israeli visitors. Stubborn rumors were told about Israelis who sold counterfeit dollars to Jews in exchange for local currency, while taking advantage of the fact that they would return to Israel and it would be difficult to settle accounts with them. Thus, despite my repeated explanations as to my source of income (research grants) real estate agents expressed their lack of confidence and inability to understand how I would pay my rent.

As the days passed, I broadened the circle of sources that I approached in requesting help in locating an apartment. I turned to community institutions and private individuals. Bureaucrats of some of the institutions cringed from the idea of cooperating with me; they feared associating with a man of Israeli citizenship. Officials in institutions that agreed to help me chose to negate my citizenship; for example, in one of the institutions the director requested that the clerk write me down as "the visitor from Texas." The need to hide the connection between us made receiving assistance all the more difficult. Many encouraged me and offered advice, but it was evident that they were not prepared to offer any substantial assistance.

A month passed and in a visit to one of the Jewish institutions I related my troubles to a high-level bureaucrat, a young man of about thirty-five.[6] He could not believe I was having such trouble finding an apartment and for such a long time, especially considering I had a grant that would allow me to pay the rent for a few months in advance. He, like many others, promised to help me. But, contrary to the others, he fully enlisted in the effort and in fact referred me to a Muslim agent who worked in central Casablanca. The second apartment the agent showed me already seemed fine, except that it was on the fifth floor in a building without an elevator. Its advantage was that it was in close proximity to many of the community offices (Alliance offices, the community health services, and the Maimonides school, etc.). Then and there I signed a lease for a year.

ANTHROPOLOGISTS WRITE ABOUT DANGER

The accommodations issue was important, though not critical to the very existence of the research. As mentioned, the question of the complex political and diplomatic relations between Morocco and Israel was the top priority during the formulating stage of my doctoral research proposal. In order to make clear the disturbance I was feeling at the time, I will bring the following disorganized, unsystematic scrawls: excerpts from my field diary from the days before I entered Morocco and in the early days of my stay there; these sections will clearly show the mood I was in:

July 11, 1990 (before the trip)
One of my most serious concerns in this journey is whether this project will at all succeed. Will the Moroccan authorities thwart—for bureaucratic, security reasons etc.—my goals? Will they let me in for an unlimited time? Will they return my passport in Spain? . . .

July 14, 1990 (one day after entry in Morocco)
Ok, that's it we got in . . .

The main feeling is one of fear, fear that comes from uncertainty, from the semi-legitimate feel of the study. One side of me says that the research is possible, and there is nothing to fear. My visa is not time limited. I could stay here all my life . . . on the other hand every time I have to present my visa I am in a state of anxiety. I feel comfortable on the street, where I am like any other tourist. It is precisely at the hotel where I feel threatened, I know they know (that I'm Israeli) and I know how easy it is for them to summon the authorities. . . .

During the flight my anxiety began to rise, and it increased as we got closer to Morocco. Before landing I noticed that on my blue bag the name "Jerusalem" was written in English and Hebrew. I found a good solution and held it upside down. A little (Moroccan) girl who was on the plane tried to guess where I was from. This added to my tension. Suddenly being Israeli is something that must be hidden . . .

Despite the warnings and worry that I heard in increasing intensity as the date of departure got closer, and although I knew for sure that I would be flooded with anxiety as we approached Morocco, I didn't want to give up the study. My previous trip to Morocco had assuaged my fears somewhat, making Morocco into a concrete place. Not only did this make a difference, but since my first trip I had met Jews in Israel who lived in Morocco; they calmed me down and promised to help me become acclimated. This is what actually occurred. One family in particular, whom I will call Elmakeyes, took care of me both by offering advice and in assisting me with material needs. But the period in which my fears somewhat subsided, was short-lived. Following difficult domestic political events and violent global developments, the sense of calm disappeared and in its place a gnawing anxiety returned. A few days after my arrival in Morocco, Iraq invaded Kuwait, and following this invasion a war against Iraq was looming. These events in and of themselves, and their implications for the internal Moroccan political scene, strengthened my sense of fear and anxiety (see Munson 1988).

The feelings of personal distress that found their way to my field diary are not uncommon in anthropological writings about a research experience. I am referring not only to personal field notes but also mainly to ethnographies. It seems that the ethnographic report of feeling threatened, detached, dependent, and transient as well as other hardships has become almost decorum in anthropology, to the point where it signifies somewhat a classic genre. Quite a few anthropologists describe the period in which they conducted their fieldwork as a time full of hardships and obstacles which threatened to jeopardize their life's work and at times (although rarely) even their very lives. Ethnographies describing these themes frame anthropological research as a dangerous and heroic journey. This construction is not new; it further solidifies an anthropological genre that began in the early days of the discipline. In fact, this writing style—this genre of anthropology as an adventurous journey—began even before the institutionalization of anthropology as a field of academic knowledge. The genre glorified the researcher and his work by his being located in a dangerous, extremely confusing, and hostile environment. The anthropologist is seen as a gallant, lonely knight, who endangers his life for the sake of obtaining precious cultural knowledge for his Western readers. This genre has been criticized by a variety of anthropologists. Note how Clifford Geertz condemns this type of story formulation by Claude Levi-Strauss, one of the central anthropologists that established this discipline. Geertz, who is himself a key figure in modern anthropology, refers to Levi-Strauss's monumental book *Tristes Tropiques:* "In the first place, it is, of course, and despite the ironic and self-reflexive denial of the famous opening passage, a travel book in a very recognizable genre. I went here, I went there; I saw this strange thing and that; I was amazed, bored, excited, disappointed; I got boils on my behind, and once, in the Amazon . . .—all with the implicit undermessage: Don't you wish you had been there with me or could do the same?" (Geertz 1988:33–34).

Part of the epic roots of this writing is ingrained in the classic feature of anthropological research itself: fieldwork. Since Bronislaw Malinowski, the researcher who is credited with founding the anthropological methodology (whose basic premises have not changed to this day), fieldwork has become the ultimate test of joining the professional guild. This, as stated, was one of the meanings behind the nickname given to me by my supervisor when he called me 'Hajj André." But not only that, fieldwork has become a crucial criterion for evaluating the quality of the anthropologist's work. This approach explains the atmosphere of distrust toward Levi-Strauss, as if he "is not really an anthropologist." The suspicion relates to the mystery surrounding the period of his research, to the point that it was suspected that it never even took place. Notice the language Geertz, who found an abundance of flaws in Levi-Strauss's work, uses: "The mystique of field work that Malinowsky founded and Mead proclaimed finds its apotheosis here, significantly enough in someone who has not done all that much field work" (Geertz 1988:37).

As mentioned, it was Malinowski who set the tone for the mental and physical difficulties inherent in doing research. One of the most famous passages in anthropology illustrates this well: "Imagine yourself suddenly set down surrounded by all your gear, alone on a tropical beach to a native village, while the launch or dinghy which has brought you sails away out of sight" (Malinowski 1961 [1922]:4). Imagine, says Malinowski, how secluded I was, how miserable, isolated, lonely, going toward the unknown, the wild, and the dangerous, without any contact to European civilization.

Following Malinowski's death, his wife published his personal diaries, and these exposed personal revelations that he probably had no intention of publishing. In these journals he continuously expresses his dissatisfaction with the "natives." Likewise, he describes loneliness, hardship, frustration, diseases which attack him morning and evening, and a physical and mental weakness that troubled him greatly. Of course, there is no need (and it is wrong) to seek evidence in diaries that were not intended for the public eye and therefore do not represent the public face of anthropology. It is enough to carefully read the above quote, designed for the readers, to entice them to join him in their imaginations on his wonderful journey to the Trobriand Islands. His methodological writings indicate that loneliness is at the heart of anthropological practice.

In order to conduct proper research it is necessary to break away from familiar surroundings. Not only is that required, but Malinowski states, it is also necessary to maintain a reasonable distance, both spatial and emotional, from the "natives." I don't want to address here the many political facets implied in these recommendations, but I do want to point out that the isolation of the researcher is painted in many heroic shades. This model of research reveals the foundation upon which anthropological writing was established: I am referring to the genre outlined by the ancestors of anthropology: the voyagers, adventurers, missionaries, and the other colonial representatives in the "Third World" colonies. Heroism was given a variety of shapes and forms in anthropological reporting: a heroic journey to the unknown, a unique encounter with strange cultures, the surprise encounter with unexpected experiences, and so on. One particularly popular form of this genre was the dangerous adventure.

Renato Rosaldo is one of those who most closely identified with the critical postcolonial and postmodern perspective in anthropology. In the opening of one of his earlier books, *Illongot Headhunting*, he relates the history of the researcher that preceded him in studying this Philippines group (Rosaldo 1980). That same researcher, Rosaldo tells us, behaved in an irresponsible fashion toward members of the tribe and in the end was beheaded. The almost *nonchalant* tone Rosaldo employs to report these unfortunate events frames his own research as heroic; he who was in the lion's mouth succeeded in escaping in peace. This is, of course, a somewhat dramatic example. It also shows no favor toward Rosaldo, since he abandoned the modernist perspective that characterized his very book. However, there are countless literary examples that are even more banal then this one; examples which insinuate great dangers, often casually inserted in the ethnographic text.

Geertz is not among the followers of this genre; note the condescending tone when he presents Levi-Strauss's (as well as other anthropologists') writings: "The anthropologist, as here, venturing where lesser souls—his café intellectuals in Paris; the orchid-elite of French-Quarter São Paolo . . .—dare not go, and penetrating forms of existence they can only read about. . . . The mystique of field work that Malinowski founded and Mead proclaimed finds its apotheosis here [in Levi-Strauss's *Tristes Tropiques*]" (Geertz 1988:36–37).

While preparing for the fieldwork, my understanding that this period would be filled with hardship and dangers and my knowledge of the colonial roots of the project did not help me overcome the feeling that my journey was indeed full of dangers. Therefore, I found myself somewhat reluctantly joining the tradition of the tormented journey. My memories from my research period in Morocco support the classic heroic story; my research, the research of a

Jewish anthropologist from Israel, was conducted in an Arab country whose constitution is based on Islamic Law. Moreover, the combination of historical circumstances which I found myself in, during the study, set into motion a series of dramatic events (see Munson 1993). Already after Iraq's invasion of Kuwait, just a few days after my arrival in Morocco, I began to feel uneasy. A long series of both small- and large-scale events seemed to place a threat on the existence of this study. It was no wonder that every knock at the door, every policeman on the street (and there are many in Casablanca!), or any unexpected gesture of a bureaucrat seemed a direct threat. I felt that these events posed a threat to me, or at least to my research. There were moments when I confused the two. As this was the state of things, I will try to keep the presentation of the hardships of my research to a minimum, while still maintaining my ethnographic faithfulness.

It is not only Malinowski's requirement for isolation that stands at the underlying difficult feelings which accompany the research; anthropological *writing* brings with it a feeling of acute insecurity: an insecurity of a different sort and scale. Life's moments are ephemeral. Anthropologists try desperately to hold onto them and to "inscribe" them into the written word, in the words of Clifford Geertz (1973c). The anthropological work is therefore in chronic need of trust in its author. In order to gain this trust on the part of the readers, anthropologists employ a variety of literary techniques that strengthen this confidence. In order to become a convincing witness, Geertz tells us, one must first establish the person behind the witness. Or, as he says in his rich language: "To be a convincing 'I-witness,' one must, so it seems, first become a convincing 'I'" (Geertz 1988:79).

The very same person who is meant to establish his credibility, according to classical anthropological tradition, is alone in the field. Usually this is a he and not a she, according to that same tradition. Except for the subjects of his study, toward whom he turns his back when he ponders his theories, there is no one to witness those ephemeral moments. Thus, the anthropologist is in a state of seclusion in foreign lands, cut off from his familiar surroundings. Within this demand, the seeds of feelings such as fear and anxiety are planted.

This style of a "working" anthropological study has deep historical roots in western European culture. Structurally, it can be paralleled to the style of grand voyagers and their stories which were published as adventure books. This modern form of storytelling preceded even the colonial project, in its type of discussion about places coined as "foreign," "mysterious," "incomprehensible," and at times "dangerous." These places were the objective of European adventurers as well as of their structural successors, the anthropologists. They, who glorified (and overstated) the cultural difference, reinforced perceptions about those same distant places that embody the ultimate "other." One may presume that in this way they cemented their credibility as anthropologists. The more dangerous it was, the less the culture was understood and the more exotic, so the anthropologist was more credible. This process resulted from the anthropologists' desire to put themselves midway between the culture, incomprehensible to the European reader, and the natives. Thus, they acquired the status of trusted cultural interpreters and overcame the lack of confidence in their unsupervised reports, while all the time paying the price of loneliness and fear while creating the heroism of the "secluded knight."

Anthropological tradition was not the only player participating in the construction of ethnographic texts combining fear and heroism. The broader political context has also been significant in understanding the genre of anthropological heroism. I will refer only to nation-states which constitute the continuous context for the anthropologist's work. The fact that nation-states have a central role, if not an exclusive one, in determining the exclusion and inclusion boundaries of national belonging has significant implications for the ethnographic genre and for anthropological practice. Anthropologists who strive for purposes of tradition and professional correctness to abstain from "fieldwork-at-home" need by definition to cross national-political borders. Simply put, they need a passport. This commodity is awarded by nation-state officials, except that in the postcolonial period this bureaucratic fact became a crucial one for anthropologists. High-ranking officials in postcolonial countries are reluctant to allow anthropological research in their countries—a memory of the close connection that existed between colonialism and anthropologists. In some places there is a tangible aversion to anthropologists. Thus, the ability to avoid doing fieldwork at home constitutes a significant currency in the anthropological community. In the case of my particular study, this difficulty was doubled and tripled due to Morocco's being a Muslim country whose cultural and political predisposition is basically Arab. Thus, I found myself joining that very same genre where the actual research was in itself an achievement. Despite the temptation, I will avoid referring systematically and in depth to this matter. It is enough that I unconditionally surrendered to the writing style of the voyager. Consequently, I will only say that throughout the months of research, I was totally disconnected from events taking place in Israel. It is hard to imagine this nowadays, but at the time there were no accessible internet connections (no e-mail, no Facebook . . .) and due to the absence of formal diplomatic relations, it was impossible to phone directly to Israel, or to send letters. From time to time I sent various materials to Israel through friends in Germany and every so often the occasional visitor came from Israel with greetings from friends and acquaintances.

In retrospect, I can state that the feelings of threat and the thoughts that I was being followed bordered on self-centered paranoia. As with any paranoid thought, there was some truth to it and a core of egocentricity. The distance, the time that passed, and the pleasant coolness of my work room made this clear to me. But, could it really just be the nature of the discipline and the tradition of anthropological writing that are to blame for this existential experience? I doubt it. I would like to offer a more specific, local explanation in which I cannot completely avoid, even with some restraint, describing some of the research difficulties. That is to say, it is unavoidable to describe these difficulties because they will assist in understanding those whom I have aimed to understand—the Jews of Morocco. I recognize a surprising structural parallel (at least at first glance) between the experience of loneliness and sense of threat to my research and one of the most basic experiences of Jews in Morocco: contraction. I will expand upon this, which is also about the structure of relations between Jews and Muslims in Morocco, in later chapters of the book. I will just say now that it is an introvert inclination of the Jews, an effort made to avoid whenever possible, an encounter with Muslims. Contraction is accompanied by a sense of vulnerability and at the same time is also the cause of it. In the eyes of many, any event that seemed to have the slightest chance of toppling the government in Morocco (and especially to threaten the royal family) was perceived as a concrete and palpable danger to the Jews. During the first few months of my research, I didn't understand this relationship whereby political internal-Moroccan, regional, or global events were perceived as a direct threat. I was especially surprised considering the tiny size of the Moroccan Jewish community, in relation to Casablanca less than one-tenth of 1 percent.

Just as I had clear signs which confirmed the sense of danger which I found myself in as a researcher, so too the Jews had clear signs that supported their egocentric perception that they were relevant, even central to public life in Morocco. They were confident that there were those who plotted their downfall. What were the signs that reinforced the sense of centrality among the Jews? I will present a few of them. The daily newspaper *Le Matin*, for example, which is identified with the then-ruling party in Morocco, to this day marks on its front page three dates; Muslim (*Hijra*), Gregorian, and Hebrew. Moreover, senior (Muslim) bureaucrats take part in many community activities, even those of minor nature, and thereby confirm that the Jews are a priority. Government representatives come every year to the central Lag Ba'omer celebration to bless the Jews. The most senior officials come to the central synagogue, Beit

El, to bless the congregation on major Jewish holidays like Yom Kippur. "They give honor to the Torah," said one of the oldest representatives of Chabad in Morocco upon seeing the heavy police escort ensuring the security of a few tens of elderly Jews who made a pilgrimage to the grave of Rabbi Raphael Anqawa in the city of Sale. I was not alone in expressing my surprise when representatives of the Moroccan authorities participated in Jewish events; often Jews from the community audibly voiced their astonishment. So it was, one night, when a celebration took place in honor of the presentation of the OSE (*œuvre de secours aux enfants*) budget. The OSE is an institution that functions today as a health center for Jews who are unable to afford private health care. This was an event that many of the city's Jews were not even aware of, yet when I arrived at the event, I came across a convoy of official cars outside the OSE. Security guards were everywhere. Disorder and confusion prevailed due to the mayor of Casablanca's participation in this event. To me his participation seemed quite unusual since this was a very marginal event, even for the community whose size, in comparison to the rest of the city, was tiny. The mayor of a major city of about 3 million people came to an event of an institution that served less than three thousand Jews, just 0.1 percent of the population. The mayor sat respectfully in the first row, showing a clear interest in the questions that came up from the budget presentation. He asked, for example, about the number of free dental fillings that were granted to poor Jews last year. His questions merited serious, to-the-point answers. Later there was a fundraising appeal, and the mayor contributed a handsome sum to the institution. His donation was received with enthusiastic applause. Beside the mayor sat his son, a young man of about twelve or thirteen, dressed as a boy his age in jeans, a t-shirt, and sneakers. At the end of the budget presentation participants were invited to go upstairs to the top floor and to partake of the rich buffet. Before they began eating, one of the city's important rabbis said a "Prayer for the Kingdom," a prayer usually said outside of the Land of Israel, wishing success to the leader of a country and asking God to protect him. The prayer was said this time with much intent and meaning for fear of the political developments that seemingly threatened the king. The mayor covered his head with a napkin and put his hand over his son's head. He was well acquainted with the prayer and knew when to respond "Amen." He, like the other guests, participated in the prayer with great devotion. After the prayer, the rabbi invited the guests to eat while reminding them not to forget to say the various blessings over the food. The mayor intervened and asked why the rabbi skipped the "Prayer for Welfare," which is the prayer for the welfare of the congregants. The rabbi smiled with pleasure and willingly obliged. Here too, the mayor covered his and his son's head, and knew when to answer "Amen." When this was completed and the participants lingered around the full table, the mayor turned to the rabbi and requested that he bless his son. The rabbi laid his hands on the young man's head; the latter bowed his head and closed his eyes with devotion. The rabbi blessed the young man, while his father, the mayor, repeatedly answered "Amen."

This episode moved me very much but also embarrassed me. It flooded me with stories my parents used to tell me in my childhood. Remorse came over me for my cynicism as I listened to my parents' stories. One can and probably should suggest explanations for such politically correct acts. Indeed, political scientists like Mark Tessler provide "rational" explanations for such governmental conduct (Tessler 1988). Some of these explanations put the Moroccans in a rather negative light, as if they were adopting a version of "The Protocols of the Elders of Zion." In other words, because the Jews control Capitol Hill in America, and because these Jews are Israel's proxies there, it would be wise to please them and to treat them with kid gloves. Thus, Morocco's interests in the United States will receive a fitting response.

There may be a grain of truth to these interpretations. However, it seems to me that they don't provide a satisfactory understanding to the incidents described above. There are a large range of behaviors that might be considered appropriate and fair toward the Jewish minority in Casablanca; there was no need for the mayor to ask for the blessing of the rabbi. As stated, Moroccan Jews emphasize the fact that these events were not the norm; the attitude toward these events was dramatic and demands an explanation. Explanations seek to establish a fundamental truth about the cultural proximity "of two thousand years that was established between Jews and Muslims," states Moshe Elmakayes, one of the central figures in a Jewish club. It is therefore not surprising that the episode with the mayor during the budget presentation elicited many explanations, all of which shared one theme: a common Jewish and Muslim history. After one of the participants expressed astonishment as to the behavior of the mayor, he added: "He was the mayor of Essawira." This was his way of arguing that because this city was known for its prominent Jewish community (Schroeter 1988), the mayor felt a strong closeness to Jews; he was familiar with their ways and respected them. Similar explanations of deep cultural affection were also expressed in regard to King Hassan II. Daniel Dadon, a community member about forty years old, offered an explanation of the king's affection for Jews when speaking about the crown prince. Like many Jews, what bothered him were the facial features of the crown prince. The latter, unlike his father, has a "Negroid look." In his racist language he wanted to express his worry that the son was not educated on the knees of Arab tradition in a love toward Jews. "I don't know who his mother is," he told me. When he realized I did not understand what he meant he added: "You know the King has a lot of wives . . . but the King loves us very much, and I'm sure he teaches his son how to behave towards us." "The King loves us very much, do you know why?" he then asked and drew close to me, as if to tell me a secret. "It is because when he was a baby, when he was just born, his mother was unable to nurse him, and they took a Jewish wet nurse. So the first food that ever entered our King's mouth was from the breasts of a Jewish woman. When her milk entered into his body, the Jews entered into his bloodstream!"

The Jews acted as though they were central players in life in Morocco. Many claimed that they worked *aux palais* (at the palace). This feeling of centrality explains why King Hassan II's speeches in Arabic on the national television station were received by the Jews with severe criticism: "It is common knowledge that we speak French." The Jews saw themselves at the heart of Moroccan existence and entitled to the kingdom's protection; this of course, entailed a relationship of dependency. Some might even suggest that this dependency was dictated by the Jews' attitude. As such, Jewish life depended on the stability of the regime. During the first Gulf War this dependency had a particularly painful reminder. Many Jews feared that they were leaning on a bruised reed; it seemed to them that the government's stability was being quickly undermined by the king's complex attitude toward the war. On one hand, the king supported the Allied forces against Iraq, and he even sent troops to fight the invaders of Kuwait. On the other hand, the king held his task forces back from removing Iraqi forces from Kuwait and did not approve the entry of his troops into Iraq's borders. At the same time that he sent troops to Kuwait, the king saw to it that his daughter led a delegation of the Red Crescent, which collected medicines and blood for wounded Iraqi soldiers. This complex position demanded frequent explanations; and it seemed that the king was compelled to appear again and again on television in order to explain them. For many Jews, this necessity was a sign of the weakening of the regime. Indeed, many of the leaders of the Jewish community decided to leave Morocco until the storm passed. Many of the senior Jewish officials left, some for a defined period of time, until the danger passed, and some never to return.

Precisely at this time, when the crisis was at its peak, as far as Jews were concerned, their sense of centrality was reinforced. As mentioned, during this time the king's daughter was the head of the Red Crescent, which delivered medicines and blood to Iraqi soldiers. The time period was the month of Ramadan. In this month there was a decline in the number of blood donations from

Muslims due to the fast, and according to the practice in previous years, Jews donated blood. This was a symbolic act of participation in the public life of Morocco. But Jewish high school students and their teachers evaded donating blood that year by stating that they "already gave at home." This refusal, explained one of the Jewish students, George Biton, stemmed from the fear that the blood would be sent to Iraq: "We should donate our blood to Morocco, who will send it to Iraqi soldiers, who send missiles into Israel?!" Their refusal was not made out loud. Jews were afraid to refuse openly, because of the sense of vulnerability that resided within them during this time.

During the war, I too felt vulnerable and exposed. A feeling of uncertainty hung over me throughout the entire research period. Mostly, I was afraid I would not be able to stay the entire time period I had planned for the research program: fourteen consecutive months. In contrast to many Jews (of the community), I did not want to leave Morocco, for two reasons. The first was purely technical: I was afraid that because of my long stay in Morocco and the ambiguous policy regarding this, I would not be permitted to return and complete my study. The second reason was essential to the research: I saw this time as a fascinating historic moment that would teach me a lot about the Jews of Morocco. Many of the Jews in Morocco did not agree with this assessment. For example, Richard Balili argued with me quietly that the study had absolutely no validity since it did not reflect routine times. Either way, a sense of unease and insecurity in being able to implement the research study enveloped me with varying degrees of intensity, all the time. These feelings were fostered by a number of events: first and foremost, as already mentioned, was the war which was taking place far away, in the Gulf. Furthermore, in the time leading up to the war, there were several violent events, some on an economic plane, which undermined the sense of both personal and communal security. During this period, the leaders of the Jewish community gathered the Jews in clubs and instructed them on how to behave. The main directive was "Do not raise your head," "Do not get into confrontations with Arabs, even if you are not guilty," and so on. These guidelines wounded the pride of some Jews, particularly the young men, but they were compelled to swallow the bitter pill and obey. Indeed, except for a rumor, for which I could not find any foundation, of an elderly Jewish woman who was murdered by her housekeeper (interpreted as a sign of the rising tensions), there was no physical harm to the Jews. However, there were Jews who received threatening letters: there was, for example, a portrait of Saddam Hussein known as "the dangerous murderer" and on the other side of the page was written "Jews Go Home." These letters were given to the police for examination. There were Jews who suspected that the Israeli Mossad was behind these actions, seeking to arouse panic among Jews in order that they would immigrate to Israel. As mentioned, I too felt that my stay in Morocco was on shaky ground and that there was at least a reasonable chance that my research would be thwarted or possibly that my notebooks would be confiscated. Therefore, I took extra precautions and wrote my journal in duplicate, one copy I sent to Israel in parts via an address in Germany or with the help of friends or acquaintances that arrived for a visit in Morocco. For a time I decided to disguise the names of people who said sensitive things. I did this even when writing in the field diary and not, as was the customary practice, to conceal the revealing details only in the ethnography.

In retrospect, I realize that, like the Jews, I was not important enough to bother anyone. But the sense of distress at the time was quite real and only dissipated upon my arrival in Israel.

THE RETURN HOME

At the completion of the research study I traveled to Ashdod to visit my mother, with whom I had had no connection throughout the entire period. She was interested in the technical aspects relating to the time I spent in Morocco. She expressed concern about the financing of the research, the weather, and so on. One of the first questions on which she lingered for a long time had to do with my living arrangements. I told her about my troubles in finding an apartment to rent in Casablanca and how I finally received help. She asked where I had lived and was not content with a general description of the area, but wanted to know an exact address. While my mother was asking for exact details of where I lived, I tried considering possible explanations for her overactive curiosity. As you may remember, I knew where we had lived before (rue de Longwy), and I also knew that in my mother's youth she had lived in a newly built area next to the mellah (the Jewish quarter or neighborhood) of Casablanca. From reading historical literature I learned that the first mellah was established in the royal (imperial) city of Fes, in 1438. Later, additional ones were established in other places. Generally, in large cities the mellah was walled and it had a large gate which was closed at night, while in small towns and villages it was usually a Jewish neighborhood, without walls. The Jews gradually left the boundaries of the mellah during the increased influence of French colonialism. In Casablanca Jews first left to adjacent houses, in order to be close to relatives who remained within the walls. My mother's family was apparently among the first to leave the mellah in Casablanca in the early twentieth century. Later, my grandfather on my maternal side moved from that neighborhood to a "more modern" area next to the ocean, in *l'habitat* quarter. I suspect that the move to this neighborhood was not motivated by the comfort level of the residence, but mainly due to its proximity to the ocean, as my grandfather was an enthusiastic amateur fisherman. Therefore, I knew that my mother spent most of her childhood years outside the mellah, first in close proximity to it and afterward next to the ocean. Later, after she married my father, she lived in a "Christian" neighborhood (the Europeans were called Nisrana, Christians). Therefore the possibility of something dramatic that would be unknown to me, relating to where I lived during my year of research, in the neighborhood where I grew up, or close to where my mother lived, didn't seem like a real possibility. My father lived in his youth in Marrakech. I pushed these thoughts out of my mind and continued answering her inquisitive questions. When I mentioned the name of the street, rue Eléonore Fournier—she insisted on knowing the number of the building. At this point my curiosity grew. My mother continued: What was the number? When I told her the number, she asked with some satisfaction: "Was there anything across the street, any interesting institution?" I thought she was referring to one of the Jewish institutions that was right next to where I had lived, the Ittihad (Alliance Israélite Universelle), or maybe the Cinéma L'arc, a movie theatre just a few steps away from the apartment on Eléonore Fournier. It was a movie theatre where they showed French and Hollywood movies when she was young. "No" she firmly replied. "I don't mean around the corner. I mean opposite, on the other side of the street . . ." After a moment's hesitation I answered: "There was some institution, but I never asked about it. From the colors of the inside walls that I could see from my window, I think it was a clinic . . ." "Yes!" confirmed my mother, "that was the clinic where you were born!"

What appeared as a rare fateful coincidence—gave me closure and closed upon me the area where I was actually born—touched, if even indirectly, on a wide if somewhat tiresome issue in anthropology of the late twentieth century: the native anthropologist and fieldwork at home.

WHERE IS HOME? FIELD WORK AT HOME

My coincidental residence precisely next to my place of birth was in itself, very surprising. But the questions stemming from the fact that I carried out my research in the place of my birth were not. Indeed, since the 1980s there had been a sharp increase in the anthropological literature that dealt with the issue of fieldwork "at home." Signs of this discussion can be found in earlier literature. In Israeli anthropology, one may see that this issue engaged anthropologists in the past, even if not that extensively. A prominent example of this is a Hebrew article by one of the leading anthropologists in Israel, Moshe Shokeid, an article whose title sheds light on the fundamental issue it is concerned with: "Anthropological Research in Israel: Involvement as Opposed to Looking from the Outside." This article was published in the book *The Generation of Transition*, which Shokeid compiled together with the anthropologist Shlomo Deshen in 1977. In the article, Shokeid points out the structural advantages that he benefited from as a researcher of immigrant Jews from the Atlas Mountains, benefits derived from his being both "stranger and kinsman" in the eyes of the people he studied as well as in in his own eyes. He relates that being an Israeli born to a family of European immigrants, he came to the study equipped with a curiosity that had been awakened by the significant cultural differences between him and the immigrants. But he believes that at the same time there are overlaps and similarities from the core fact that both the researcher and the subjects are Jews and Israeli. Moreover, unlike anthropologists who traveled far from their homes in Europe or North America for research, the limited geographic distance within Israel does not allow for a sharp detachment in the relationship between researcher and subjects upon completion of the fieldwork.[7] In his article Shokeid demands that anthropologists maintain a distance necessary to "have the ability to observe their own society from a position of detachment" (p. 43), but he also strives for intimacy as the "test of anthropologists and their future prospects, lies precisely in their (the anthropologists) ability to conduct research within their societies" (ibid.).

Even though in earlier years discussions were held about fieldwork "at home," since the 1980s the discussion concerning this type of research had changed in its scope, importance, and emphasis. The discussion was less about questions of the strategy with which to obtain the most complete and reliable information than it was about the analysis of the implications which stem from the fact that the researchers have preconceived positions on culture, class, gender, politics, and more. This awareness turned the discussion toward how these "positionings" affect the questions being asked and the way in which the anthropologists perceive the social and cultural lives of the subjects they are interested in observing. This is also bound to the recognition that the border that distinguished between the familiar home and between the other far away, which in the past anthropology carefully maintained, is blurred. At its core, this recognition is the result of historical-political developments: the liberation of "faraway" provinces, which were subject to the inquisitive eye of anthropologists, from the yoke of colonialism. The people in these districts refused to be passively displayed and took harsh critical and politically aware stands concerning the way anthropologists portrayed them, sometimes even opposing the conducting of any research within their communities.[8]

The developments that arose as an outcome of the blurred distinctions between the familiar and the Other are more relevant to anthropology in affluent countries, such as England and the United States. They are less typical of anthropology that has grown from "intermediate" or small-size countries or of anthropology that was shaped in countries under colonial rule. In the absence of economic resources, anthropologists in these countries tended to conduct research within the confines of their own nation-states. Not surprisingly, in countries where anthropology was in want of resources, recognition of the penetration of the borders between researchers and the fieldwork was more obvious. The boundaries were already blurred, even if intensive efforts were made to clarify them so that the research would resemble hegemonic anthropology.

In Israeli anthropology of meager resources (both in prestige and in material assets) the situation is similar.[9] Anthropologists found it difficult to raise funds for research outside the country and therefore concentrated their efforts on research "at home."[10] However, mainstream anthropology defined its mission as an effort to understand what was taking place in the "Other" districts in Israel (mainly among north African immigrants and Palestinians in Israel) and thus divided "the house" into "main tenants" and "secondary tenants." The division was expressed in the insistence to strengthen the borders separating "field research" and the "academic homefront," although this border was not preserved over long periods of time. The fact that the "subjects" could read the language of the anthropologist made maintaining the barrier difficult. A clear expression of the challenges posed by the blurring of borders is found in Yoram Bilu's book epilogue, where he shares a story about his inability as an researcher to maintain the boundary between his "house" (i.e., academic institution, his duties, functions, and a rationale for his actions) and his "field" (Bilu 2000). In his epilogue Bilu tells of the surprising appearance of the "folk healer" by the name of Rabbi Yaakov Wazzana, about whom he wrote the book, which retells the wonderful biography of Wazzana through the memories of different people who met him during his lifetime. Seemingly, Wazzana was supposed to sink into oblivion following his death in Morocco on the eve of the great emigration of Jews from there. As Bilu claims in his book, Wazzana was "entombed in another place, in another time" (Bilu 2000:121). It was therefore difficult to imagine the appearance of this phoenix, this legendary healer, in Israel in the late twentieth century. Without stating so explicitly, Bilu lets his readers understand (and I think quite correctly) that had it not been for the book's publication, then "nothing of his [Wazzana's] remains," as is stated in one of the titles of the closing chapters of the book. It appears that it is precisely the publication of this academic manuscript that triggered a desire among his admirers to memorialize him through activities. The early Hebrew version of the book received remarkable coverage both in the press and on single-channel television. Shortly afterward, Bilu, who was partly pulled in and partly came by his own desire, became involved in a series of meetings with different agents who desired to bring the memory of Wazzana back to life, using the academic legitimacy that Bilu had granted as leverage. Waqnin, a central player in the reawakening of the activity surrounding Wazzana, established an institution in memory of the healer in Be'er Sheva, the capital of south Israel, with most of the activity revolving around festivities commemorating the anniversary of his death. It is possible that the anthropological research about the healer is what brought about the phenomenon, which might otherwise not have come about were it not for the book. Thus, Bilu's assumption was undermined: an assumption that cultural realities are waiting for the anthropological researchers "out-there," realities that are disconnected from the actual research itself.

In retrospect, Bilu describes a struggle concerning the rights to Wazzana's story: a struggle as to the question of how the legendary healer is represented, while each side (Bilu the anthropologist and Waqnin, the "key informant") has its own unique sources for conducting a struggle for the profile of the character. Unsurprisingly, it appears that the modern anthropological divide between the "field" and the "academic homefront" that Bilu insists on preserving allows for the relatively peaceful coexistence of two stories that seemingly do not sit well together. Bilu relates that while the relationship between the anthropologist and the informant was preserved, on the content level there was a division; Bilu and Waqnin each wove a different ethnographic story about Wazzana. Each of the sides sought to perpetuate in a different way the winding story of Wazzana's life. In other words, the people in the anthropologist's study are not (*always*) passive in this dynamic research, especially if each of the players has a separate audience toward whom he is conducting his struggle for credibility.

Along with these issues is the question of ownership of cultural property. Let me briefly comment that this issue arises often, in a very clear and straightforward manner, in studies that focus on countries that were under colonial rule. Researchers have been asked to return cultural assets which they stole for their own benefit, as part of the colonial pillage. This claim is based on the resistance of postcolonial countries to the implementation of the "discovery doctrine" that originated in the European Middle Ages. The European countries had seen in North America a barren land and therefore gave its ownership to the representatives of the first country to "discover" it. Legally, the claim of refunding ownership is divided between claims of "real" assets (mainly material possessions, such as a claim for the refund of property stolen under Napoleon's occupation) and claims of spiritual/intellectual property (poetry, songs, folk tales, language, and so on, claims concerning which are often filed against anthropologists). Claims of the latter type emphasize that the transfer of spiritual/intellectual property is also an act of thievery that must be compensated. These claims have been recognized by UNESCO, which asserted that "cultural property constitutes a basic element of civilization and national culture."[11]

It should be noted that the claim on spiritual/intellectual property is quite complicated when the boundaries between the two sides ("exploiter" and "exploited") are not sharp, as is the case of fieldwork "at home." It is then difficult to base a claim on the act of stealing from one member of the community by another. The attempt to define the collective boundaries through ethnicity is futile due to the embedded essential assumptions about "culture," as well as the omnipotent stature of the national discourse. Indeed, in the case of Israel, the success of Zionism, the assertion that Jews constitute a nation, is so convincing that a demand is barely heard for anthropologists to return spiritual/intellectual property (except for weakly voiced claims made by individual activists from the spectrum of the Mizrahi Democratic Rainbow Coalition).

The issues that result from the blurring of the modern boundaries that divide between "field" and "academic homefront" are not unique to anthropology "at home." But the research "at home" intensified these issues, due to both the geographic and the cultural proximity and also to the absence of a collective colonial experience, which inspired sweeping opposition to anthropological research because of the identification between the colonial and anthropological projects (Asad 1973). Despite the different political contexts, Israeli anthropology clung for a long time to the Anglo-American model (with its colonialist traditions), which draws a clear distinction between the researcher and "his" subjects. One of the major political mechanisms for creating a border was established from the unspoken division of labor that relies on the ethnic identity of the participants. That is to say, the field of anthropology in Israel was mainly "Oriental" ("Arabs," "Bedouin," "Palestinians," "Sephardim," "immigrants from Islamic Countries," "immigrants from north Africa," etc.), while the researchers were mostly "Israeli" (namely, Jews whose family origins are from eastern Europe). However, this professional distinction was not consistent with the Zionist ideology that rejected the relevance of categorical boundary distinctions differentiating between non-identical Jewish populations. This position, which was adopted by the majority of the immigrants, affected their ability to voice significant opposition to cooperating with the anthropologists, similar to that which occurred to the researchers that arrived from colonialist countries. In the end, the most significant distinctive category, agreed upon by anthropologists and "Mizrahim" both, was shared Jewish nationalism.

In this context, Lavie and Swidenburg's article (Lavie and Swidenburg 1996) is interesting because of their desire to abolish the colonial distinction between "researcher" (usually a white European male) and the "field" (mostly Third World countries). According to them, this goal can be achieved by making anthropology itself into a field of research. Thus the research would strive to undermine anthropology's embedded authority. Even if politically and morally I adhere to this position, the underlying assumption is problematic because it obscures the presence of a boundary that is constituted from the very activity of the research. That is, the very decision to study a particular topic, even the most intimate of topics, turns it ipso facto into the "Other." One doesn't have to go as far away as the "African tribes" in order to construct Others. Distance is inherent in every (anthropological) study, even those the most empathic and close. I find more satisfactory the conclusion of anthropologist Kirin Narayan, who seeks to entirely eliminate the distinction between "ordinary" anthropologists and "native" anthropologists conducting "at home" research (Narayan 1993). The distinction, in and of itself, between different types of anthropologists, Narayan argues, harms the professional authority of "native" anthropologists, to the point of making them into some kind of professional informants. They become figures of authority on ethnographic data only, information providers for the white anthropologists, while the latter have the prestigious responsibility of providing theory and abstraction.

My argument somewhat continues Narayan's: even if anthropology would amend its ways and accept cultural knowledge derived from "native" anthropologists as "regular," in any case the act itself and even the intent to conduct research establishes a distance. So it is that I understand my mother's revelation; although I had reached the actual place of my birth, despite my reaching my intimate *axis mundi* (so to speak), the distance remained, a distance that hadn't allowed me to realize that I had found my own private foundation.

Issues that touch upon distance, estrangement, and alienation are one side of the Janus face of this book. The other, complementary side is longing, nostalgia, and yearning for unification of memories that will surface from the severed past, following the movement to other destinations. Indeed, my efforts to connect to the past and its spaces are nothing more than a manifestation of this disconnection. I will tell stories of tragic heroes who yearn to integrate their pasts and spaces, yet through this realize and understand in moments of insight that this yearning is the purest expression of that disconnection. The research literature and public image assume that these gaps between coherence and innocence, on one hand, and partiality and incompleteness, on the other, are part of postmodern experiences. After all, the existence of postmodernity and the philosophy standing at its foundation contrast themselves to the modern past (not to mention the traditional) by claiming an exposure of alienation and dissolution that disappeared or perhaps was obscured from the modern and traditional views (Baudrillard 1975, 1994).

Already in the next chapter we will see the existence of self-imposed distance and a certain alienation, created by the hero's desire to draft ethnography at home, for Jews that lived "far away." The chapter will focus on one Jew who lived in Morocco at the end of the nineteenth century. Even if the theoretical and methodological issues of self-ethnography are not found in the forefront of the discussion in that chapter, they are interjected and appear from time to time. These issues are fascinating not because of their analytical innovation, but because of the period to which they are relevant; the chapter deals with the period marking the stage in which European modernity is gaining momentum and the postmodern name is still unknown. Particularly, chapter 2 will discuss Yitzhak Ben Yais Halevi and the way in which he sketched the image of his community before eastern European Jews, while trying to overcome barriers of space and culture between the communities. Thus, our journey takes us toward Morocco, to a Morocco that meets with a new reality of an invasive Europe threatening to undermine the social and cultural order. Specifically, these are the social orders upon which relations between Muslims and the Jewish minority are based.

CHAPTER 2

"Amongst Our Faraway Brethren": Surfacing Memories of Suppressed Colonialism

I first became acquainted with the figure of Yizhak Ben Yais Halevi while I was still a student. I came across his writings thanks to the recommendation of Michael Abitboul, an influential historian of north African Jews in modern times. He suggested that I write a paper about Ben Yais Halevi's approach to the worship of holy men in Morocco. In addition to his polished and clever style, his writing fascinated me for a number of reasons: first, because it is clear that Ben Yais Halevi is keenly aware of the political dimensions of his writing and uses them toward political goals.

Second, his texts revealed connections between worlds that in my eyes, as a layman in relation to this period, seemed disconnected: worlds of religious Jewish content on one hand and ideas of Enlightenment on the other; there were unexpected connections between the religious and the secular. But above all, he fascinated me for two other reasons; one, because of the gap between the way Maghrebi Jews (a general term for Jews in Morocco, Algeria, Tunisia, and Libya) are portrayed in the writings of social scientists and the way they appear in his texts.[12] Mainly I am referring to the common and sharp distinction that exists between "tradition" and "modernity" and the different geographical usage of these terms in relation to north African and Asian countries, on one hand, and to Europe and America on the other. I will discuss this issue first, primarily to demonstrate how the character of Ben Yais Halevi deconstructs this image.

The second reason his writings fascinated me was the manner in which he revealed the complexity of the colonial experience of the Jews as a minority in Morocco. These two reasons are bound together by the symbolically

FIGURE 1. Early influences of Europe (circa 1900s). Notice the cartridge at the right serving as a flower vase.

peripheral place where Ben Yais Halevi's editors placed his articles. It is my opinion that this positioning is a historical foresight of the attitude of eastern European emigrants toward Maghreb Jews upon their arrival in Israel. But my criticism of the scholarly and popular attitude toward Maghrebi Jews is one that is bound by discomfort. In this chapter I will expand on these areas and clarify them.

SOME COMMENTS ON THE STUDY OF NORTH AFRICAN JEWS IN ISRAEL

From the beginning of the great immigration, in the nineteen-fifties, to Israel, the Jews of north Africa have been the subject of much research in the social sciences and the focus of anthropological and sociological curiosity. I will not take issue here with the critical, mostly justified opinions that have been written about the epistemic, ontological, political, and ideological failures of "Israeli society" in general and the implications of these writings on studies about the great immigration from north Africa to Israel. For my purposes here, I will just note that this criticism was being made against the recruitment of social sciences to the Zionist enterprise. Uri Ram—one of the most significant and prominent indicators of this critical trend—claims without any embellishment: "From its establishment as a defined area of study and research, Israeli sociology has been connected by the umbilical cord to the ruling establishment, has adopted its viewpoint and provided it with an intellectual seal of approval, or seemingly 'scientific' authorization" (Ram 1993:7), strong words.

Despite the skepticism of critical research in relation to "empirical reality" which is presented by institutional sociology, a number of rather surprising nonreflexive expressions has been revealed. The first among them appears minor, almost petty. I am referring to the tendency of critical sociological writing to swallow up anthropology, to the point where it is indistinguishable as a unique discipline with its own history, writing style, and independent academic institutes. Critical sociology in Israel overshadows anthropology, mainly by not distinguishing between the two disciplines, thereby continuing the prevailing trend of disregard that was set by established sociology. This disregard is significant precisely because in all universities these disciplines are institutionally partnered; they share quarters, something forced upon both disciplines as a result of historic developments (whose details will not be discussed here); they are partnered, but always unequally. Anthropology in Israel is subordinate to sociology. Symbolically, this inferiority is expressed in the department names of universities in Israel, in each and every one of them, sociology appears first.[13] In concrete political university affairs, this is expressed in the fact that in all the departments among the four main universities in Israel, there are a majority of sociologists. The subjugation of anthropology allows for the deep divisions that exist between the disciplines to be ignored, while relating to both disciplines as "sociology." As such, anthropology becomes a satellite to sociology at best, or as an unwanted afterthought at worst.[14]

Even the longtime disproportionate institutional proximity has not succeeded in lessening the disciplinary allegiance of the researchers (even if some sociologists and anthropologists may be found who somewhat deviate from the rule). Historically, the roots of the differences derive from several sources: different interpretations of similar theoretical-social approaches on which the disciplines relied; differences between areas of research (traditionally, sociologists studied Europe and America and anthropologists mainly studied the rest of the world) and the separate methodologies of the disciplines (anthropological fieldwork as opposed to the reliance of sociology on quantitative methods and historical research).

Precisely because of the profound differences between the disciplines even at the most basic level, I would first like to emphasize some similarities regarding the study of the north African immigrants in Israel; most researchers—whether sociologists or anthropologists—related to the Mizrahim, the Easterners, as a "problem." A clear example, even though far from being exhaustive, is a collection of articles in the *Megamot* Journal which was published in 1984. Its declared goal was to propose a rectification of the volume that had appeared some decades previously (in 1952), where a discussion was presented about immigrants from north Africa and Asia. As the editor of the later edition, Moshe Lissak notes, his desire is to "disengage from all a priori normative-ideological assumptions" (Lissak 1989:147–55) which were characteristic of the *Megamot* Journal in 1952. But the title of the journal in 1984, "The Ethnic Problem in Israel: Continuity and Change," in itself indicates that this disengagement was unsuccessful, as the majority of the research articles studied Mizrahim and only a minority were directed at Israeli society at large. Ashkenazim are discriminated against; they were not a subject of interest for the researchers. In contrast, the Mizrahim were regarded as "problematic." Another similarity, no less important, between the disciplines relates to the unfounded assumption that the encounter between the immigrants from the Islamic countries and the veterans in Israel is always an encounter between a traditional and a modern society. Thus, for example, writes sociologist Moshe Lissak: "The meeting between the veterans who built the relatively modern social institutional system and between the immigrants from the East, most of whom had strong ties to the traditional cultural system did not take place on an equal and symmetrical basis" (Lissak 1989:135).

Today some social scientists are attempting to release the Mizrahim from their "problematic" status. A prominent example of one such attempt can be found in a book published within the framework of the Forum of Social and Cultural Studies by the Van Leer Institute in Jerusalem. The book, edited by Hannan Hever, Yehuda Shenhav, and Pnina Mutzafi-Haller, includes a collection of articles by anthropologists, sociologists, political scientists, and other literary people, who from a postcolonial perspective attempt to suggest a new critical style of studying Mizrahim (Hever, Shenhav, and Mutzafi-Haller 2002). A quick browse through the book reveals a sad truth: the existence of a significant "class" division among Mizrahim. Immigrants from Iraq are presented as the highest class, and they merit a disproportionate representation in the book relative to their numbers in Israel. They are presented as active individuals

FIGURE 2. Early influences of Europe (circa 1930s). My maternal grandfather in the streets of Casablanca.

and not as a wide social group. In contrast, the remaining immigrants, including those who arrived from north Africa, are presented as one general mass, without faces or names.

Despite the significant common interface found in sociological and anthropological writings, there are distinct differences between them in regard to what has been known by various names such as "Sephardim," "Eastern Jews," "Orientals," or "Mizrahim" (the differences in name reflect, among other things, a process of refinement of speech and a blurring of politics embodied within research and language about this particular Israeli group). One of the innate theoretical differences is connected to the different assignment of status for the "culture" of the immigrants to Israel (See, for example, Goldberg and Bram 2008). While "established" sociologists—as part of their theoretical and ideological understanding of the "melting pot"[15]—saw culture as a residual category, destined to disappear over the years due to the immigrants' integration in state institutions, anthropologists regarded culture as a critical player, shedding light on the lives of the immigrants. According to anthropologists, the cultural differences between "veteran Israelis" and immigrants from Islamic countries are at the heart of the life experiences of the latter. Culture was seen as a set of values and expectations, clearly ethical, moral, and religious, which guided the actions of the immigrants and constituted an interpretive framework that helped them make sense of their experiences in Israel. According to these anthropologists, culture, as an interpretive framework or, in any case, as a system that served to guide their actions, arrived with the immigrants from their countries of origin. As far as they were concerned, even if the immigrants' social reality changed overnight upon their arrival, the degree in which the cultural system adapted was slow.[16]

The different analytical views of culture are associated with another crucial difference between sociology and anthropology: a difference connected to the attitude toward the time frame under discussion. Sociologists tended to focus on the present, and on the dynamics taking place between the different cultural groups in Israel, while anthropologists looked at the immigrants' past experience, when they were still in their countries of origin, as an important key to understanding the present (see, for example, Goldberg 1985). Ironically though, the disregard for the past in the critical post-Zionist sociological writings, in fact mirrors the Zionist outlook which denies its diasporic past (Raz-Krakotzkin 1993, 1994).

Since anthropologists attached great importance to the culture and past traditions of the immigrants as a contextual interpretive factor, they were accused of being indirect contributors to the preservation of new variations of old traditions. These, according to the secular Zionist perspective and according to the established sociological model of modernization, should have been disappearing or vanished altogether. The comprehensive work of the anthropologist Yoram Bilu, for example, regarding the jarring emergence of "worshiping holy men" in the Israeli public arena in the mid-1980s was an object of strong condemnation to the point that his study itself gave legitimacy to the phenomena and contributed to a regression of Israeli society into (ghetto-like customs) a type of "diasporization."

The focus of anthropology on the north African immigrants' past contributed in an essential and positive way to understanding their life and experiences in Israel. Yet the image of the past itself as portrayed in anthropological writings was lacking and problematic. Reading anthropological manuscripts

FIGURE 3. Migration (1962): separating from family grave. Left to right: my mother at her mother's grave with her brother, sister, and father.

about these immigrants, even as recently as the nineteen-eighties, revealed a portrait of their past which characteristically undermined the stated mission of anthropologists, which was to challenge the negative image of these same immigrants.

From my point of view, the most problematic feature was that by focusing on Jews who lived in the Atlas Mountains, the anthropological studies largely ignored the colonial experience of Maghrebi Jews in general, and in particular of those from Morocco. In this way, they ignored the fact that due to the early influences of colonization, even before France took over Morocco, the Jewish population of this country was essentially urban. Indeed, in this context, attention should be given to the words of Michael Abitbol, a historian of north African Jewry, who notes that when calculating the number of Jews who in the beginning of the twentieth century lived in the new coastal cities (such as Essawira, Al-Jadida, and Casablanca) together with those in the more established cities within Morocco (such as Fez and Marrakech): "It becomes clear, that the Moroccan community was an urban community on the eve of the French Protectorate" (Abitbol 1985–86:307).

The consistent disregard of anthropologists of the colonial experience is not accidental, even if not necessarily intentional. Let me briefly mention that all of north Africa was under the colonial rule of France, Britain, Spain, and Italy beginning in the nineteenth century up until the middle of the twentieth century. Algeria was conquered by France in 1830 (it gained independence in 1962). The establishment of the French Protectorate in Tunisia was in 1881 (it gained independence in 1956); a year later Egypt was taken over by Britain (and gained independence in 1922). Italy invaded Libya in 1911 (independence was gained in 1952), and a year later the French Protectorate spread to Morocco (ending in 1956).

The different styles of colonialism had a diverse influence on the subjected populations. These disparities were a result of different policies adopted by the various colonial regimes as to their degree of involvement in the life style and management of affairs in the countries and provinces under their control. Often there wasn't any uniformity even within the various regions ruled by a particular colonial state. Thus, France adopted a relatively involved style in Algeria and a lesser one in Morocco and Tunisia. Despite this policy and despite the fact that Morocco's period of direct colonialism was relatively short, in comparison to other north African countries, lasting only half a century (1912–52), it underwent a profound change due to the *mission civilisatrice* (civilizing mission). Half a century before the French Protectorate began, already in 1862, the first Jewish educational institute of Alliance (a Paris-based international Jewish organization founded in 1860 to promote the ideals of the *mission civilisatrice)* was established in Morocco, and gradually more and more similar institutions were established throughout Morocco. The Jewish community underwent rapid changes, mainly due to the establishment of a comprehensive educational system, from kindergarten to high school, which operated according to a curriculum which matched that of France (Laskier 1983; Rodrigue 1990). It is important to emphasize that, for the most part, Moroccan Jews were willingly exposed to the new socialization through the Alliance Jewish educational network and saw in it an instrument of liberation.

As such, many of the Moroccan immigrants to Israel were exposed, in varying degrees of intensity, to the French educational system. However, as the Israeli public has, at best, largely ignored this fact, so too anthropologists didn't apply any special significance to the influences of the colonial past. I think that this disregard on the part of the anthropologists was a result of a number of deeply rooted assumptions, disciplinary and political, which were often overlooked even if they were consistent with the spirit of the times. I will not expand on this issue here, but just comment that the lack of reference to this period is consistent with the anthropological legacy that searched after the exotic and sought to obsessively engage with emphasizing cultural diversity. Not in vain do some anthropologists ironically testify that anthropology is a discipline of over-exaggerated cultural differences. This exaggeration was purely rhetorical and was meant to argue to what extent diversity is misleading and is really nothing more than a different form of social knowledge similar to that of the West. Apparently the classic anthropological exercise of making cultural diversity into something familiar likewise served the anthropologists in Israel.

In American and British anthropological studies in Morocco, which profoundly influenced many Israeli anthropologists, the search for the cultural core is noticeably evident, just as the French-European colonial influence placed a stain on the Maghreb "authenticity." An example can be found in Paul Rabinow's book, considered critical and revolutionary at the time it was published (Rabinow 1977). In his book Rabinow describes the structural process of his work in Morocco. The research structure is described as a journey that was born out of his disgust with America's entanglement in a war not hers. He felt the hopeless despair on American campuses in their criticism toward the nation's policies. In his journey, Rabinow turns toward France, and upon discovering the "student's rebellion," his flame of hope is rekindled. After a short stay he continues to Morocco, where he meets *colons* (French colonists in north Africa) who remained in Morocco after the protectorate ended. The highlight of his trip is an unmediated encounter with the "authentic" Morocco, the one yet untouched by France, which he discovers through a "key informant" who goes by the name of Ali. Only from the time he meets with Ali, does the study become significant for him. Beforehand, the encounters are veiled by the presence of the French, who cover up the long-desired ethnographic reality: Morocco without the French presence. At the same time, Clifford Geertz, Rabinow's teacher (and the object of Rabinow's sharp criticism), carried out his studies in an urban environment, in Sefrou, Morocco (Geertz 1968), and thus didn't give in to the dictate of a search for the "authentic" Moroccan experience. Israeli anthropologists studying immigrants from the Maghreb countries continued this trend of searching for Moroccans who hadn't met with (or been contaminated by) France. Thus, this study offered a part-romantic and part-orientalist perspective, which unintentionally echoed commonplace images of the Israeli public such as "two fingers from France/Paris," "Farangi/Frankie," "the Moroccan Knife" (knife-throwing/wielding

Moroccan), "primitives," "not nice," and so on. Even if anthropologists had tried with all their strength to destroy these harmful images, their very disregard of the influences of French colonialism undermined their moral goals. Therefore, it was not enough that the anthropological expertise did nothing to undermine the common image of "Moroccans" in Israel: it actually worked to strengthen it. Let it be noted, that this duality is not unique to Israeli anthropology. It is deeply rooted in the tension between the European colonial and humanist sources in anthropology in general (Asad 1973).

COLONIALISM AND ENLIGHTENMENT: ANOTHER PERSPECTIVE

Unlike Israeli social scientists, their fellow historians (of modern times) did not overlook the colonialist influence on north African Jews in general and Moroccan Jews in particular.[17] Perhaps this can be explained by the conservative tendencies of major Israeli historians who studied Maghrebi Jews. The modern history of north Africa is described most often by conservative historians as an outcome of its encounter with the emerging European states. Accordingly, most of the historic references to this period are influenced by (naïve or sophisticated) theories of modernization. Only a handful of historic works present a multifaceted account of the relationships that existed between the colonial powers and their subjects.[18] Most of them describe Maghrebi history exclusively from a European modernist perspective. Few are the works that do not treat modernization as a desirable process, unidirectional, universal, and dichotomous: dynamic modernization on the one hand and static traditionalism on the other.[19] In this chapter I wish to join the steadily growing number of anthropologists seeking to overcome these orientalist assumptions. I will do this by presenting the worldviews of one Jewish community in Morocco. I want to focus on the city of Essawira from one person's perspective, as stated—that of Yitzhak Ben Yais Halevi. This man, a nineteenth-century metropolitan Jew, fully understood and embraced the exciting changes that were taking place in his community (in Morocco) following the deepening and expanding influence of western Europe on his personal life, as well as on that of his community.

I would like to present the formative experience of the oppressed, in view of the growing European colonialism in north Africa: I will emphasize how surprising, varied, and contradictory are the faces of this experience. This emphasis is not entirely new; the most prominent literary figure representing this view is, of course, Frantz Fanon. But, rather than referring to his work, I will discuss a different thinker who is often overshadowed by Fanon. I am alluding to the most outstanding representative of this perspective on the Jews of Maghreb, Albert Memmi. Memmi shows that in the context of north African French colonization the Jew was subject to a unique subordination, full of contradictions and not at all similar to that of the Muslim experience. Mostly, the Jews aimed to tie their fate to the French; they identified with the cultural ideas that colonialism represented, and most importantly, with the universal message used to justify the colonialist regime. In this way, the Jew was radically different from the Muslim, and this identification with the colonialist culture created a process which in the end only increased his suffering. However, politically, says Memmi, Tunisian and Moroccan Jews were part of the larger group of subjects. Such was the will of the oppressor: without saying so openly he carefully rationed legal and political portions of "Westernization" for the Jews. Naturalization was permitted only in tiny amounts. The fact of the matter was, Memmi claims, that the Jew was partner to the oppressed in the oppressed land in the colonial restrictions and harassments. But Memmi immediately continues by stating that the Jew also felt this historical oppression, which was absolutely real, and he felt it differently than the Muslims. From a social and psychological standpoint, the Jew's problems were more complicated than that of the Muslim (Memmi 2003).

According to Memmi, the problem of the Jews stemmed from the unique historical process of colonization itself. At the beginning, colonization, which was a catastrophe for the Muslims, served as a de facto release of the Jews from their low class position as a *dhimmis* (dependent, referring to non-Muslim monotheistic minorities in Islamic states). The Jews benefited from this situation and looked positively toward the optimistic possibilities that this new model might offer. Thus, Carlos De Nesry wrote, from a semi auto-ethnographic perspective with a touch of orientalist nostalgia, about the changes taking place before his eyes in his city of Tangier in northern Morocco: "The Jews of two generations are leaving the Mellah, marching before my eyes. Here is the older generation: He has a long beard, a dark Jellabiya (traditional Arab garment), a skullcap of disgrace upon his head. However, his behavior demonstrates proud contempt. This is the royal misery of sages" (De Nesry 1958:12). In contrast, the next generation walks thus: "He carries a mock existentialism of this century's young men, his hair is shorn in Marlon Brando style. His shiny shoes are dainty as he walks mincingly on the paths of Gomorrah. He aspires to be at the forefront of progress, even though he stands at the crossroads of snobbism (De Nesry 1958:12). The metaphor of the journey out of Mellah is in itself the entry to modernity.

In Memmi's opinion, this enthusiasm for the liberating aspects of colonialism explains that, despite the criticisms the Jews had against colonialism, there remained a degree of moderate forgiveness toward it. The forgiveness did not, of course, derive from the acceptance of colonialism, but from the fact that as representatives of Europe, French colonizers carried with them the message of liberation. However, even though they had felt this gratitude, the Jews were enslaved just like the Muslims. For, as suggested by Memmi, the situation of a slave is to be in a state of misfortune: political bondage, economic exploitation, and cultural degradation. This enslavement was especially difficult because parallel to the physical exploitation and oppression, he (the oppressor) formulated a position of moral, spiritual, and cultural superiority toward the enslaved. In places of darkness such as these, Memmi says, the oppressor embodies the luxury and the power, the material comforts and the spiritual superiority when, openly or secretly, a passionate desire is awakened within the enslaved to become like the oppressor.

In this historical process, the Jew, unlike the Muslim, cannot go back to who or to what he was before (or at least, to hold onto that illusion the way his Muslim neighbor can). He also cannot become assimilated into the oppressor. Memmi, of course, refers to a particular oppressor—the French one—that acted according to specific cultural premises. One of the colonialist traits of the French was their ambition to implement the *mission civilisatrice*, which in the Jewish case was implemented mainly by the Ittihad. Yet, albeit its universal rhetoric of *liberté, égalité, fraternité,* French colonialism was nothing more than an illusion. It didn't intend to change the basic cultural identity of the enslaved, transforming him into a full fledged Frenchman even if he would recite words of praise about the national history dating back to "*nos ancêtres les Gaulois*" (our ancestors the Gauls). This rhetoric of an embracing liberation is, according to John Comaroff, "thin varnish" for the main task of colonialism in its classic form: the desire to discover the expanse and to occupy the territory, in the name of "redemption" and "modernization" (Comaroff and Comaroff 1991).

Indeed, according to Memmi, one must not assume that there are uniform responses to the European colonialist violence. The response varies according to one's religious or ethnic category. This argument will serve me only as a starting point. Based on Ben Yais Halevi, and as a refinement of the above argument, what I would like to show is that even within a specific ethnic category there were varied colonial experiences. The degree of exposure to colonial violence differed depending on the social status within the group. Some within a specific group had it in their ability to channel this power for their benefit.

It becomes evident, then, that there is an emancipating component in the colonial experience. Thus colonialism does not completely define the enslaved person, even though it disrupts the previous social order. The failure of the colonialist program to civilize its subjects does not only stem from overcoming the exploitive rationale, because, as Homi Bhabha claims, the colonial process was not lacking in self-skepticism, as some may have thought. It does not even operate from a large master plan that it has set out for itself.[20] It also does not actually implement what it set out to do. I am suggesting that sometimes there are positive results that will benefit the downtrodden. These may come about unintentionally, as the by-product of contradictory logics that unfolded from an intricate and complicated process of implementing a colonialist plan. Such cracks provide options for action among weak individuals and groups; they recruit colonialism for their benefit in order to achieve goals that otherwise they could not obtain. This capability is the real freedom of the enslaved, a limited freedom that sets into motion the beginning of the erosion of colonialism, and heralds in its replacement with a postcolonial state.

*

As stated previously, in this chapter I will focus on one place, on one historical time, and on a single character. The place: the port city Essawira, located about three hundred kilometers south of Casablanca, on the Atlantic coast. The time: the last years of the nineteenth century (specifically between the years 1891 and 1894). The character: Yitzhak Ben Yais Halevi (~1850–94), a young man of the city who is captivated by the ideas of the European Enlightenment.[21]

I became familiar with Ben Yais Halevi through his letters and through Daniel Schroeter's writings. Schroeter, a social historian who studied and wrote extensively about the Jewish community in Essawira, based his studies on archive materials and on a column Ben Yais Halevi wrote in *Hatzfira*—one of the Hebrew-language publications of the Jewish Enlightenment, located in Warsaw, Poland.[22] From the accumulated knowledge about him we see, as noted, that he was influenced by European Enlightenment ideas. Indirect evidence of his affinity for the Jewish Enlightenment can be found in his occupation: he was a modest bookseller in his hometown. This profession also testifies to his complex and contradictory position in the social fabric of the Jewish community in the city: on one hand, he is educated, he is aware of global developments, and he possesses an impressive knowledge of world Jewish culture (it is worthwhile to pay attention to the wealth of references he uses in his writings, based on diverse fields and disciplines, as I will present below), and on the other hand, his occupation as a book salesman is not highly profitable and his financial status is not particularly impressive. Evidence of Ben Yais Halevi's low status relative to the education he possessed was expressed in his place of residence; he lived in the mellah of the city, as opposed to the more comfortable area—the Kasbah, where the wealthy Jews lived (such as the Elmaliach, Corcos, and Abatan families, and others).

Embodied within Ben Yais Halevi's writings is the clever recognition of how powerful are the political and economic European forces and their superiority over Morocco. Indeed, Ben Yais Halevi's initiative to write a column stems from his desire to recruit this political influence in order to change internal decisions in Morocco that concerned a certain village where Jews lived.[23] I will quote his first letter in its entirety:[24]

> Mogador (Morocco). A twenty-hour journey from our city lives the government minister l'a qaid Iyad l' Menbehi; he governs three tribes: Nafifa, Damsira, Saksawa, and within his administration are two Jewish streets, Yeludzan and Abdallah, which encompass six hundred people. Our fellow Jews have resided in these regions for seventy years, and have known quiet and tranquility in this province; they built homes with their money and God blessed them with sheep and cattle etc. They do their business honestly, and lived in peace with the people of the land and were not oppressed by them. Last month, the Minister went to receive the Lord our King, Moulay Hassan [1873–94] on his visit to the city of Muakyis [probably meaning Marrakech], as did all the ministers with a gift worthy of his dignity. After ten days the Minister returned home and brought with him a cruel and terrible dictate, he sent for the Jews, who were living without worry, and told them the King's decree, that an irrevocable decision had been made and that they must leave all the places under his jurisdiction immediately, that not a single Jew would be allowed to be seen or remain within the kingdom. The words that came from his mouth were like a stab in the hearts of our brothers. There was terrible grief and sadness, to which nothing can be compared, which filled the chambers of their wretched hearts, and they stood in stunned silence, helplessly caught in their own passing thoughts with fear taking hold of them and their eyelids dark with gloom. I do not have the strength to describe their state. When the first moments of panic subsided they pleaded and prayed. They burst out with cries and their eyes filled with tears, but no ransom could avail them, and they begged the Minister for pardon, or that he should give them a little time in order to try and salvage their properties and belongings, but he closed his ears to their pleas, and would not go back on the words, and he placed twelve officers over them to force them out

as quickly as possible. How terrible this is! The unfortunate people, they, their wives and children, with dying hearts and eternal pain, left their homes in such a weak state. They managed to save some of their property and went to hide at their Mohammedan [Muslim] neighbors, until the danger passed and the remainder of their lives they depended on G-d to send them salvation. A terrible thing as this has not been seen from the time that the Moroccan kingdom was established until today, and we are in great fear, lest all the other village ministers follow suit, since the majority of Jews in this province live in the villages.

The heart of our Lord the King is kindly towards Israel, but his ministers and advisers are at the root of this damage. My dear brothers, the honored Minister, the Austrian-Hungarian Consul, "who seeks the good of his people," Mr. Reuven Elmaliach (May the Lord preserve and keep him well) tried with all his strength to help his unfortunate brothers and wrote letters of appeal to ministers and rulers of lands. He spoke with the consuls of kingdoms in an attempt to prevent this terrible thing; he also wrote to the Alliance organization in Paris and London to request their assistance in facing this disaster. May G-d be with him, and reward him with good things.

Therefore, Mr. publisher Sir, I request that you bring this letter to the readers of "Hatzfira" to inspire pity and compassion in the hearts of our elder brothers in other kingdoms towards their brothers scattered and oppressed by savages without righteousness and without justice.

YITCHAK BEN YAIS HALEVI, (*Hatzfira*, 1891, 67, p. 269)

And so, the first time Ben Yais Halevi addresses the newspaper he seeks the support of European Jewry. He hopes they will use their influence on their respective colonialist governments to intervene and improve the living conditions of Moroccan Jews. These steps affirm his support for colonialism much more than the passive support of the Jews as described by Albert Memmi. Ben Yais Halevi's belief in the power of influence Europe has is unlimited. He encourages the intervention of both influential Jews (such as Edmond de Rothschild or Moses Montefiore) and the European governments. Ben Yais Halevi demands the involvement of influential Jews in Europe because he recognizes their ability to act and to have a positive influence on Jewish life in Morocco. Thus, in contrast to the accepted opinion of historians as to the negligible impact of Moses Montefiore's renowned trip to Morocco, Ben Yais Halevi saw it as having substantial benefits:[25]

In times past, Jews, men and women, would go barefoot throughout the city, except on the Jewish streets, where they had permission to wear shoes.[26] And

> if there was any Jew who was guilty in the eyes of the City Minister, the police would attack him; they would push him to the ground and beat him with whips and ropes of sewn leather until his blood was flowing into the ground. From the year 5624 [1863] the Crown of our Glory, Lord Sir Moses Montefiore (May his merit protect us) got up and took the long journey and came to our country to ask mercy from the King for his beaten and tortured brothers; and the King promised to watch over us kindly. From that time on, the Jews walk around the entire city in shoes, and for any crime or sin or iniquity, and for anything that is said it is, until the Minister hears them both, there is no greater or smaller punishment then imprisonment. However, with a reasonable bribe, he will be required to sit in jail for only a few days. Money releases prisoners, and if the captive doesn't offer money, he will not be released.
>
> (*Hatzfira*, 145, p. 589)

Shortly after his first letter, Ben Yais Halevi writes a long series of reports, which appear in his column in the *Hatzfira* newspaper. He writes dozens of reports over three years. The column receives the unsurprising title of "Amongst Our Distant Brothers." I will not waste words on the contextual framing of Ben Yais Halevi's writing in this title that transforms Moroccan Jews into exotic, ethnographic, distant subjects. I will only point out that the conceptualization of "close" and "far" depends on one's political stand as to the place of the center. Although Essawira was far from Warsaw, the emphasis in the title on distance as central indicates that the editors were intent on more than just marking geographic distance without any hierarchical meaning.

Ben Yais Halevi's column abruptly stopped in 1894. A few months after the last column was published a brief article appeared, signed by two friends, announcing the untimely death (at age forty-five) of Ben Yais Halevi.

COLONIALISM AND ITS EFFECTS ON ESSAWIRA AS VIEWED BY BEN YAIS HALEVI

Essawira was intended to be a central port city in Morocco, a city of "nationalities of merchants" (an international city based on commerce) in Ben Yais Halevi's words. It was established by Sultan Sidi Muhammed Ben Abdallah in the mid-eighteenth century (1764), who requested, in addition to the profits of the port taxes that he collected, to be allowed to compete with well-established port cities over which he didn't have control. At this time his rule was not very solidly based, and like many Moroccan rulers before and after him, he could not fully control all the areas of Morocco. The boundaries of "Blad el-Makhzen"—that is, the areas where the ruler succeeded in imposing his authority (expressed both symbolically and concretely in his ability to collect taxes)—changed from ruler to ruler and from period to period. The actions of weaker rulers, concerning "Blad a-Siba" (the strips of land which the monarch had no control), diminished the areas under their control. By constructing a large and new competing port, Ben Abdallah sought to increase his hold on the Atlantic coastal region. Additionally, he wanted to create economic dependency of the rebel tribes around Essawira by establishing through the port a new economy (Schroeter 1988). Ben Abdallah attained considerable success, such that until the establishment of the modern port in Casablanca by the French regime, Essawira was the largest and most important of the ports in Morocco. The port reached the peak of its success during the period when the hero of our story lived (Schroeter 1987). Just as sea ports open new horizons, so too they invite new economic pressures, and so the independence that the Sultan Ben Abdallah sought was quickly replaced by economic dependency on Europe. The beginning of the colonial presence in the city is not marked by direct expressions of political or military control, but rather by an intensifying process of expanding economic influence even before there was a direct hold on the city. The Moroccan rulers realized that their country was exposed to growing and varying pressures from the European countries. This is vividly evident in commerce. Ben Yais Halevi is aware of the booming trade with Europe and even knows the details of the coming and goings of the ships arriving at his hometown.

> Each month, on a regular basis, two English steam ships, a Spanish ship and two German ships arrive [at our port]. They bring various goods to different merchants and carry the grain of our land to Europe. This is in addition to other ships that sometimes come to private traders. All European leaders trade here [at our port].
>
> (*Hatzfira*, 143, 581)

"Most of the merchants and the wealthy are from amongst our brothers the Jews," he writes later, in continuation of the above letter, and immediately, in order to emphasize the Jewish character of the trade, adds, "and the European trade is mostly in the hands of the Jews. On Saturdays and Jewish Holidays there is almost no one working and all of the simple people celebrate with us, '*none went out, and none came in.*'"

Even though Ben Yais Halevi was not counted among the elite in his community, he provides his readers with many informative details concerning the economic activity of the wealthy merchants in the city.[27] He appears to have had a panoramic perspective; he knows which cities trade (London, Marseilles, Lisbon, Hamburg, the Canary Islands) and knows the goods exported ("abundant amounts of olive oil . . . sweet almonds, bitter almonds, cattle skins and goat skins in large quantities . . . sheep wool, wax, cumin, sesame, citron, ostrich feathers, nuts, dates, beans, peas, maize, durra (sorghum) and sometimes gold dust or ivory"). These goods, he reports to his readers, arrive in Morocco from all over Africa, flowing through Morocco to the city "and from there goes off to many different places." He also knows what is imported from Europe ("Cloth, sugar, coffee, tea, perfumes, iron bars, solid iron, tin, wool clothes, silk clothes, flax threads, wool, silk threads, gold thread, mercury, sulfur, buffalo skins, medicinal drugs, smoking tobacco . . . but the main goods are imported from London"). Not only was Ben Yais Halevi knowledgeable about the comings and goings, but he also understood the method of distribution: "The rich merchants have agents and partners in every city and village, they send them European goods on camels and in their place merchandise from our land is sent out."

Like any other port city, and in fact like any community located on the border, Essawira soon discovered smuggling: "Weapons, gun barrels, swords . . . all forbidden by the government to come into the city, but by various schemes they found their way into the city, as *money answers all things*. Once in the city they were permitted, and they could be sold in broad daylight" (compare McMurray 2001).

It is evident in Ben Yais Halevi's writing that he is excited about the commercial encounter with Europe and the opportunities it offers. But his great detailing of the goods exported from Morocco also shows that he was proud of the goods produced in his country.

Although Ben Yais Halevi sees the positive influence and impact of the fertile commercial encounters with Europe, he is not pleased with the division of wealth among the Jews. Somewhat bitterly, he reports to *Hatzfira* readers on the class division within the Jewish community: "The very wealthy from al-kasbah live in the upper part of town with large courtyards and, do their business in the lower section. The middle class have shops throughout the city streets; and even though the Jews do not have permission to live wherever they choose, they can trade and do business anywhere they desire."

In other words, Ben Yais Halevi claims that even though the Jews are dhimmi, and as such are forbidden to live outside the walls of the mellah, their high economic status as the king's merchants allows the wealthy to ignore this prohibition. This exception was directed particularly at three important families: the Corcos, Elmaliach, and Afriat families (Abitbol 1977, 1978).

Elsewhere, he provides further detail of the economic structure of the Jewish community in his city:

> Our town has two thousand Jewish families and they do not reside in one area. The wealthy dwell among the high status residents in al-kasbah together with the Christians, city ministers and representatives of the Kingdom. The middle and lower status live on al-Mallah, Jews' Street, at its lowest most dreary point, in narrow quarters, mostly with two families sharing a house. The dirty streets and market places where they dwell arouse the disgust of anyone who chances by them. The rich Jews living in our town know nothing apart from their trading and transactions, their days are laden with strife, and they know no peace. Only a small number of them watch over our poor brethren with compassion, while most take no notice of them. There are those to whom G-d has been kind, who own lavish homes and courtyards, and earn more from their properties than from their trade. In addition to their own property, they have real estate that they rent from the King cheaply and rent out to others at high prices, through this they make a good salary without having to work hard.
>
> The people of the al-Mallah are artisans who live off their labor and their hard daily work. There are some who trade, each according to his means, though the majority is poor and do not own any property.

Ben Yais Halevi is not always so candid in his criticism. He can be careful and subtle. But, despite the language of courtesy and caution that he sometimes employs toward the leadership of his community, his criticism of the economic abyss that exists between the rich and poor is piercing. In his opinion, stratification is a result of political capability, which is mainly expressed through access to local sources of power; the wealthy Jews in Essawira have access to the king and the heads of the colonial administration in the city. They rent real estate from the officials at cheap prices and, in turn, rent them out to Jews of Mellah at exorbitant rates. But the main resource of the king's traders lies in their ability to acquire the protection of European countries. "Anyone working in commerce should endeavor with all his strength to be under the auspices of a European government—that is, an acquaintance or partner should send him a letter from the government through the delegates in Tangiers, stating that he is an agent authorized on their behalf, and is hereby under supervision of the consul, in order that nothing bad should befall him. Without this his life hangs by a thread, and his money is in jeopardy" (*Hatzfira*, 143, 581).

Elsewhere he employs quasi-prophetic language; "In a few years our city will be exalted and become the main city of trade. The King has given an order to his ministers and officials to build houses and courtyards for dwelling and trade for the Europeans coming to settle in our town; and the command of the kingdom is powerful indeed" (*Hatzfira,* 146, 593).

The results of historical research coincide with what Ben Yais Halevi sees from his unique perspective; historians tell us that Jews served as representatives for European countries and thus were protected by those countries who wanted faithful representatives who would promote their economic and political interests (for example, Abitbol 1985–86). This patronage, in the form of official protection, was an item in high demand among the wealthy Jews of Morocco because it bypassed their limiting status as dhimmi, though this thereby sparked anger among the many Muslims in the city (Stillman 1979).

Of course, only a small minority of Jews were able to enjoy such benefits. Essawira, as typical of Moroccan coastal cities, should have been more lenient in its attitude toward Jews. But, Ben Yais Halevi regretfully points out, that in contrast to other coastal cities his city still meticulously maintained the limited dwelling areas for Jews. Except for a few lucky individuals, who served as representatives for colonial powers, the vast majority of Jews lived within the confining walls of the mellah. This confinement to the mellah was difficult. As the weighty words of Ben Yais Halevi reveal, the demographic problems were compelling when the Jews were unable to expand their borders. So the Jews appealed to the European representatives in Morocco with a request to expand the area of the mellah: "When the French emissary, Lord Papnuter (May the Lord preserve him and keep him alive) was in Marrakesh, at the King, he spoke with the King about expanding the Jews' boundaries, and the King welcomed him and promised that when he gives permission to European merchants to build houses and courtyards, which he already promised he would, he will also remember the Jews kindly and widen their boundaries" (*Hatzfira,* 181, 733).

Annulling the prohibition of transferring real estate between Jews and Muslims or, at the very least, permitting Jews to rent outside the walls would have substantially alleviated the economic stress of the Jews living in the crowded streets of the mellah, where the demand was great and the supply low. Interestingly, it was the wealthy Jews who opposed an improvement of the Jews' living conditions, simply because the lack of room drove rental prices higher.

> One thing have we asked of the Lord, that will we seek after, that our aristocrats and noblemen sitting in al-kasbah will heed our call and establish honest

> rulings and just arrangements for the good of our brothers in need of their assistance, and they should be quick in performing a good deed. And that the people of Mellah should live in comfort and peace, and be able to spend their days sitting idly. But if the people of Mellah dare not be courageous, and establish no rulings, then it [the promise to enlarge their boundaries] will be canceled completely and be as the dust of the earth, because the poor man's wisdom is despised . . . because the location [we live in] is also a factor, because a beautiful dwelling is one of the things that increases a man's self-esteem. And if G-d expands the boundaries of Jews, then the earth shall be full of the knowledge of the Lord, and the wall that separates the people of Yeshurun will be destroyed to its foundation, and everyone will have one heart and be of one mind and all the factions shall unite.
>
> [. . . .] But on account of the opponents nothing was done, and unfortunately also some of our fellow Jews opposed this, because they owned homes and courtyards in the Mellah, and if G-d widens the borders of the Jews, then the price of rent will drop, because rent paid to the King was cheaper, Every man is considered a relative to himself [and will not make a ruling to his own detriment].
>
> [. . . .] Our brothers, the land owners, opposition to expanding the Jewish boundaries was well documented in the Memoirs of the Alliance Israélite Universelle in Paris in 1873 (in the holy tongue).
>
> (*Hatzfira*, 182, 737)

Opposition to expanding the borders could have continued for as long as the Jewish socioeconomic system in Morocco remained relatively closed. But the evolving connections in Europe, and the ability to mobilize influence there, allowed even the weak to free themselves from this economic siege. Thus, Essawira Jews from the "lower section" managed to deliver a letter to the British consul sitting in Tangier, through a Moroccan Jew named Moshe Lugasi, who had moved to London. In this way they managed to circumvent the opposition of the wealthy community members to expanding the residential area. Moreover, Lugasi helped these Jews to establish a branch of the Alliance Israélite Universelle in the mellah, where they could approach the Jews of London directly to ask for assistance. So it was that quite quickly Mr. Lugasi had a letter deposited in his hand, with a request for help: "On the seventh day of this month, Lord Lugasi (May the Lord preserve him and keep him alive) travelled on a steamer to London and promised to do anything in his power for the good of his people, may G-d bestow upon him His blessings for the goodness of his actions" (*Hatzfira*, 86, 352).

The efforts of Lugasi and his friends bore fruit, and after many hardships and setbacks the Jews of Essawira slowly succeeded in going beyond the borders of the mellah.

MODERNITY, EDUCATION, RELIGION, AND EVERYTHING IN BETWEEN

Ben Yais Halevi's correspondence with the European Jewish newspapers stemmed from an inclination toward Westernization, Europeanization, and modernization that was prevalent among the educated classes in north African countries (Schroeter and Chetrit 1996). It is apparent that Ben Yais Halevi himself, as an educated Moroccan *maskil*, was strongly influenced by the Jewish Enlightenment movement in Europe. He read the published literature of different Jewish thinkers and writers. He followed the Hebrew press of the movement, and these readings clearly shaped his patterns of thinking. However, the manner in which these concepts were translated into the Moroccan cultural context teaches us how flexible and subject to a unique local design they were, inasmuch as the framework for Enlightened thought dealt with, among other things, outcomes that were location specific. An example of this was hagiolatry in Maghreb. One of the points of view adopted by Ben Yais Halevi from the European influence was rationalism. In this spirit he condemns, for example, what he calls belief in the righteous people of dreams. Again and again he denounces the increasing intensification of people worship amongst his townsmen. According to Ben Yais Halevi, this phenomenon spread with no force stood against it.

> The belief in nonsense, spells, charms and incantations, in dreams and fantasies, and in frivolity prevails in this land. I will briefly describe some of it. Nearly 15 hours away from the city, there is a high mountain, called Ait Bayoud. Within thirty-two years, this mountain rose to prominence in a magical way. This is what happened: a woman had a terrible and awesome dream that the wonderful Holy man Rabbi Nissim ben Nissim was buried in this place. This righteous man (who never really existed) caused the entire land to tremble. All the townspeople in their masses came to visit the grave of this wonderful saint at the top of the mountain. A man who had no sons went with his wife to ask for sons from the righteous man; someone who became sick, struck with madness (it is believed that he was compelled by a demon or that a spirit had entered him), was tied with ropes and brought to the righteous man to expel the spirit. Also those who have become hard-pressed and are lacking came

> to the mountain to request their livelihood. But this righteous man was not well versed in the Book of Creation, and was not a medical specialist or a great receptacle. The demon or spirit does not leave the body—since it hasn't entered, it cannot leave; and yet, through all this the people of Israel are believers, children of believers. . . . In time, this mountain will rise higher and higher, and eventually will be filled with any number of righteous men. Three years ago a woman dreamt that in this place another righteous man was buried, not beneath the first in stature, whose name is Rabbi Yitzchak Halevi, and last year another woman dreamt that another righteous man, last but not least, named Rabbi Shimon Abitan, may they blossom out of the city like grass of the earth. How good and pleasant is the fate of the Mohammed's inhabitants of the mountain, who receive gifts from all those who come to the graves of the righteous. Most of the people of this city are devoted admirers of the righteous men that were created in dreams. They hold this belief and forbid any inquiry. There are those who say that these men are saints buried in Jerusalem, who have been reincarnated from a decease and came to this place in order to bring merit to the multitudes. One day I was talking with a scholar who knows much about these foreign beliefs, and about the poor people who sell their clothes so they can go to the righteous dream men, and he replied that he too once had his doubts about this, but one night he also had an awesome dream, he saw an honorable old man and described him as an angel of G-d, who told him: "I am Rabbi Nissim ben Nissim and my family is called Tzarfati", and from that day on he has had no doubts, G-d forbid.
>
> (*Hatzfira* 81, p. 331)

Hagiolatry is at the forefront of Ben Yais Halevi's criticism of everything connected to "nonsense and stupidity." He even ironically summarizes the dispiriting rise of appearing righteous by saying: "And in a short while the number of dream saints *shall be as the sand of the sea, which cannot be measured nor numbered*" (*Hatzfira* 141, p. 573). Indeed, many studies that examined this phenomenon, place its significant expansion historically at the end of the nineteenth century. The concurrence of the growing influence of European modernism and the venerating of saints is, of course, not accidental. One can see in this contingency evidence of an "invention of tradition." The sense of threat raised by the enormous influence of the secular modernists triggered a reaction in the traditionalists that was anti-modern or perhaps "excessively" traditional. Goldberg (1983) sees it differently; he sees hagiolatry through symbolic lenses. According to him, the only way Jews could express nostalgia for the villages and small towns they abandoned in favor of big modern cities was through a cultural idiom mutual to Muslims and Jews, the holy man. Since Jews, as dhimmi, could not claim ownership over land they left, even land that they and their parents lived on for many generations, they stuck a symbolic stake in the ground, in the form of a holy tomb. This appeared in a dream and required the dreamer to establish and mark a site that had been abandoned. Thus, the Jews could visit places that no longer had a Jewish presence. Schroeter and Chetrit (1996) present a prosaic explanation: Modernity carried on its wings new technology, paved roads, cars and trucks, and additional aids that facilitated the realization of an old religious practice. Holy sites were never so accessible; if in the past a great physical effort and a significant financial investment were required in order to make the pilgrimage to someone's grave, indeed the changes caused by European influence in Morocco made the Ziyarah (pilgrimage) so much easier, so that now many could join.

Apparently, hagiolatry turned central in defining Maghrebi Jewish identity (Bilu 1984). Yet, Ben Yais Halevi's criticism was not limited to the "righteous men of our dreams." He also gave details of other "superstitions" elsewhere. In one place he described the beliefs associated with healing:

> And there are other disgraceful and revolting practices that brand Jacob for a spoil and Israel to the robbers. And this futility did not help anyone, for what is considered important is the belief itself: if one does not benefit from his faith in this world, he will benefit from it in the next. Once I was at a gathering with many of my acquaintances and I asked them: until when will this foolishness continue to trap us? Let us try and remove this evil from our midst, this nonsense, quackery and falsehood? And one answered me: the customs of our fathers are like Torah [commandments], and forsake not the teaching of thy mother. And another answered triumphantly: it is much better to believe even in foolishness and lies, in order to [learn to] believe in the truth, then to deny everything including foolishness and lies and eventually come to deny the truth as well.
>
> (*Hatzfira* 83–84, p. 341)

To Ben Yais Halevi's regret, "irrational" behaviors are not limited to hagiolatric practices. He also tells of the use of amulets in different contexts. For example:

> When a son is born, amulets are brought with some strange names written on them, and they are plastered onto the walls of the house. Shapes that have five edges are painted inside and outside of the house, with tar or black paint, to ward off the evil eye. This is because anything with the number five is a remedy

> against the evil eye, and drawing the Star of David is even better. All seven nights before the child is circumcised, the house is closed up and a large steel knife is brought out and passed over all the walls of the house. Pieces of steel are also held and beaten together because the demons are afraid of steel and when they hear that sound they will not kidnap the child. And outside of the window they hang the neck of a red combed rooster with five pieces of meat and small mat and pieces of steel with some rags and the demons also are afraid of this, and they will not enter the house, like the sea monsters which are afraid of the [horrific] shapes made for ships.
>
> (*Hatzfira* 81, p. 331)

Ben Yais Halevi's despair concerning the practice of saint veneration deepened upon realizing that it could even be found among scholars. His despair is intriguing because he himself was a believer; and while he adopted the values of the Enlightenment, he rejected secularism. To be sure, secularism was to eventually become an integral part of the Enlightenment, so much so that religious belief and the Enlightenment movement were seen as polar opposites. However, like some of the Jewish *maskilim* in Europe, not only was Ben Yais Halevi a believer who adopted Enlightenment values, he likewise showed no discomfort toward what may be seen as an internal contradiction between these values.

Despite Ben Yais Halevi's enthusiasm toward the modern, the rational and technological tidings it carried on its wings, he was not blind to the price that this European influence might demand if it was not implemented appropriately. In one of his reports in *Hatzfira*, he tells of how distorted information in medical technology led to a great disaster among local residents:

> With a heart full of grief I will tell my brothers of our troubles from the chickenpox. . . . After this bitter sickness left us . . . it revisited our city and added disaster upon disaster. Every place it laid its eyes upon and entered, it came out with its hands full, and took children and youth to the grave after great agony. Bitter sorrow was in the hearts of the poor parents and it left behind wailing and weeping. May the All-merciful save us.

This epidemic, according to Ben Yais Halevi, was a result of inaccurate medical information regarding the idea of a vaccination. Healers who heard about the concept of a vaccination, tried to implement it without taking any precautions: "There are also people who have given the liquid to their children, but not . . . by the prescription of a doctor, but only by imposters, who know nothing, but bring spoiled chickenpox liquid . . . and place their fingers on the young child's skin in a large cut made with a scalpel, a broken piece of glass or the flint of a rock and they place cotton wool on the cut." By doing this, those same healers only exacerbated the plague, which claimed many lives.

BEN YAIS HALEVI AS AN ETHNOGRAPHER

Ben Yais Halevi's success in bringing his varied opinions and detailed positions to the awareness of Jewish readers in Europe was not lost from the scrutiny of his community members. Also the success he and his comrades had in handling the issue of extending the boundaries of the mellah, which implied criticism toward some of the community leadership, received attention. Ben Yais Halevi himself reports to the readers of *Hatzfira* of the dissatisfaction of some of his community members.

> There are some illiterates, who see themselves as intellectuals, who saw my previous letters in Hatzfira, and the people were as murmurers, speaking evil in the ears of the Lord, saying: who permitted this one to exaggerate and to misguidedly write about the customs of our city which they of old time have set, and made them into ridicule and disgrace as if he was born in Paris or in London? He too is from the land of darkness and deep shadow like us, and how many opinionated, intelligent and wealthy people are there in our town that allows him to write in this manner?
>
> I will not deny the truth that in our city there are intelligent, important people, with opinions and talents. But the reader will judge, if those who are not born in Paris or London have any authority to tell the truth? And the truth is, that had I been born in Paris or in London, I would speak even more, but because I am from the land of darkness and deep shadow, I therefore conceal more than I reveal.
>
> (*Hatzfira* 182, 737)

As it turned out, members of his community were concerned by "his washing out the dirty laundry in public"; that is, by his violating the "cultural intimacy" of the Jewish community in Essawira by inviting a foreign gaze (compare: Herzfeld 1997). The social obligation that stems from this imperative which serves to preserve cultural intimacy is, of course, for the sake of the property owners and the men of power, who seek, in this way, to silence any hint of criticism.

In addition to a description of internal community dynamics, regarding a community requesting to preserve its unity and to limit the threats toward its policy makers, another significant point is being made in this section. It relates to the question of how ethnographic texts are read. I will explain: the common images about the "other" in the embryonic years of anthropology were deeply entrenched and thus continued in the later years of modern anthropology and fused between "distance" and "cultural development" (Auge 1998). This exact image was reiterated in the title of Ben Yais Halevi's column (Amongst Our Far Away Brothers). Indeed, the energy of modern anthropology's research was directed toward "faraway" lands and accordingly compensated for the irreversibility of time. In other words, anthropologists implicitly assumed that the journey to do fieldwork in a distant land would offer a glimpse into what happened at an earlier time, in their own courtyard. This assumption was based on evolutionist thinking: the development of different cultures in a linear sequence, with the peak of development being reached in Europe. Thus, if all cultures evolve linearly, then an inferior culture in the present is similar in its foundation to that of the Europeans in earlier periods. Although evolutionist theories in anthropology had already lost their luster in the early twentieth century, this logic continues to shape the thoughts about the "other" to this day.

The story told by Ben Yais Halevi about the reactions to his column in *Hatzfira* are, of course, not compatible with that image. Apparently, his fellow city-men were not naïve subjects unaware of his writings about them "far away" in Europe. Like Bilu's research on Rabbi Yaacov Wazana, Ben Yais Halevi performs a type of fieldwork at home, but with a very different type of public scope. Bilu's work was widely publicized in Israel, and therefore it can be most likely assumed that the subjects of his study were exposed to the publication. Ben Yais Halevi's articles were published far away, in Europe (and I am deliberately reversing the Archimedean point from where the distance is measured). Thus, not only is Ben Yais Halevi's writing a testimony to refuting the "distance" (between "East" and "West"), but also his community members, who in his words are "illiterates," even they are aware of his writing about their community in "faraway" places.

A FEW WORDS ON COLONIALISM AND EMBARRASSMENT

In this chapter I suggested looking at one man, as a person but not as an individual. That is, as a unique human being yet as one who is highly integrated in his socio-cultural fabric (compare: Crapanzano 1985). Therefore, his writing can be seen in a somewhat general light. Through him we are able to understand the implications of the colonial experience for the social group that Albert Memmi claimed were developing dual-consciousness regarding their state of enslavement. This historical experience was not a minor episode, a fleeting moment or unknown. However, as I argued earlier in this chapter, this experience was overlooked by many anthropologists and sociologists who studied Moroccan Jews in Israel. They determined, without hesitation or reservations, that this was (a "faraway" place) a "traditional" society. The perspectives offered by the hero of this chapter are, of course, not in keeping with this assumption.

Notwithstanding the public and political ramifications of sociology and anthropology's ignoring the colonial history of the Maghreb Jews, it seems to me appropriate to view it from a social-cultural perspective. A closer look offers subtle insights on the implications of a colonial regime. One cannot (and should not) deny that this was indeed a violent, despotic, and cruel power that oppressed many large populations. However, it brought with it freedom for oppressed groups, such as the dhimmi Jews in Morocco, offering them new horizons. This dualism was previously noted by Albert Memmi. What a look at Ben Yais Halevi's writings illustrates even more is that the colonial power is not experienced equally, especially *among* those enslaved by a dual-consciousness. Ben Yais Halevi emphasizes the implications of hierarchical stratifications of colonialism on his community in the city of Essawira; however, with this he warmly embraces the social messages it carried. The wealthy Jewish merchants, the *toujar as-sultan,* gain power because of their political connections and even suppress the Jews beneath them, at a time when the intellectuals like Ben Yais Halevi are beginning to use their newly acquired knowledge in order to influence internal community processes as well as (not always successfully) processes in greater Morocco.

My criticism of the Israeli sociologic and anthropologic disregard of this colonial history is not simple for me: I find myself embarrassed by my own criticism. This embarrassment connects me to various episodes in my life. I will mention two of them briefly. The first was when I was on my way to elementary school in Ashdod; on my street one of the neighborhood kids cursed me, calling me a "stinking pork-eating Ashkenazi." As a boy of nine or ten years old, I experienced a sense of pride immediately followed by a burning shame. I was proud that in the eyes of this neighborhood boy where we grew up, I resembled someone better than us. I was proud that I didn't look like "everyone else in the neighborhood." But the shame that covered my body instantaneously afterward was harsher. I realized how my reaction denied my very lifestyle, not to mention the condescending attitude it implied toward my community and my own family.

The other incident to which I would like to refer occurred many years later. It took place when I screened a film for close friends in which one of my uncles in Morocco, then a five-year-old boy, appeared playing a piano. I felt uncomfortable with the cries of exaggerated admiration. I was first embarrassed and then surprised with the inherent racism which came in the remark "I didn't know there were pianos in Morocco!" I was embarrassed by the situation and then embarrassed by my resentment, as there was an element of implied acceptance of the Western standards of criteria for "Culture": playing piano.

This chapter itself is all the more embarrassing for me because of the implicit stamp of approval given to colonialism. My request to invoke the memory of colonialism in order to refute the claims of traditionalism (not to say primitiveness) of Moroccan Jews, positions European colonialism as a liberating and civilizing force. This results in my opinion both as adopting nonmoral colonial rhetoric and as justifying its regime. The exposure of Moroccan Jews to colonialism transpires to have had positive historical merits, while on a deeper level, the invocation of the memory of colonialism gives an implicit seal of approval to the European/ Western value system as a universal set of values. West remains West.

CHAPTER 3

Contraction: Immigration and the Jewish Community in Morocco Today

The winds of colonialism that blew stronger and with greater intensity during Yitzhak Ben Yais Halevi's lifetime eventually led to the constitution of French bureaucracy, which, both directly and indirectly, oversaw and managed the public, political, and economic life in Morocco. This regime, known in its deceptive name as the "Protectorate"—implying that the Moroccans were in need of patrons to care for them—in practice ruled Morocco. As we learned from Ben Yais Halevi in the previous chapter, this powerful regime had already begun making extensive changes in Morocco during his lifetime, and during the lives of the Jewish minority living there. Toward the end of the century in which Ben Yais Halevi lived, more and more changes in the lives of the Jews took place and began to take root. These changes happened in a wide range of both public and private spheres, including the organizational spheres within the community as well as changes in the Jews' relations with Muslims. In many ways, these changes marked, if not caused, the beginning of the decline of the largest Jewish community in the Muslim world, and one of the largest Jewish communities in the world at large. At the present time, this decline has extended to the brink of extinction of the entire community. A community which at its peak numbered about a quarter of a million people is estimated (somewhat generously) in recent years as only about three thousand people. Most of it, more than 70 percent, dwells in Casablanca.

This chapter will begin with a concise presentation of the historical twists that preceded the transformation of the face of the Jewish community. I will mainly focus on those changes that concern relations between Jews and

Muslims. Later in the chapter, I will expand the topic that contemporary history has neglected to study; that is, I will focus on trying to decipher the logic behind the present configuration of the community following its dramatic decline.

Before I turn to the past, I would like to say a word about what seems to be the end, about the present historical moment; if there is a concept that more than anything else, expresses the collective life experience of Moroccan Jewry following the great migration, it is "contraction." With this concept I wish to tie together two crucial trends in Jewish life: the first—continued demographic depletion (a result of migration from Morocco mainly to France, Canada, and Israel), and the second—an increasing tendency toward self-isolation and detachment from the Muslim surroundings while simultaneously converging into consolidated social-cultural enclaves. It is important to emphasize from the start that the convergence into cultural enclaves is not a new and modern version of a past and traditional existence, that is, a relative seclusion between the walls of the mellah. I am not suggesting a division between past and present, one which also holds within it a binary distinction, between traditional and modern: Likewise, I do not see the unraveling of past stories as a determined linear sequence from the past to the present. Moreover, I don't assume the presence of deep cultural or psychological structures which repeatedly shape, throughout history, permanent forms of existence. Certainly, it is possible that contraction is partially influenced from the collective memory of past patterns, but I am referring to a different pattern. As far as matters concern contraction, as I understand and phrase it, and which has been formulated more recently in modern times: it is a process influenced by comparatively recent local and global contexts.

In order to understand the novelty in the configuration of contraction, it is important to consider, even briefly, the past, especially anything concerning the relationships between Jews and Muslims throughout the generations and the way in which these relationships were influenced by global developments. Serving in an existential Jewish context, I will present and clarify some historical turning points of how contraction became a central social and rhetorical device to manage Jews' lives in Morocco in recent years. In addition to using different historical contexts as interpretive tools, the account which I will present of the Jewish Moroccan past will serve as an important key for readers who are not familiar with the complexities of stories about Morocco and its Jews, in order to understand various concepts and issues that will serve me in the rest of the book.

A BRIEF HISTORY OF RELATIONSHIPS

The relatively few historical studies that attempt to date the early Jewish settlement in north Africa are not in agreement about the time period. According to Haïm Zeev Hirschberg—one of the most prominent Israeli historians of Jewish communities in north Africa—the first known document indicates the existence of a Jewish community west of Egypt in approximately 300 BC (Hirschberg 1965).

Dating Jewish settlement in such early times hints at an interesting fact, even if it is far from being revolutionary for those familiar with north African history; Jews lived in the area of Maghreb about a thousand years prior to the arrival of Arabs and Islam. Without expounding too much, I'll mention, however, that the mere indication of this date may imply a political-rhetorical strategy: transforming this information into a provocative weapon in the context of the Israeli-Arab conflict. In other words, Jews can also claim a deed on north Africa and undermine the seemingly self-evident assumption that Arabs "naturally" belong in the Middle East and north Africa. For me however, pointing out this date is intended to emphasize a different matter altogether; I wish to highlight the extent and depth of immersion of Jewish communities in this region.

The majority of these first Jews settled around Egypt and slowly wandered from there to the western part of north Africa (in the Talmud—*Africki*). This distancing from the Land of Israel during the periods of the First and Second Temples did not harm the continued interaction with it or affect participation in journeys to and from the Land of Israel. One of the more famous journeys for Israelis was the trip made by Rabbi Yaakov Abuhatzeira from Morocco to Israel that abruptly ended at the beginning of 1880 when he died in Damanhur, Egypt, while on his way to Israel. Voyages such as this were not rare at all, and testimonies of these journeys exist from even hundreds of years earlier. For example, Yaakov Moshe Toledano writes in his book *Candle of the West* about two sages who "lived in Fez at the time of Dunash [Dunash ben Labrat (920–990), a commentator, poet, and grammarian who lived in the Tenth Century AD. A.L.] . . . traveled from Fez to the Land of Israel," in order to meet Rabbi Saadia Gaon the Pithomite (Toledano 1910:26). Not only did voluntary and private journeys connect between the regions over the years, but also religious obligations: throughout the generations Jews aspired to observe the commandment of making pilgrimage to the Temple (Safrai 1965).

The Jewish communities which slowly formed in north Africa thrived and flourished under Roman rule. They were so successful that the Roman historian Philo of Alexandria claimed that the Jews of north Africa (including Egypt and sub-Saharan Africa, but not the areas west of Libya) numbered close to 1 million. Hirschberg offers an educated and fairly reasonable guess that about one hundred thousand of them settled in the area of Cyrenaica (in the area north of Libya today). Following the destruction of the First Temple in 586 BC, new waves of Jews began moving toward Africa. Most of them were tempted to leave their country in light of the attractive opportunities the Roman government offered (Hirschberg 1974; Zafrani 1983); some had already arrived in north Africa, as prisoners of war whom the Sidonians had sold as slaves.

From the second century CE, the Jewish community in north Africa grew significantly. Many Jews settled in the major cities, and these urban Jews peacefully accepted the fact that they were under Roman rule. In contrast, those who settled in rural areas opposed the rule of the empire. Socially and politically the rural Jews were organized as tribes and were spread out among the interior areas of Africa, where they waged guerilla wars against the Romans. From about the sixth century CE the pattern of Jewish settlement—in the tribal model–became rooted, and Jewish "kingdoms'" rose in the Draa Valley and in other areas south of the Atlas Mountains. Topographically, these areas were almost inaccessible, so that they, together with those called "Berbers" (Amazigh—the free people—in their language, recorded as the earliest inhabitants of north Africa), were able to establish autonomous rule.

Unlike the invasions of various conquerors or intruders up until that time, the entry of the Arabs and Islam in the seventh century CE had critical influence on both the depth and breadth of people's lives in north Africa. The repeating waves of infiltrating Arabs changed the face of the region beyond recognition. For the first time in this region, the conquerors brought with them an uncompromising demand for a complete change of lifestyle of local residents. The Arab conquerors demanded that *Dar-al-Harb* (literally: The House of the Sword; connotatively: the world that is meant to become Muslim) be transformed into *Dar-al-Islam* (House of Islam: a region dominated by Islam and administered according to its laws). This decisive and uncompromising stand did not include the conversion of all other religions; according to the doctrines of faith, Islam could tolerate the presence of Jews under their patronage. Judaism, like Christianity and Zoroastrianism (Mazdaism), was recognized by Islam as monotheistic and therefore Muslims were not required to convert Jews. Such was not the fate of the Amazigh, who were considered heretics because of their belief in several gods; therefore, their fate was to convert to Islam or die by the sword.

Within a relatively short time, religion became a critical determining feature in distinguishing between groups and an important, but not exclusive, criterion in shaping the nature of the relationships between social groups. If a sweeping generalization is to be made, it can be said that in north African *Dar-al-Islam*, Jewish-Muslim relationships were organized around an interchange that was clear to everyone; in exchange for religious autonomy with specific restrictions, granted to Jews in their provinces, they were regarded as dhimmi, "under [Muslim] patronage." In practical terms, the status of dhimmi offered protection in return for submissiveness marked by symbolic and economic discriminatory and humiliating characteristics. For example, Jews were not permitted to ride horses, wear shoes in the vicinity of mosques, or bear arms. Islam's symbolic display of superiority also had architectural expressions: for instance, Jews were prohibited to build synagogues that stood taller than mosques, and at times they were not permitted to build synagogues at all. The same applied to the location of cemeteries; on principle, they weren't supposed to be situated between Muslim communities and Mecca. However, there were endless exceptions to dhimmi rules. The social customs relating to this dhimmi status were irregular. Various actions expressing subordination and discrimination were implemented or enforced differentially in different periods and in different regions of *Dar-al-Islam* (see Lewis 1984). Furthermore, for the Jews at least, some of the discriminatory symbols lost their oppressive and humiliating meaning. For example, Jews were forbidden to dress in bright, colorful clothing like the Muslims. On the most part, they had to wear brown or black jellabiyas. But Jews had their own symbolic meaning for the wearing of dark clothing: a sign of mourning for the destruction of the Temple. This is one of many examples that may express the complexity of interpreting the Jew's situation in Maghreb.

The formation of suborned relationships did not begin immediately upon the arrival of Islam to north Africa: the Arab occupation of these vast areas was not simple, and certainly it did not take place with the swift wielding of a sharp sword (to use Orientalist language). The Arabs encountered opposition from the local residents in north Africa, from the Amazigh and the Jews alike. A most fascinating founding myth of Maghreb was woven surrounding this resistance. The myth tells of its Jewish leader—Dahiya-Al-Kahina (Dahiya the priest)—who headed a coalition of Jewish and Amazigh tribes, which fought fiercely against the Arab conquest. However, over time the Jewish-Amazigh resistance wore down. According to the myth the end of this period came when Kahina died in battle after a young attractive Arab prisoner of war, whom she adopted (some say turning him her lover), betrayed her.

In approximately the ninth century CE, a unique political entity, distinct and relatively centralized, slowly congealed in the region of today's Morocco. Simply stated, but perhaps not entirely accurate, the appearance of the first dynasty—the Idrisid (789–974) marks the beginning of the entity we now call Morocco. According to Moroccan historiography it is customary to count seven dynasties that have ruled since the Idrisid and up until the current Fillali dynasty (from the Tafillalt District). During this long period there have been significant changes in Jewish life, which in this context can be mentioned only briefly. I will comment solely on the great drama that took place following the arrival of the refugees, many of whom settled in Morocco, after the expulsion of the Jews from Spain in 1492. As a result of this development two distinct communities–"residents" and "exiles"—were formed, who were careful to maintain the socio-cultural boundaries between them.

The myth about Al-Kahina is not an isolated exception, demonstrating the Jews as being interwoven in the general Moroccan fabric, and their being an integral part of the Moroccan historiography. There is another important founding myth in which Jews are involved; this myth is known as "The Tale of Ibn Mish'al," a story that comments on the establishment of the rule of the current Fillali Dynasty. Following a period of governmental chaos (more than ten rulers within forty years), the Fillali Dynasty rose to power. One of the main features of the governmental chaos (some might say—decentralization of power) that preceded the formulation of this ruling dynasty was the establishment of multiple small centers of power. One of them was ruled by a wealthy Jewish merchant, named Ibn Mish'al. His wealth, as well as stories of how he humiliated Muslim virgins, encouraged Er-Rashid ben Muhammed al-Sharif (1666–1672), one of the most significant founding rulers of the Fillali Dynasty, to deceive the Jew. Er-Rashid dressed up as one of the Muslim maidens designated for Ibn Mish'al and in the folds of his female costume he hid a dagger. The moment of opportunity was not long in coming, as soon as Ibn Mish'al came close to him, assuming he was one of the maidens offered to him, Er-Rashid rose and killed him, and then pillaged his property. Thus, literally on the ruins of a Jew, his money and his blood, the most recent and most stable dynasty in the history of Morocco arose.

The crucial relevance of Jews in the founding myths of the collective Moroccan historical memory, as in countless other life spheres, testifies to the intricate entanglement and intimacy of Jews within the fabric of Moroccan life. Precisely because of their deep involvement in Morocco they were harmed during periods of political unrest and enjoyed prosperity and security when the government was stable. During both routine and troubled times,

Jews maintained, at different levels, rich and complex trade relations with the Muslim majority.[28] Hence, it is impossible to understand the experience of Jewish life without understanding the general social-political and cultural framework to which Jews were subjected (Rosen 1984). One cannot understand the developments of the collective life experiences of Moroccan Jews throughout the ages without linking them to the wider socioeconomic and political contexts. This claim is of course an overused anthropological cliché. There is nothing remarkable about the claim that one must understand human groups, including minorities, in their wider context: because inasmuch as groups may aspire to completely isolate themselves from their environment, they are still subject to its influences and similarly influence their surroundings. I see it fit to emphasize this cliché due to a tendency of Israeli Jewish conservative historiographers (particularly those affected by European Jewry historiography) to describe Jews as separate from other "nations." But as previously stated, just as any other cultural group that is differentiated by and distinguishes itself from the majority with symbolic, organizational, political, and other means, the Jews of Morocco were also exposed, even if in different ways unique to their own structural social and cultural situation, to the same processes that affected their environment. Their language, poetry, faith, economy, and many other areas of life were deeply affected by their intimacy with Islamic Morocco. I am not suggesting that this influence was one-sided or that it was impossible to distinguish between the groups, but only that more than the Jews influenced their Muslim environment, they, as the minority under Islamic rule, were influenced by it. This influence was, of course, translated into the rationale of Jewish existence.

If I were required to provide a more focused characterization of the lifestyle of Moroccan Jewry amongst the Muslims in the era up until the French Protectorate, I would note in a very general statement that the Jews had an ambivalent relationship toward their Muslim neighbors. This was a built-in ambivalence, characterized by intense trade exchanges with Muslims together with a simultaneous tendency to withdraw from contact with them (Levy 1994). Indeed, the uniform and relatively sparse historical records of daily life (Bashan 2000) confirm this generalization.

In the 1960s and 1970s there was a heated debate about the quality of life for Jews, both generally in the Muslim north African context and particularly in Morocco. The debate revolved around the question of the impact of the symbolic mechanisms of exclusion and inclusion, and the depth of their political significance. There was also an intense dispute on the question of whether historical events that were difficult for the Jews were specifically directed toward them. There were researchers who saw in the exclusion (and inclusion) mechanisms of Moroccan society in general, and those directed towards Jews in particular, an outcome of internal processes resulting from the ethnic-religious character of both groups (Ayache 1987; Flamand 1959; Hirschberg 1968; Kenbib 1987, 1994). Some understood the relationship between Jews and Muslims from within the framework of the general Moroccan existence, and not as mechanisms directed against the Jews (Rosen 1984). Others saw the mechanisms of demarcation between the groups as an expression of legal and religious inferiority of the Jews as dhimmis (Deshen 1984, 1989). An extreme and somewhat simplistic example of understanding the relationship between Jews and Muslims is presented by Bat-Yeor, who analyzes the status of Jews as a direct religiously discriminatory legislative function on the part of Muslims (Bat-Yeor 1985).

As mentioned, the different approaches regarding the influence of inter-religious boundaries on the Jews' quality of life and the nature of their encounter with Muslims are deep and extreme. One may offer a variety of interpretations for these differences. For the sake of brevity I will enumerate only two interpretations as the source of differences between these approaches: The first is political-moral and the second disciplinary. The first approach, based on the political-moral axis, is simple and fairly self-evident. In this context, understanding the relationship between the two groups is analyzed by the effect of the political framework of the Arab-Israeli conflict. In other words, adopting a "darker" approach toward the relationship between Jews and Muslims might testify, among other things, to the desire to defend the Zionist idea (things are not generally good for the Jews in the diaspora, and particularly in Arab countries) while simultaneously critiquing the regimes in Arab countries for their negative attitude toward the Jewish minority. This approach also tends to justify the claim that due to ill-treatment, the Jews were forced to flee their countries. Besides the benefit derived in accusing Arab countries of oppressiveness toward the Jewish minority, there is also a concealed message which seeks to rectify the historic balance: the founding of new states in the Middle East generated a stream of refugees. Thus, the rule of law for [Arab] refugees fleeing Jaffa and Acre should be the same as for the Jews who fled from Iraq and Morocco. As such, the demand to compensate Palestinian refugees will have a corresponding demand to compensate Jewish refugees from Muslim countries. This position also weakens the degree of attachment which Jews from Islamic countries feel to the Zionist ideology; they immigrated to Israel not voluntarily but because they were expelled from their countries. Thus, this position might serve (or is capable of serving) a double benefit: first in the area of international relations (Israel as the only democratic country in the Middle East) and second in the area of internal-Israeli-Jewish matters (an indirect justification for the negative attitude toward the immigrants from north Africa in Israel). The contrary approach, which "lightens" the Jewish and Muslim relations, may imply, and most probably does, opposite political views.

As mentioned, one may add a disciplinary aspect to this political interpretation of the differences in researchers' approaches. I am mainly referring to the differences between historical and anthropological approaches. This difference is well reflected in a long and exhaustive debate between the historian Norman Stillman (Stillman 1974, 1976, and 1978) and the anthropologist Lawrence Rosen (Rosen 1968a, 1968b, 1972a, 1972b). Briefly I will state that the "darker" perspective tends to be historical while the "lighter" one tends to be more anthropological (Bilu and Levy 1996). Anthropologists argue that historians (at least the conservative ones) tend to focus on climatic events which are occasionally events of political turmoil, changing regimes, wars, and so on. In crisis situations Jews, like everyone else, suffer. Indeed, as they are a religious minority it is possible that they suffered more than the Muslims, though for the most part the violence was not directed deliberately toward them. Thus, over-reliance on texts of Jewish rabbis, for example, might present an impression that the political turmoil was entirely directed toward Jews, because the harm to Jews was the central question concerning them. Furthermore, the routine periods which offered both personal and collective safety may not have warranted documents that might catch the eye of conservative historians. However, neither were the anthropologists free from restrictions. The limitations of anthropological research relate mainly to the depth of the study and to the confining of its context: that is, typical anthropological research lasts for about one continuous year or two at most, and it is limited to a relatively small geographic area. If during this time the collective life in that area is running smoothly, then the researcher might be misled by the calm. The researcher's perspective is limited both spatially (as noted, he does research in a limited area which at times does not reflect what is taking place in adjacent areas) and socially: he may succumb to his informant's perspective. Thus, in his research, Lawrence Rosen focused on Muslims but assumed that the conceptual framework that he formulated also fit the Jews.

However, even the profound differences of opinion do not undermine the wide range of agreement that the Jewish existence in the Moroccan-Muslim context throughout the generations (until the arrival of European colonialism) was characterized by close and intimate socio-cultural exchanges between Jews and Muslims. By employing the concepts of "intimate" or "close" I wish to avoid the idealization of those relationships. Jews were, after all, a subordinate cultural group.

JEWS AND MUSLIMS: COLONIALISM AND POSTCOLONIALISM

French colonialism disrupted the existing sense of social order. In the previous chapter we learned from Yitzhak Ben Yais Halevi about the budding influence of the French Protectorate. Here I will address the continuing aftereffects of that influence. One of the most immediate and pronounced changes that took place at the beginning of the protectorate was that of demography; the massive human influx, which included Muslims and Jews, who moved from the small villages in the hinterland to the large cities, grew and grew. Mostly it was directed toward the coastal cities of western Morocco.[29] Everyone sought to benefit from the economic opportunities offered by the French economic regime. The large numbers of Jews in this trend were evident; in addition to the weighty considerations of livelihood, they also sought to integrate into the new urban areas the French colonialists built for themselves. They aimed, if not to walk shoulder to shoulder with them, then at least to stand in their shadow and to enjoy the profits that were promised in the equalitarian rhetoric of French colonialism. The Jewish enthusiasm toward this promise (and for modernity in general) generated tensions, not only among different sectors of the Jewish community, which Ben Yais Halevi discussed, but also between Jews and Muslims. The French ethnographer Pierre Flamand sorrowfully portrays the implications of this tension in the summary of his book:

> At the start of the [twentieth] century, the Jewish-Muslim symbiosis maintained some sense of balance. Each of its constituents nurtured feelings of superiority and indigenousness over the other, causing a separation which had tangible implications—separate and sealed off living arrangements—and moral implications: haughtiness and contempt. The Muslims were regarded as fanatics, prosperous and cruel, the Jews as weak, limp, dirty and with corruptive characteristics . . . together with this, each accepted the other as a neighbor; . . . a question mark was placed on this *modus vivendi* in our time.
>
> (Flamand 1959:324)

These are the romantics of the conqueror, the romantics of the ethnographer on the destruction generated by his country.

Despite the short period of direct colonialism, the changes it created were profound. The historian Michel Abitbol writes: "The effects of the colonial period on the Jewish community were apparent everywhere: they were accompanied by a long series of political, economic, social and cultural rewards such as changes in the legal status, rapid urbanization and migration from villages to new centers, changes in employment patterns, improved sanitary conditions and a rise in natural increase in population, dissemination of European education and the formation of new patterns of social mobility" (Abitbol 1985:32).

Shortly after its withdrawal and the establishment of independent Morocco in 1952, some of the changes the protectorate had brought developed further and were joined by new ones. Together, they deepened the rift created in relations between Jews and Muslims. The latter group accepted one of the main ideas of modernity: nationalism—which deepened the aforementioned rift even more. After all, the tendency of those holding power in Morocco to shape the national identity of the old-new state through rhetoric and social-political ideas of "Arabization" (Entelis 1989) and Islam (Bourqia 1987, 1999; Suleiman 1989; Tessler 1978, 1981b) further deepened the rift between Jews and their [Moroccan] homeland; the Jews certainly found it difficult to identify with the Muslim component.

A simple but illuminating example of the commitment of Moroccan politicians and policy makers to Islam and Arabism was manifest in the changing of street names in various cities. For example, the street where I lived during my childhood in Casablanca was changed from rue de Longwy, after the city Longwy in the southern strip of Luxembourg bordering France, to Saad Ben Abi Wakkas, marking one of the first converts to Islam and a legendary warrior who participated in efforts to deploy to the Mashraq (East). Ben Abi Wakkas was the head of the army who in the seventh century conquered Persia and ruled it. The street's new name therefore reflects a commitment to Islam. But like other social-political processes, the trends are not as unambiguous as they may seem at first glance. If we stick to the example of converting street names, it appears that the commitment to Islam in the public sphere of Morocco at the least has an impressive degree of flexibility. A casual visitor to the large city of Casablanca can easily see that the central streets of Casablanca maintained their colonial names, such that one of the main arteries of Casablanca bears the name boulevard de Paris. Its continuation is none other than boulevard de Bordeaux and at the other end it is boulevard de Strasbourg. They are not the only ones. Adjacent to them, our visitor will come across boulevard de Bourgogne. Not only that: the majority of streets (possibly even all, but I'm not certain) whose names were changed after the French period have their old names written below the new Arab/Muslim name.

Another brief example of the ambivalence toward colonialism can be seen in the design of open spaces in Casablanca. The design of the urban landscape reveals a complex relationship with the colonial past. One example of this is the attitude toward the statue of the omnipotent ruler of French colonialism in Morocco, Field-Marshal Lyautey, which during the colonialist past was situated in the middle of a main plaza in Casablanca. Inconsistent with the custom of destroying statues of fallen colonialist tyrants, Lyautey's statue was not destroyed after Morocco received independence. It was moved, with due respect, to a corner of the plaza, within the boundaries of the French consulate.

Detection of ambivalent expressions toward the colonial past does not require a particularly sensitive eye or interpretive virtuosity. The ambivalence is deeply rooted in the popular Moroccan discourse. Even in jokes, there are significant expressions of this dualism. For example, during the first Gulf War there was a popular joke about a request from King Hassan II to the popular Iraqi ruler Saddam Hussein to buy Scud missiles like the kind he was launching into Israel. The Moroccan king wanted to direct them toward Paris—in revenge for decades of colonial humiliation. The Iraqi ruler responded enthusiastically and a launch site was quickly erected in the heart of the Sahara Desert. The order was given from the authorities, the launch was in place, and the countdown began: 10, 9, 8 . . . 2, 1 and . . . nothing! The missile did not launch. The wiring was checked, the electronic circuits scanned. Once again they attempted to fire the missile toward the exalted goal, but without success. They sent an expert from the air-conditioned control center to examine what was stopping the missile from leaving the launch pad. To his surprise, he found dozens of Moroccans hanging onto the missile, hoping to reach France along with it.[30]

These examples, like many others that could be presented, indicate that despite the fact that both official rhetoric and literary research emphasize an ideological turn toward Islam and Arabism as part of the establishment of Moroccan national identity, this ideological mobilization is not necessarily unequivocal. Therefore, it would be imprudent to ascribe the commitment to Islam and Arabism as the entire rationale for the Jewish motivation to migrate from Morocco. In addition to those factors which were pushing them out, one must examine the factor which was pulling them in, namely, Zionism. The question as to the role of Zionism in the migration out of Morocco (and not necessarily to Israel) is complicated, and I do not intend to present it here in detail. Various historians of modern times such as Michel Abitbol, Yaron Tzur, and Haim Saadon have dealt with it. I will only mention that Zionist activists in Morocco (*les sionistes*, as they were called) took fairly aggressive measures toward encouraging Jews to migrate to Israel (Segev 1984). Without any connection to the impact of these Zionist activities in Morocco itself, there is no doubt that the very creation of Israel and the activities of its early leaders in defining the new state as the homeland of Jews everywhere had a profound impact on Jewish life in Morocco, as well as on the Jews' relationships with the Muslims. Even today, Israel, which for the most part is perceived as a homeland, both in the Jews' own eyes and by the majority Muslim environment, has a dramatic impact on Jewish life and on the Jews' relations with Muslims. For example, when the State of Israel celebrated Independence Day, Jews in Morocco secretly gathered in one of the clubs, and after ensuring the dismissal of all Muslim workers (from the building), they closed the shutters and windows and softly sang "Hatikva," the Israeli national anthem. It is important to emphasize, in this context, that for many Jews, Israel was not (only) an obstacle, but offered a political solution for the heavy pressures increasingly placed on them at home (Laskier 1990; Rosen 1968a; Stillman 1991).[31]

Without defining Zionism's role in the awareness and decision-making process of Moroccan Jewry to emigrate in the 1950s, or defining the impact of the political process in formulating the national Moroccan-Arab identity, and certainly without defining the mutual influence these two national movements had on one another, I think it can be argued with great confidence that the combination of these processes, and many others that I have not mentioned, did not leave the Jews with much choice but to consider the concrete possibility of migration. That is to say, the majority of Jews did not have the freedom to redefine their relationships with Muslims in light of the liberation from the yoke of colonialism.[32] Therefore, migration seemed to be the only and inevitable solution to the integrated and intensive attacks on Jewish daily life. The issue of migration became so central that toward the end of the 1940s and during the 1950s each and every Jew had to consider this question. The majority chose to migrate. The great migration created a situation which weakened the usually unexamined definitions of space.

Between the 1940s and the end of the 1950s, Israel became the main destination of Moroccan migration. Second in line was France.[33] The number of Jews in Morocco dwindled at a dizzying speed. If at its peak (in the 1940s) the population numbered about a quarter of a million Jews, today it numbers approximately three thousand (see fig. 4). The scope of the Jews' migration from Morocco expanded in parallel to the urbanization process taking place in that country; the more the Jewish population in Morocco dwindled, the

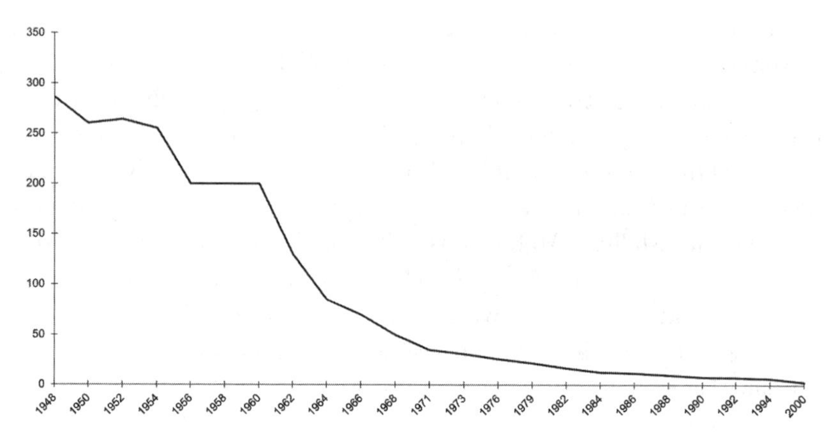

FIGURE 4. The reduction of the Jewish population in Morocco (in thousands): 1948–2000. Source: *American Jewish Yearbook* (1948–2000).

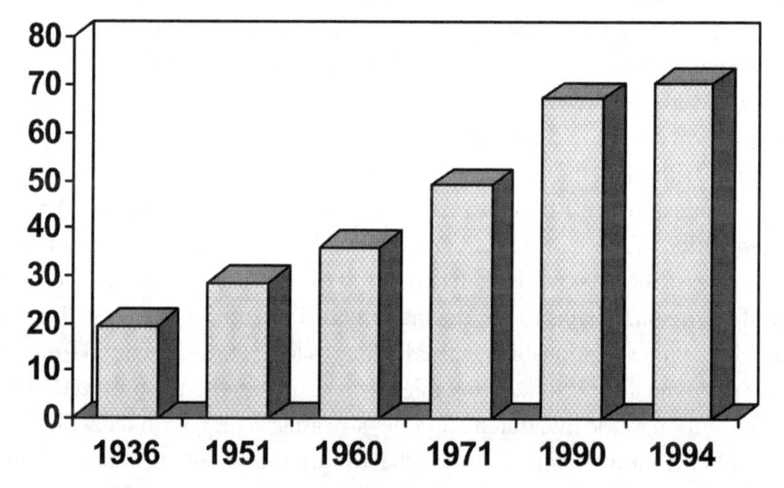

FIGURE 5. The percentage of Jews in Casablanca, relative to the estimate of the general population of Jews in Morocco (1936–94). Source: *American Jewish Yearbook* (1936–71); *AJDC Reports* (1994).

more its relative proportion in the larger cities increased. This is especially true for Casablanca (see fig. 5). In 1951 approximately 20 percent of the Jewish population lived in Casablanca, while in the 1990s nearly 70 percent of them lived in the Moroccan metropolis. The demographic contraction and the convergence toward Casablanca continue to this day.

COMMUNITY, MIGRATION, AND NATIVITY

Hence, migration from Morocco, which was a fundamental condition for the birth of the contraction process, is also one of the central keys to understanding the collective life of Jews in Morocco in contemporary times. Therefore it is important to dwell upon the various facets of migration and its consequences. Migration, in and of itself, is not a new field of study in the social sciences; for decades it has been a widely popular research topic and remains so today. Researchers in this field focus primarily on either the economic context or the establishment of ethnic identities. Unfortunately, few studies seek to understand the impact of the stable and constant migration process on the population that remains in place (Bottemley 1992; Pattie 1997). Mostly, researchers follow the route and paths of the migrants and how they integrate into their places of destination. They examine the process of how they form into minority groups. These groups may take the form of temporary communities, ethnic groups, etc.[34] These studies choose to focus on the very unstable (usually) and intriguing encounter between migrant communities and the indigenous population in the destination country. They typically ignore the social-cultural, economic, and political mechanisms being formed anew in the country of origin following the rift caused by the migration.

One of the key concepts relating to questions of migration is "community," which describes or explains the way in which the migrants assemble in their destination country. While using the term "community" I would like to distinguish between several levels: the *experience* of being part of it, its *organizational* apparatus, and its *sociopolitical structure*. Rather than being innovative here, I am using Anthony Cohen's definition which indicates that a community is "a conceptual structure," whose "objectivity" in locality and ethnicity are what give it its credibility. For him, a community is quite symbolic, and the implications of this situation are that its members can invest their very selves into it (A. Cohen 1985). According to this approach, a community is not a steady and permanent reality, nor is it an organism or an object. If so, how can researchers grasp onto "it"? How can one research the nontangible? One theoretical strategy examines unsteady research sites such as cultural border zones, fragmentation, hybrids, and political defiance (Appadurai 1990, 1991; Lavie and Swedenburg 1996a; Lavie and Swidenburg 1996b; Rosaldo 1989). In other words, a strategy such as this rejects the assumption that cultural communities are static, distinct, and separate entities that have sharp and clear boundaries; at most it may be argued that people work hard to make their worlds appear stable. In order not to fall into the trap of "the tangible," which denies its own essentialism (Herzfeld 1997), anthropologists, like other social science researchers, enlist border areas as their research sites where one may examine the rustlings of activities of political forces that construct the "actual community realities." The labor that goes into creating this appearance of "real reality," the sweat put out in an effort to deny the objectification and essentialization, brings about opportune times and places to observe the rifts that are found behind the façade of a clear, undisputed ontology.

With this said, the basic dispute of the ontology of community does not detract from its epistemological reality. In most cases, it is understood as natural and genuine at any given historical moment. Therefore ontological invalidation does not detract from the real implications of the actual experience. Thus, the actual experience denies the intangible character. Its expressions, which are characterized in the public's eye as objective-authentic, have profound and long-term implications. One should not underestimate the reality of the imaginary community and the moral problems it might pose for people. One of these is the adherence to ethnic chauvinism. Such chauvinism is often revealed in people's efforts to create agreement between the existence of a cultural group as actual, with clearly defined characteristics, and a specific and defined territory. The violent expressions of these efforts are summarized in the term "ethnic cleansing." The structuring of violent clashing between different social groups on defined, bordered territory is a significant characteristic of modern times.

A growing number of postcolonial communities live today in defined and demarcated spaces (Shields 1991; Sibley 1995). Together with this, and somewhat paradoxically, there is discordance between spatial and cultural borders. These are associated with, on the one hand, social, economic, and political processes and, on the other, processes that increasingly drive additional social groups and individuals not to attach themselves to a territory, but to integrate mobility into their lifestyle. That is a precise depiction of "globalization": an outcome of all sorts of movements, including migration. And so, we reveal a dialectical relationship between migration and community; migration breaks apart communities but also constructs other cultural communities in the destination countries.

Social scientists frequently attribute the rationale for the formation of cultural communities in destination countries to the immigrants' feelings of alienation. Thus, according to various researchers, the migrants attempt to minimize, as much as is possible, their feelings of strangeness in a new place. The unstated assumption of these same researchers is that the migrants need to adapt themselves to their new environment. Thus the strangeness is perceived as a central existential experience. The sense of being a stranger can elicit both fear and anxiety from the unknown. Strangeness is the consequence of the irrelevance of the cultural knowledge they arrived with from their country of origin to the new environment. Drawing on Alfred Schuetz's (Schuetz 1944) pioneering work, "The Stranger," Erik Cohen, for example, claimed that the strangeness to an unfamiliar environment is a key element in the experience of an exile, as well as the main problem that he, or his community, are meant to deal with (E. Cohen 1977). Cohen concluded that expatriate communities are structured around their efforts to solve the problem of alienation. This phenomenological position assumes that the solution (even temporarily) to strangeness is in the constitution of cultural enclaves. These enclaves provide the basic needs of individuals and groups and substitute, even partially or temporarily for those that are meant to be provided by the host country. These enclaves likewise minimize exposure to unknown and incomprehensible characteristics. According to Cohen, the enclaves that constitute migrant communities are not necessarily identical (E. Cohen 1977); their unique design is the outcome of the type of encounter between the host community and the migrant population. The rigidity of the boundaries of the cultural enclaves, for example, is a result of the migrants' degree of readiness or ability to be exposed to a foreign environment.

What does this general discussion on migrants have to do with Jews living in Morocco? Seemingly nothing: after all, Jews did not migrate from their own country. In spite of this, it seems that their connection to the discussion about migration is relevant to the process that was behind the architectural design of their community. In explanation, as mentioned, the Jews strictly maintained the enclaves that separated them from the Muslim majority, even after living in Maghreb for many generations. The depletion of their numbers exposed the Jews to situations which strongly emphasized their fragility and political vulnerability. Their main response to such situations was a constant retreat into their social-cultural enclaves, which preserved their unique existence, their autonomy, and alleged autarchy. Thus, in their eyes, their weakness becomes reversed; contraction turns into a powerful tool in their hands. The Jews take advantage of their enclaves in order to manage their relations with the Muslim majority from a position of control. The enclaves allow them to maintain familiarity in the complex social-cultural field they find themselves in and provide them with an ability to predict the unfolding interactions with Muslims.

A Muslim perspective of these dynamics would surely offer an important contribution to this discussion. But, due to my being an Israeli in Morocco, political restrictions prevented me from performing this research, and it was therefore not to be included. Compensation for this absence may be found in numerous anthropological studies which examine the relationship between Jews and Muslims in Maghreb. What is missing in the research on this topic is the opposite; anthropological studies tend to ignore the Jewish point of view.[35] Researchers from other disciplines who related to the Jewish perspective tended to ignore their activities as social players. They described the Jews as passive subjects facing huge historical and political forces, such as Zionism and Arab nationalism (Tessler 1978, 1981a, 1981b, 1988; Tessler, Hawkins, and Parsons 1979).[36] Common to all is the disregard of the Jews' ability to at least partially shape their own lives. There are a variety of explanations for this neglect. For example, the small number of Jews makes it tempting to assume a surrendering to the logic of the Moroccan-Muslim cultural activity.

The scarcity of research on Moroccan Jewry following the great waves of migration is not limited to describing them as passive. Due to their small numbers, historians and political scientists saw the Jews as an insignificant minority. Thus, for example, in his book about the history of Jews in Islamic countries, historian Bernard Lewis concludes thus: "There have been many chapters in the long history of the Jewish people. Greek Alexandria was the home of Philo, Babylon of the Talmud, medieval Spain of a rich Hebrew literature; the Jews of Germany and Poland wrote major chapters in modern Jewish history. They have all gone, and only their monuments and their memory remain. The Judeo-Islamic symbiosis was another great period of Jewish life and creativity, a long, rich and vital chapter in Jewish history. It has now come to an end" (Lewis 1984:191).

Likewise, the historian Michel Abitbol, in his introduction of the historical review of the fate of the Jews of Maghreb, concludes with the following words: "This was the background for the destruction of the North-African exile and the end of a long chapter in the history of the Jewish people in Islamic countries" (Abitbol 1985–86:303).

Historians have not expressed an interest in examining the events of the few that remained in Morocco. In contrast, anthropologists almost fully ignored the impact of migration on the Jews in Morocco. For example, in one of his more famous articles Clifford Geertz dryly notes that Cohen, one of the heroes of his story, "left last year, part pilgrim, part dying patriarch, "home" to Israel" (Geertz 1973a:19). He left it at that, adding nothing more.

Unlike the approaches that eliminate, whether implicitly or explicitly, the theoretical and intellectual aspects of the few Jews remaining behind, this chapter, like the entire book, seeks to dwell specifically on those few Jews.

The consequences of the migration are seen as a central theme, not as a final outcome that seals the entire issue.[37]

CONTRACTION

On the surface, contraction appears to manifest itself as a twofold unidirectional complementary process: a numerical decrease on one hand and a turning away from the Muslim environment on the other. But this schematic picture conceals even more ambivalent and complex life experiences. Despite the Jewish rhetoric of disconnection from Muslims, the retreat from encounters with them was not absolute for two basic reasons. The first reason was economic; as a small and ever-dwindling group, Jews are unable to provide for all of their needs by themselves. They are unable to maintain a self-sufficient governing body—be it cultural, political, or material, or otherwise. The second reason is connected to a long-standing history shared by Jews and Muslims. This history has shaped practices and shared worldviews which appear again and again in Jewish life and sabotage the Jew's ability to stubbornly cling to the ideal of hermetic separation. The Jews have been forcibly sentenced to come up against, and encounter Muslims in a variety of circumstances. It is no wonder that complex issues frequently arise as a result of the tensions between the necessity to meet with Muslims and the declared desire to withdraw from them into private enclaves. Generally, the fundamental solution to this tension lies in limiting the encounters with Muslims to strictly defined social-territorial areas where Jews seek to gain control.

Indeed, it was evident that Jews in Casablanca went to extraordinary efforts, in a wide range of areas in their lives, to gain control over their interactions with Muslims. It appears that this effort supports the phenomenological interpretation, that contraction is a symptom testifying to the deep experiences of a stranger. But focus on the emotional experience of strangeness cannot explain other significant aspects of occurrences in Jewish life. First and foremost, the perception of strangeness minimizes the importance of power relationships between the groups and within them. And note, power relationships have many expressions, both overt and covert, in social life. Monopoly over space is one of them, and through space, power can both be demonstrated and used when desired (Bahloul 1996; Herzfeld 1985; Mernissi 1975; Rabinow 1989a).

Even if, in principle, the (spatial) power sources are not symbolic, but in fact, economic-material, it is fairly common to find that dominant groups employ symbolic demarcation to control their social-cultural boundaries.

Precisely because of this, it is intriguing to consider how politically weak groups, such as Moroccan Jews, establish exclusive spaces by symbolically marking spatial boundaries. Simply put, the border is not the exclusive weapon of the powerful (whether speaking about economic or political power, or both). Various studies have shown how groups of vulnerable and weakened migrants close themselves off into confined spaces (such as homogeneous ethnic neighborhoods in cities). But migrant communities aren't the only ones which adopt such strategies. In situations where indigenous groups were vulnerable or weak and the migrants (mostly, colonizers) were the strong and dominant ones, it was found that the native groups retreated into social-cultural enclaves. However, despite their weakness, emphasis of one's indigenousness grants symbolic rights to claim ownership or possession (metaphoric or concrete) both on land and in spatial identity. Therefore, contrary to the phenomenological approach which emphasizes strangeness, it becomes evident that the historiographical claim to indigenousness is not a guarantee against negating their strangeness; these people may find themselves alienated from their countries, expelled both politically and symbolically—a consequence of different types of colonialism. As a result, the group develops characteristics that parallel migrant communities in their structure.

We learn, then, that the widespread (and highly fashionable) comparisons in research writing between dominant and familiar groups, on one hand, and groups that are ruled over and are innately foreign, on the other, is not the only possible experience for societies that have a majority-minority relationship. A fairly well-known example from the history of the late twentieth century is racist South Africa, where the whites were the dominant group while at the same time they were a demographic minority. Despite their power, they isolated themselves in social-cultural enclaves out of fear of the majority. The South African whites felt an existential threat to themselves and their surroundings by the sheer numbers of the oppressed black majority. This trend intensified toward the end of the apartheid era, a time when the whites found themselves "forced" to defend themselves against the political minority (Crapanzano 1985). Moroccan Jews, in contrast, never enjoyed the status of a dominant minority group; however, they established separate cultural enclaves whose boundaries became very rigid following the process of de-colonization from France.

SMALL NUMBERS, BIG PROBLEMS

Denial of the ontology of social structures in no way diminishes the critical impact of the players-bureaucrats acting "on behalf" of those structures. As central actors, their power is derived (for example, as Ben Yais Halevi testified about his time period) from their proximity to those in power in the Moroccan regime. The contribution of both municipal and state bureaucrats acting on behalf of the Jewish community committee was evident in their management of the contraction trend and in their nurturing it. For in the end, the trend of contraction preserves the vitality of the community organization.

An overused sociological truth is that every bureaucratic organization seeks to preserve its continued existence. To put it differently, and more consistent with my theoretical perspective: bureaucrats always struggle against the disintegration of the "real" structure on behalf of which they work and for which they are given authority, or legitimacy, for their activities (Herzfeld 1992). Thus, in Casablanca, bureaucrats work hard to preserve their political maneuverings behind rhetoric of "the community organization," this in the shadow of the daily and continuous demographic shrinkage. They do this in the name of need, which they define as essential, to cope with the steady reduction of the number of Jews. Community council officials of Casablanca have designed different economic, political, and cultural mechanisms within which they operate, whose declared purpose is to reduce, or even altogether stop, the demographic erosion. This motive did not go unnoticed by many of the Jews. Thus, for example, Mr. Elkayam claimed that "our leaders . . . the important people [he makes quotation marks with his fingers], the self-important, are afraid we will leave. They need to have enough Jews for their clubs . . . for their jobs, so that they can travel to Rabat [the administrative center of Morocco] and feel important. They try to convince us to stay in Morocco; it doesn't matter to them if it is dangerous or not to live here. The most important thing is that there are enough Jews in Morocco."

Mr. Elkayam, of course, was not the only person who adopted this bitterly ironic standpoint. In the shadow of the impending and nearby war in the Gulf, many community leaders left. Many Jews did not spare them the poison of their sharp tongues: "Now, when there are troubles, they run away! But when someone else wants to leave, they are offended," said Moshe Alkobi. This realistic or cynical attitude toward the Jewish leadership is not a mere conspiracy worldview; it finds expression in the attitude of high-ranking community officials on issues that are defined as threatening to the well-being of the community. In the chapter "To Be a Community That Is Both Homeland and Diaspora" found later in this book, I present a story about a Jew's murder. I was told about the murder by, among others, the victim's son. He said that following the murder, which was committed by Muslim workers employed by his father, the family wanted to migrate to Israel. This decision, he told me, was met with an unambiguous negative response from community leaders. The son explained that this attitude stems from the way these leaders interpret the act of leaving. They saw the migration of the grieving family as criticism of one's choice to live in Morocco in the shadow of an existential threat. They, explained the son, were afraid of a domino effect. Robert, the victim's son, was probably correct in his assumption; due to the tiny size of the community, every migration, even of just one family, was noticeably felt by those who remained and triggered discussion on the wisdom of their decision to stay.

One of the main daily expressions of the distress over the continued collective existence was the preoccupation with the size of the community. This issue endlessly worried the Jewish community bureaucrats. But not only them: this was a subject that everyone spoke about. I too, as an "expert-researcher," was frequently requested to express my opinion on the number of Jews in Morocco. However, despite the tiny size of the community, my efforts to establish a reasonable estimate of the number of Jews in Casablanca were unsuccessful. I encountered endless problems, some of which were fundamental. Alongside the heavy and essential issue of "Who is a Jew?" another difficult question emerged: "Who is a Moroccan?" Namely—How do you know a (Moroccan) Jew when you see one?! Both of these questions about collective (be it ethno-religious or national) identity are indirectly related to the modern distinction of the principles of belonging to a nation-state: belonging according to the "law of blood" or according to the "law of land" (respectively). Mostly, the Jew's position in Morocco in regard to the first question about genealogical belonging ("who is a Jew") was essentially social; blood is societal. Namely, the Orthodox Halachic definition (according to Jewish Law, those born to a Jewish mother or who converted according to Orthodox Jewish Law) is not sufficient. For many, Jewishness is defined as those who participate, in various ways, in the community life of the group or exclude themselves from it. As such, the connection toward a Jewish woman who married a Muslim man was abruptly severed (at times, even by family members). Even though according to religious law she remained a Jewess, socially and symbolically, she ceased to be a Jew in the eyes of many Moroccan Jews. Of course, the boundaries do not only exclude but also include. Contrary to the trend of contraction, and occurring rather infrequently, the boundaries also embraced Muslims. Well-known examples which are documented in folklore literature relate to symbolic struggles over the identity of a righteous man: the Jews claimed that a particular figure was a *tsaddiq* (pl. *tsaddiqim*)—the holy pious rabbi, and the Muslims determined that he was a *marabut* (Muslim holy pious). But there were also situations that included social discoveries; in the next chapter, " Controlling

City Spaces, Essentializing Jewish Identities," the character of a young Muslim by the name of Nantes, who is warmly embraced, will be presented: "He is no longer an Arab," it was said of him frequently. "He is one of ours [*les nôtres*]." This statement, even without the explicitly patronizing implication, likewise included a message of adoption and acceptance: "Because he's like us, he can't be one of [them]!" More than once I heard stories about Muslims (usually men), who secretly went to their Jewish neighbor and showed him a Jewish prayer book, praying shawl, phylacteries, a *mezuza,* and so on, that were hidden in his house for many generations, evidence of his family's Jewish roots. The rhetoric surrounding these stories usually reinforced the boundaries of belonging to the Jewish community, specifically by avoiding the need to clarify the source of these holy Jewish objects, or even by expressing contempt for the jealousy Muslims feel toward Jews. However, there were a few cases in which Jews complained that there is no possibility to embrace the Jewish convert, because according to law, Morocco is a Muslim country.

In contrast to social adoption, the strategic-rhetorical adoption of Muslims as Jews was a routine activity. For example, Juliet Elhayat proudly told me that in her daughter's class "there is an Arab student who knows more about Judaism then the Jews! She knows Hebrew even better than Rachel [her daughter]. You should have seen this, André, how last year on Purim she played the role of Queen Esther! An Arab played the character of the one who saves the Jews from the evil Haman!" The rhetorical use in this conversation of a Muslim girl was twofold; on one hand, Juliet expressed her dissatisfaction that her daughter Rachel didn't demonstrate fluency in Hebrew as was expected of her. But the mother was also trying to say something else; she expressed her satisfaction that "even an Arab girl" values the Jewish religion. This assessment, particularly in the context of the political weakness of Jews in Morocco, served to strengthen the mother.

Determining the status of belonging according to territorial residence is no easier than the former; for what does it mean to be a Moroccan in Morocco in general and in Casablanca in particular? How does one quantify one's being in a place? Quite a number of Jews that I met spent a third or a half of their time outside Morocco; their base of belonging was not constant. A typical example of this was Morris Shukrun, a pensioner and widow of some forty years, who jealously guarded his loyalty to his late wife's memory. He was careful not to replace any of the furniture in his home after his wife passed away. The furniture was full of holes where termites had devastated it, but Morris refused to change anything in the apartment. It would appear as though Morris was a man who clung loyally to his home and never left it. But Morris spent half his time with his family scattered in different parts of the world. In the fall, at the beginning of each Jewish year, he spent three months in Casablanca, in his rundown house. He preferred to spend the Jewish New Year and the other holidays of this season in Morocco. He then traveled to Paris to visit the home of his oldest son, where he spent around three months. Morris then returned to Casablanca for a comparable period of time and then once again renewed his travelling. This time he went to his youngest son, living in Manhattan, and stayed there for three months and then repeated the process. This nomadic wandering was not unusual within the Jewish community scene of Casablanca. I was acquainted with quite a few businessmen who lived in Casablanca, but parallel to this, lived full lives in other places outside of Morocco. These people were careful to maintain a regular routine as long as they remained in Morocco.

Mobility did not always maintain an organized form. At times it was quite erratic. For example, one day I spoke with Robert Elmaliach and made a plan to meet with him the following day; he wanted to tell me additional details about his father's murder. The next day I waited for him in vain. About two weeks later I met him by chance while strolling in the streets of Casablanca; he told me that on the morning of that day he had had the strong desire to order a suit from France by phone. At the last minute he changed his mind and instead decided to fly to Paris and meet the tailor in person in order to be measured for the suit. "It took about a week for him to make the suit for me," he said, explaining his disappearance with a half-smile. This frequent sort of disorganized mobility made it even more difficult for me to determine who should be defined as a Jew living in Morocco.

In the attempt to overcome the difficulty of determining belonging according to permanence in a defined space, I decided to define the "Moroccan Jew" according to the place of residence of his or her nuclear family. But even this option did not solve my practical problem, since there were those who lived full lives separate from their nuclear families. I do not mean families that were formally broken and divorced, but a model of a split nuclear family. For example, when I arrived for fieldwork in Casablanca, I met George Buskila. Then a man in his late fifties, Buskila told me he had plans to liquidate his business and join the rest of his family members, who had already moved to Montreal; "I need to sell my upholstery shop, and then I'm getting out of here. That's it, I'm tired of Morocco!" he declared. "My wife and daughters are already there . . . and I miss them so much!" Much to my surprise, even at the end of my main research period in Casablanca, he was still there. Even upon my return to Casablanca for shorter periods, every year or two I would meet him at the club and he would be telling all the skeptics there how he was about to close a business transaction.

In a moment of truth, George told me that it was difficult for him to move to Canada—"The weather is very cold for me there," he explained apologetically. On my last visit several years ago, he was still living in Casablanca.

My efforts to obtain official data that would help to clarify the size of the Jewish population in Casablanca also failed. For example, I tried to acquire figures for the number of Jewish students in various schools. I came up against a brick wall; the officials who ran the schools refused to give me the information. For example, the database for the Alliance educational system was closed to me. I approached the Alliance management and requested that they provide me with their computer list. I knew that this list included not only the number of students studying in the various network of schools but also the number of people in each family, the ages and addresses of each, as well as other data which was important in understanding the local distribution of the Jews in the city. A senior official at the Alliance, from whom I requested assistance, claimed that the request needed to be discussed at a meeting. Much to my surprise, my request was granted and I was asked to go to their offices. On the said day I went to the offices of the Alliance and met the clerk who was meant to give me the prized information. At that very moment, the senior director of the Alliance appeared and confiscated the computer printout without a word. He didn't confiscate them because of the strict privacy of the documents, but because of the desire to hide the information. After all, the allocations of various institutions, including the American Joint Distribution Committee (AJDC), was contingent upon the number of students. However, even if I had succeeded in obtaining this data, I doubt how much I would have learned from it. Even had I known (and I didn't) the average number of people in a Jewish family in Casablanca, in many families a critical age range was missing: between ages eighteen to thirtyish. This was the result of a typical route taken by boys and girls after they graduated from high school. Many of the younger Jews turned toward higher education in Paris. On the other hand, some of the thirty-year-olds returned to Casablanca.

The number of Jews *remaining* in Morocco was, as mentioned, an acute and existential subject. At any gathering with a large number of participants within or without Casablanca, the question of the size of the community came up, and especially how much it had shrunk relative to the previous gathering. So it was at large funerals, at celebrations, and at the prayer services for major holidays, and so forth. Efforts to evaluate the size of the community were also related to practical, technical needs such as planning bureaucratic activities (opening or closing classes in schools, budget allocation for assorted activities, etc.). The AJDC, for example, determined that in the late 1980s there were 5,500 Jews in the city. In those same years, various spokespeople for the community repeatedly mentioned the number 5,000. Conversations revolving around the question of the logic of the committee in investing in future entertainment and recreational facilities for youth likewise reflected concerns over the size of the community. Moshe Dadon, who ran an organization for Jewish youth in the city, complained that community leaders "prefer to invest in the dead and the elderly rather than in the youth. They are investing a lot of money into renovating cemeteries, in the graves of the tsaddiqim—not that I mean God forbid, we shouldn't invest in the tsaddiqim—but no one is investing in the youth! Look at how beautiful The Home (nursing home) is! But the 'Scouts' get almost nothing." According to him, community officials choose to invest in commemorating the past instead of securing the future.

In another conversation, which took place about the future of the city's schools, some of the participants stated that there were almost no Jews that remained who would reap the benefits of investing in the youth; and the future, they added, does not promise much more. Morris Saado, who listened to the conversation taking place between Max Elmaliach, Mark Vaknin, and David Levy, intervened and fervently argued that in his opinion, there is a very good reason to invest in the youth, because according to his estimate there are about fifteen thousand Jews in Morocco. Elmaliach, Vaknin, and Levy jumped up as if they were bitten by a snake: "No! There are only six thousand," Levy said, while Mark and Max vigorously nodded their heads in agreement. Saado accepted this assessment of population size without argument, while trying to offer an explanation for his mistake; he quoted (with slight changes) a biblical saying:

SAADO—"Of course I'm mistaken. It's this way, because with us Jews, it's as written in the Torah: 'We will be as the dust of the earth.' This means that even though we are few, it will seem to everybody as though we are many!"

LEVY—"No, that's not true . . . I told you, we in Morocco are only six thousand, and in Casablanca, about five thousand. This is why what you are saying is not true for all of Morocco. It's true only for Casablanca. Here we are many, five thousand. But, for example, a few days ago I walked around in Rabat. For an entire day I walked around Rabat and didn't meet a single Jew! I also went to the market, and there asked the Arabs. They told me that Jews don't come to the marketplace anymore. No! There is almost no one left."

The agreement between officials and ordinary Jews about the size of the population was rather surprising. It appears that this agreement, among other things, stems from the intense preoccupation with this issue. Among those agreeing were elementary and high school principals; worshipers in the synagogue, who were concerned about the number of worshipers for a quorum; kosher butchers afraid there would be too few customers; managers of clubs who catered only to Jews; and many other parties who had an interest in these numbers. The most overt and prevalent expression of this interest was expressed in the constant pointing out of Jews on the streets of Casablanca. Almost every Jew who I walked with along the streets took the trouble to point to someone and inform me or someone else that so and so who was walking in front of us or passing by was a Jew.

The constant interest in the changing size of the student population in Casablanca is, in no small measure, one of the most important factors in formulating the surprising consensus. The information available to those same bureaucrats is transferred informally, in gatherings with friends and acquaintances. The information moves like lightning, precisely because it is an issue that disturbs their peace. The brief conversation that took place between Saado, Elmaliach, Vaknin, and Levy demonstrates how the information gets around and how it is reinforced. Levy, who had been a teacher for car mechanics at the "ORT" School, retired several years ago. He however remained on friendly terms with Sassi, a teacher for building design at the school, whom he would meet daily at the CA club (Cercle d'Alliance Israelite) to play cards with.

The wider consensus concerning the size of the population is not based on a systematic collection of data; no internal Jewish population survey has been conducted. As stated, this has been a result of oversensitivity to the issue and does not necessarily reflect knowledge-based information or even rest on a vague sense of solid information. On the contrary, the widely excessive occupation with this matter suggests just how fragile the sense of security is about it. Moreover, the continuous exchange about the size of the Jewish population in Morocco is bound to the wider issue concerning the economic consequences of the demographic contraction of various community institutions. The AJDC, which provides economic support for various projects in the Jewish community, has never taken upon itself to carry out a population survey. For many years no other responsible body did so either. The AJDC does possess annual estimates, but these are kept confidential. My repeated requests to the organization's offices in the United States were denied. The last population survey of the Jewish community was taken decades ago and was carried out within the framework of a general population survey of the Royal Bureau of the State of Morocco (Attal 1963; Gouvernement 1953). Since then, no population survey distinguishing between ethnic groups has been carried out in the Maghreb Kingdom of Morocco.[38] One of the high-ranking officials in the Moroccan

AJDC claimed that the Jewish community leaders themselves asked to avoid the negative implications connected to a population survey of the Maghreb Jews. He added that "respectable people on the Community Council told him that the last Jewish population survey took place during World War II, during the Vichy regime. . . . The survey was for the purpose of property registration and for organizational purposes . . . and for transferring Jews under the regime to labor camps." I am not convinced that this is the underlying reason for the secretive behavior, even if the said event actually took place. Indeed, in Algeria and Morocco some thirty labor camps were established during this period. But these had no connection to the question of the survey the Vichy regime carried out. These two historical events were mixed up and intermingled with each other, and they became as one historical fact that served the Jewish community leaders as an excuse for their strong and continual opposition to counting the Jews of Morocco.

CONTRACTION: A TANGIBLE SOCIAL REALITY

I never met Jews who denied the process of demographic contraction. On the contrary, I came across countless comments such as: "In the end we will be finished," or "In the end there will be no one left after us!" The numerical reduction was not only felt by professionals who were concerned by the slow and steady exodus from Morocco due to their positions. Even in the daily flow of life the process was clear to everyone. Thus, when a Jew publically announced (in the C.A. club for example) that he and his family were leaving Morocco, his declaration disturbed those who heard it. The sense of threat was clearly evident. Worshipers in small synagogues experienced this reality closely, due to the increased difficulty in filling a quorum. I often heard anecdotes from people who, in self-mocking irony, told how they would "ambush" innocent passersby (who did not regularly attend synagogue) and enticed them to stray from their path and come to the synagogue.

Vaarda, for example, came to the CA club one Sabbath and jubilantly shared his exciting news: "Today there was a miracle from heaven, thanks to the tsaddiqim! Really! We thought we would never again have a quorum. We had given up, because everyone is old and many are leaving to go to France. We should have closed down the synagogue by now and have already discussed it. Today, suddenly, six young men arrived together, and said that they would come and begin to pray with us regularly!"

Contraction is not only felt in narrow circles such as synagogues or school classrooms; it is also evident in larger spheres. One of the more noticeable events that illustrate the process of contraction is the annual tsaddiqim celebration which many of the city's residents attend.

The main *hilulah* celebrations, and especially the central Lag Ba'omer festivities, are unique public events that bring together a substantial number of Moroccan Jews to one clearly defined place. The circle of participants diminishes yearly, and the celebrations provide the disturbing opportunity to observe the entire community as a whole. At the Lag Ba'omer celebrations in 1990, Edmond Elmaliach sadly commented:

> I think that there is maybe only a quarter of the number of people that I saw at the last celebration I attended four years ago. Since then the amount of participants has fallen to twenty five percent! I think that the celebrations [the main ones] are not so important here anymore, things here are finished. I think that the most important, the celebrations that is, the most important ones, are those we have in Israel. There, masses of people come! But I was also told that many make pilgrimage to ziara, to the celebration of Rabbi Amram Ben Diwan, in Wazzan.

The small amount of participants at the celebrations troubled many. All those whom I spoke with who participated in the celebrations began our conversation with a discussion of estimates as to the number of participants. An exchange of assessments took place not only in conversations with me but also among themselves. It was apparent to everyone that the *hilulah* celebrations served as a census. The contraction in the numbers of celebrants is not only a question of demographics. It is also expressed by a change of the central symbol of the ceremony, the tsaddiq. In contrast to the impressive number of tsaddiqim that were previously renowned when the majority of Jews were scattered throughout Morocco (Ben-Ami 1998), now most are lost in oblivion; they fluttered out of the minds of Moroccan Jewry and were forgotten. The existence of these tsaddiqim is entirely dependent on the memory of members of the Jewish community who are almost no longer found throughout Morocco. They (the Jews) came together to the big cities, but they didn't take their tsaddiqim from the countryside with them, and so many who were greatly admired in the past, are now lost and forgotten.

In actuality, there are only about ten tsaddiqim today whose grave sites are regularly visited by Moroccan Jews at least once a year. The most important among them include

A) Rabbi Yihya Lakhdar, who is buried next to Benei-hemad. His gravesite serves as the central site for Lag Ba'omer celebrations. The site is about three quarters of an hour's drive from Casablanca. The tsaddiq's grave site is far enough away that one has to make an effort to get there (Turner 1973); this, as opposed to the grave site of another tsaddiq–Rabbi Eliyahu—who is buried in the new cemetery in Casablanca. This site (of Rabbi Eliyahu) is not far enough away from Casablanca that the efforts both of the pilgrims and of the organization committee from the community would be enough to make it worthwhile. In addition, the grave site (again in contrast to the site of Rabbi Eliyahu the tsaddiq) is far from the population centers, and the temptation to have a picnic outdoors is too enticing.

B) Rabbi Amram Ben-Diwan, who is buried close to Wazzan (in Asjan). This righteous man's grave has become a focus for Lag Ba'omer celebrations for Jews living in northern Morocco, who have difficulty attending the celebrations at Rabbi Yihya Lakhdar. In addition, relatively many Moroccan Jews visit his grave site for his *hilula* on Tu B'av (the day attributed to his death), and on Rosh Chodesh Elul, the beginning of the new month.

C) Rabbi Haim Pinto, also known as "the great" (as opposed to his grandson Rabbi Haim Pinto "the little," who is buried in Casablanca) is buried in Essawira. Many people from Casablanca come to these festivities which begin on the 26th of Elul, but the "hard core" celebrants come from Essawira.

D) Rabbi Nissim Ben Nissim is buried in Ait Bayyoud South East from Essawira. This anonymous tsaddiq has in recent years become very central to Moroccan Jews due to the intense activities of native Essauirians, who are spreading hagiolatry traditions about him.

In addition to these four saints, there are others, but they have achieved a more modest scope of visitors. I am referring to saints such as Rabbi David u Moshe, Rabbi Avraham Wazana (Bilu, 1987, 1993), and Rabbi David Halevi Draa. It should be noted that the latter were all "local tsaddiqim" at most, to use Goldberg's terminology of classification categories (Goldberg 1983).

The contraction process of the number of tsaddiqim that remained in people's memory—and more important, the decrease in the numbers of those who merited visits—seems logical and self-evident, in light of the fact that likewise the number of Jews in Morocco drastically diminished. The process is even more understandable, and this is being said especially due to the discontinuation of visitors to the sites, if we recall that many of the tsaddiqim's burial sites are in fact distantly situated from urban centers. A large percentage of the tsaddiqim's sites are situated in southern Morocco, in small villages in the High and Middle Atlas Mountains. These villages were abandoned by the Jews during the internal migration process in Morocco and during the great migration from Morocco (Chouraqui 1968).

STRUGGLING WITH CONTRACTION: BUREAUCRATIC ASPECTS

The main strategy of officials and policy makers in confronting emigration is concentrating Jewish institutions in restricted and defined areas in Casablanca. The reasoning behind this action is framed in terms of bureaucratic efficiency. Committee bureaucrats and community activists of the many institutions and organizations strive to maximize the scope of services they offer, as well as how these are practiced. The more the scope of services grows, the greater the Jewish population's dependence on the community's institutions and organizations. This dependency reinforces the isolationist tendencies of the Jews, because they are then in less and less need of contact with the Muslim population, since the Committee tends to the various needs of the community.

The retreating *modus vivendi* of the Jews of course intensifies the necessity of community organizations for the Jewish population. It appears, therefore, that the smaller the Jewish population, the more essential (in both its connotations) the Community Committee ("*le comité de la communauté*"), the most prominent and strongest Jewish institution in the Moroccan Jewish community, becomes. This necessity is reflected in the range of institutionalized services and in their degree of activity. The community has many organizations which serve the Jews: there are lively social clubs such as the CU (Cercle de l'Union), the CA, and the SOC (Stade Olympique Casablancais), a youth club of the DEJJ (Département éducatif de la jeunesse juive), where much of the activities for Jewish youth takes place. Committee members are involved either directly or indirectly in these clubs, as they are in the extensive educational system, which tends to the Jewish population from kindergarten through, elementary and high school (vocational, dormitory, prestigious, and regular).[39] The community also has a medical system (a type of HMO sick fund), the OSE (*œuvre de secours à l'enfance*), which provides basic medical care as well as dental care. Medical services are provided by The Home for the physically and mentally infirm. Included in these organizations and institutions, which are under the watchful eye of the committee, is the network of synagogues, the slaughterhouse, the kosher supervision system, kosher butchers, *hillulot* (annual death celebration of a tsaddiq; pl. for *hilulah*) organizers, and so on.

The monetary capital involved in both direct and indirect control of these same organizations affords the committee a degree of control to the amount of exposure the Jews have with the Muslim population. Moreover, in practice these service providers function as a mediating tool and buffer between Jews and Muslims. Therefore, even poor Jews are exposed to Muslims to only a relatively limited extent. They are protected by the services the community provides for them and which envelop their lives from cradle to grave. It should be noted that much of the committee infrastructure, its branches and affiliates, are all concentrated in an area no larger than a single square kilometer; here also contraction takes on a dramatic spatial expression (see figure 6). These mechanisms of social and spatial contraction intensify the feelings of self-isolation among the Jews.

As such, the Community Committee tends both to the living and to the dead. The committee, together with the Ittihad and other educational systems, runs daycare centers, elementary and high schools. The committee supports the institutions responsible for running informal activities (such as the "Scouts" Youth Group). The committee also indirectly and partially controls the Jewish social clubs. With the support of the committee, the community operates a health system for Jews as well as The Home. This institute cares for the elderly and chronically mentally ill, providing them with a variety of social and financial supports.

The variety, scope, and intensity of services provided by the committee members and other bureaucratic organizations are impressive, especially if you consider the minute size of the community. In fact, the range and scope of committee services grows as the community shrinks. As mentioned, the increase of the scope of committee activities contributes to the disengagement process, because these institutions in fact, act toward the establishment of a quasi-self-sufficient autarchy. Together with others from various satellite organizations, the committee members benefit from the partition between Jews and Muslims, which they themselves contribute to establishing, because these walls make it easier for the committee members to govern the Jews of Morocco. This control is crucial, because without it the committee members risk the dissolution of the community. The more the Jews are dependent on committee services, the more they refrain from leaving Morocco, and the more the committee members provide services, so the fear of the Jews toward Muslims increases. These are seemingly contradictory processes, because it would seem that fear would encourage Jews to leave Morocco. The fear from Muslims stems (among other things) from the services provided by the committee, because the services raise the walls of separation between Jews and Muslims.

It is important to remember that the educational system, which the Community Committee oversees, also contributes to the isolation of the Jews. Jewish students learn French as a first language and Hebrew as a second language, while Arabic in Morocco becomes only the third (and not at all preferred) choice of language. It is no wonder that few Jews know Fusha (classic Arabic), and few of the young people speak Darija (Moroccan-Arabic) very convincingly. For the foreign observer it is surprising to discover, that except for a small number of intelligentsia, the majority of Jews do not watch the (Arabic) news on television, which is broadcast in Fusha. Their day-to-day experience is also shaped by their lack of Arabic literacy; Jews cannot read the street signs or billboards unless they are translated into French. The lack of proficiency in written Arabic isolates them from their surroundings.

The self-isolation of Jews leads not surprisingly to growing fear and anxiety from the Muslim environment; and these feelings, in turn, encourage the trend of separation even further. This becomes a vicious cycle in which these difficult feelings are sanctioned and cultivated by detachment, which then accelerates even more the disengagement process of Jews from their Muslim surroundings. These circumstances feed into each other: the fear leads to self-seclusion, which again leads to fear, and the seclusion in turn makes it more difficult for people to leave. The more Jews rely on the generous services the Community Committee members provide, the more it becomes harder for them to leave; they recognize that in no other place will they receive benefits like the ones provided by the community's institutions, not even in Israel, which encourages Jewish immigration.

Despite these efforts of self-isolation, the Jews cannot exist in complete seclusion from their surroundings. Not only does the small size of the community make self-sufficiency impossible, but it would be equally impossible to avoid contact with Muslims on a daily basis. Jews meet Muslims on the streets, in marketplaces, in coffee shops, and on the beach. They meet with housekeepers, employers, colleagues, and neighbors, etcetera, all of whom are Muslims.

CONTRACTION AND CONTROL

Contraction acquires some rather diverse spatial expressions. For example, Jews avoid entering the homes of Muslim neighbors and thereby avoid the need for reciprocal visits. The bureaucratic mechanisms of the Jewish Community Committee (henceforth: Committee) also contribute to contraction, by an extensive provision of services that allows community members to refrain from bureaucratic interaction with Muslim officials. An enlightening example of this is the function of Committee officials in issuing passports to Jews. Through this service the Committee contributes to further reducing contact with Moroccan bureaucracy. The example of passports is not accidental; visas and passports are an important topic in Jews' conversations, especially at times of political tensions. For example, during the Gulf War (which over the years became the "first [Gulf War]") Jews held intense conversations about the advantages and disadvantages of different passports. Canadian, American, and French passports were considered especially good; Israeli passports were considered inferior. The rather tiresome discussion about passports was for Jews associated to the severe stress they were immersed in during that time. The passport tangibly expressed their ability to maintain continuous contact with remote centers of identification, as well as their ability to leave Morocco during a time of crisis. Indeed, just before the first Gulf War many of the Jewish leaders escaped to Europe to find refuge there, as they feared that the regime was unstable. According to the passport official of the Committee, "The passport is the modern wandering stick for the Jew."

Without the authorization of the Committee it would be difficult for Moroccan Jews to receive a passport. That is, Moroccan state institutions cooperated in establishing an intermediary bureaucratic mechanism within the Committee. However, as the organization responsible for maintaining the size of the community, the Committee strove to prevent emigration. This surprising authority awarded the Committee, as an intermediary for issuing passports, gave the senior bureaucrats enormous power and control over the members of the community. The power was intensified even more because of the Jews' desire to avoid contact with the Muslim environment: "Never did we feel the involvement of the Committee in our daily lives as we do today," noted-complained to me a member of the Ittihad. The Jewish educational Ittihad organization has made efforts in the past, and also today, to maintain its organizational independence from the Committee (Laskier 1983). As could be discerned from the criticism of that same senior member of the Ittihad, these efforts were most often doomed to failure.

Disengagement from the Muslim surroundings, characterized by inward movement—is a result of Jewish activities of both individuals and the Committee. This was made clear by one of the Committee members, Moise Ladani, who told me with great pride about his successful effort to "kidnap a Jew." Moise spoke French garnished with biblical Hebrew words. His appearance as well as his language was starched and somewhat formal. In spite of this, it was evident that he was clearly excited by the adventure he had taken part in:

> I heard from someone that there was a solitary Jew living in Tadla. I was told that he was neglected, dirty and that he regularly looks for food in garbage cans; never bathes, and that he sleeps in the streets, outside. . . . I traveled there together with Mrs. Aflalo (one of the organization's social workers) and with my wife, Babette. But when this Jew saw us . . . when we first approached him, he began yelling that he doesn't want to see any Jews. "Well," I said to myself, "I must find an appropriate tactic . . . I must use my head!" First of all, I pampered him. I paid for a cup of coffee for him and got him a haircut. Meanwhile, I sent Mrs. Aflalo to the local police to get permission to take him by force. Then, I spoke to him softly, gently, and coaxingly. The police approached him slowly and carefully and in a single moment all of us hastily grabbed him and pushed him into my car. Poor Babette, she had to sit next to him in the back, she had wanted us to bathe him before the trip, because he smelled, but I said "No." It was better to take him directly to Casablanca. You should see him today—he has clean clothes, and he lives in The Home . . . you can visit him there—he is in the psychiatric ward.

This story is yet another lesson of many, almost universal in modern times, concerning the employment of emotional mechanisms of embarrassment and shame, by officials who speak in the name of national responsibility, and the need for proper behavior in cultural surroundings that are not within the confines of the group. This is a story about the power of cultural intimacy (Herzfeld 1997); besides teaching us a lesson, it shows that the very existence of a Jew outside of the control of the Committee, "without reins," is a thorn in the eyes of Committee members, and his very freedom is a challenge to the Jewish retreat into themselves. This unnamed Jew slipped from the control of the Committee, endangered the imaginary but rigid borders of the community, and rejected the accepted position that demands contraction. From the perspective of the Committee heads, it is preferable that this same Jew be locked up in the walls of a Jewish psychiatric institute, doped full of psychiatric drugs rather than that he be allowed to remain "without reins." Moreover, as legitimate representatives (in their eyes and in the eyes of many Moroccan Jews), the Committee members benefited twofold from the kidnapping of this Jew: they demonstrated their power and their ability to eliminate the possibility, even a negligible one, of a Jew existing in the general Muslim surroundings, that is, outside of the boundaries of control of the Committee members (and they even received the help of Moroccan authorities for this purpose). They also publicly showed [their community] the damage inherent in an existence such as this. As for Moise Ladani, the practical outcome of a Jew living in Muslim surroundings without community supervision and control is a life of denigration, resulting in the inevitable necessity to forage for food scraps from Muslim garbage cans. The existence outside of the Jewish enclave therefore means an existence with no self-respect, on the margins of society, in the "wilderness." I am not suggesting, of course, that all Jews in Morocco or even Casablanca are under the absolute rule of the Committee. But individual cases that evade the community's nets demand an explanation. For example, cases of marriage between a Jewess and a Muslim (I know of no opposite situations) are usually explained as resulting from acts of sorcery on the Jewess. Namely, the explanation removes responsibility and awareness from the "victim" so that this impossible action, as far as the Jews are concerned, didn't actually take place.

The next chapter will closely examine the territorial mechanisms that served Moroccan Jews, while focusing on their operation in the Moroccan metropolis: Casablanca.

CHAPTER 4

Controlling City Spaces, Essentializing Jewish Identities

During a conversation in one of the Jewish clubs, Daniel Balil told the people he was sitting with about his trouble on the streets of Casablanca; he once got so confused, that he ended up in a completely unfamiliar neighborhood; and this in spite of his being a native of Casablanca! The place where he accidently ended up was filthy, neglected, falling apart, and teeming with utter poverty: "You could be walking quietly through these streets . . . and suddenly someone can spit on the ground, right next to your feet! In this part of town, Casablanca is really an Arab city!" Somebody else associatively reinforced his words and reminisced about the "good old days," when one could walk in the city streets and not fear for his personal safety. In those days, he said, Muslims "did not dare raise their heads . . . [and] they stayed away from many of the city's quarters." The discussion took on a romantic-nostalgic twist, with all the participants expressing their longing for the time when Morocco was a well-developed colony under the French. The club's chairman summarized the afternoon conversation with a deep sigh: "Ah! The good old days!"

The more I became acquainted with the Jewish community of Casablanca, the more it became clear to me that nostalgia of this type revealed an increasing and crawling process of alienation from the surrounding society: a deep and substantial process that found its expression, among other things, through the conceptualization of Moroccan spaces. Extensive areas of the city turned dangerous in the community's eyes. Spaces ranged from *terra incognita* to *terra non grata*.

Jewish conceptualization and perceptions of the urban space, their daily life in it, and the rhetoric about it are at the heart of this chapter. I will address the shaping of conceptions, of practices, and of the rhetoric about space as it stems from a feeling of belonging to a group. As a most general argument, I will point out that this shaping stains the urban spaces of Casablanca in black and white islands, accessible and inaccessible areas (compare: Engle 1981). I will demonstrate how space demarcation, with boundaries and dividers on an ethno-religious basis, allows for the use of rhetoric that maintains the distinction between a marginal minority group and its surrounding majority.

Anthropologists, as moral socio-cultural scientists, strive to make the marginalized and excluded voices heard. They do so, in part, by exposing the cultural markings that push the minorities into these marginal spaces. The markings are mostly based on socio-cultural categories such as gender (Herzfeld 1985; Mernissi 1975), ethnicity (Bahloul 1996), or status (Rabinow 1989a; Shields 1991). Spatial exclusion is perceived as a powerful tool for maintaining control and for continued manipulation of the weak minority. For example, researchers have shown how a powerful social class can use cultural capital (Bourdieu 1986), creating symbolic gatekeepers that prevent access to specified spaces, thereby defining the group being prevented entry as marginal, as unworthy of entrance, etcetera (Crapanzano 1985). This marginality is defined by a variety of rather creative parameters in different cultural contexts (Shields 1991).

Allegedly, the capacity to define spaces as prohibited or as accessible is in the hands of the dominant group. Its members use it to create a sort of homogeneous cultural enclaves. In using the term "dominant groups," I am referring to social groups that hold a significant measure of control over the political, economic, or symbolic spheres (Bourdieu 1986). Quite often such groups develop socio-cultural mechanisms that reinforce their borders in order to monitor the entrance to them. This is what the whites in South Africa did when they locked themselves in cultural, political, and economic enclaves in order to preserve their status as "lords of the land." Their impressive success in this was self-defeating; these enclaves obstructed their ability to offer alternative solutions to the changing political circumstances. The more the political pressure increased, the more the whites closed themselves off into their enclaves. As their self-confinement increased, so too their feelings of fear and anxiety intensified, as they waited for a future shrouded in uncertainty, whose only inevitability was that they had reached the end of their reign (Crapanzano 1985).

Note that the constitution of cultural enclaves is not limited to ruling groups (E. Cohen 1977). Dominated groups (Kasinsky 1978; Rubchak 1993) can also close themselves into cultural enclaves in order to cope with fear and anxieties of real or imagined violence of the ruling majority. The conversations presented at the beginning of this chapter demonstrate it well; Moroccan Jews close themselves off into enclaves not only because they constitute a weak or insignificant minority in Morocco but also because enclaves are a tool for fighting the gradual but constant process of demographic reduction which threatens their very existence.

The process of numerical decline forces Jews to move within limited spaces and within a small number of places in Casablanca, while disconnecting themselves from the faster pulse of life in the big city (Rotenberg 1996). This disconnected existence feeds into a vicious circle that, at the moment, cannot be stopped; the restrictions Jews impose upon themselves intensify their fear and apprehension regarding unfamiliar urban areas. These fears, then in turn, intensify the ethno-religious separation.

Collective identities in a city are not an outcome of a momentary situation. They are continually molded and organized, while relating to past concepts of social, political, and cultural life (Bunzl 1996). Possibly, a stable and continuous collective identity may crystalize; and at the same time it is possible that in the same sociopolitical context these relations will lead to a fluid, dynamic, and fragmented identity. Even "primordial" symbols, such as blood ties or ties of kinship, that clearly appear as stable and permanent are subject to manipulation and adaptation according to political events or social circumstances. For example, political processes in eastern Europe in the late twentieth century led to fairly rigid collective identities. As a result, a demand arose for different ethnic groups to separate from broader political-state frameworks. Among Moroccan Jews, the reaction to demographic decline due to historical circumstances and political changes of modern times integrated in a complex way two intertwined trends of self-isolation: a desire to disengage from the Muslim environment and the creation of autonomous cultural enclaves. In contrast to what took place in eastern Europe, Moroccan Jews are not emphatically and publicly demanding political rights. On the contrary, they have retreated from the public arena as much as possible. They gathered and shrunk into themselves at a time when their collective identity hardened with their reluctance to discuss its contents. As part of the contraction process, they avoided close-by spaces in Casablanca in favor of expanding relations with distant cultural and political centers: namely, France and Israel. The tension inherent between the desire to withdraw and the necessity to interact with Muslims, even if in restricted spaces, led the Jews to erect complex and opposing arenas for interaction.

To understand how interactions are conducted in these areas, it is best to first understand the urban context of Casablanca, the place where these interactions transpire.

MODERN CASABLANCA

The prevalent image of the city, nurtured by the Hollywood film "Casablanca," is far from the actual experience of the average wanderer on the streets of the Maghrebi metropolis. The Orientalist desire to find a perfect mix of cosmopolitanism and "Oriental charm" in this big city is doomed to failure, even though the city was built under the Orientalist logic of colonial rule. The aimless roamer—the flâneur—will find wide streets that intersect the central squares (the French avoid stationary intersections at all costs, says the flâneur to himself). He or she will walk along the central boulevard adorned with long continuous lines of straight-standing palm trees in harmony with the fantasy of the Orient. Upon lifting his or her head the flâneur will see high, but not too high, above the official apartments and luxury apartment houses, which likewise imitate classical Western-European aesthetics and architecture. But, as in many "third world" cities, the wanderer will quickly notice the cruel mixture of great wealth and miserable poverty, separated from each other spatially. The poverty is located far from the uninterested eye, in the outer circles of the city. Along with the extravagant and blinding wealth of the high socioeconomic class, the wanderer will also meet the poor: street dwellers, drunks, and beggars garbed in clothes that have seen better days. At almost every street corner the flâneur will encounter the piercing and pleading look of a homeless or limbless beggar exposing his disability to all in order to receive some compassion or even a little money. The wanderer will notice without a doubt beggars carrying young babies or newborns on their shoulders while their older children assist them in begging. All these examples clearly demonstrate the cruel divide between the dirt poor and the thin layer of the filthy rich.

The city map will show that the city is clearly divided into quarters according to the different socioeconomic statuses of its residents. The rich reside in Anfa—the upscale neighborhood of the city. This neighborhood stretches along the *cornice*, the "cliff" of the Atlantic Ocean shore. Bearing the name of the fishing village on which Casablanca was founded, the neighborhood serves as a resort village for wealthy people from distant Arab countries. These sojourners annoy the residents of Casablanca, who are blinded by the huge ostentatious villas which hide behind the high walls that surround them. In contrast to this extreme wealth are the recently arrived immigrants living in *bidonvilles*—neighborhoods built from tin shacks, on the outskirts of Casablanca; there is no running water and electric power is a distant dream. A sewer system does not exist. Tens of thousands live as mere visitors to the city, residing in those tin shacks. The less fortunate do not even have a roof such as this over their heads.

In its colonial past, and in accordance to its own internal logic, the city was divided into three quarters corresponding to its ethnic-religious lines: the *medina*, the Mellah, and the New City, whereby lived the Muslims, Jews, and Christian colonialists (respectively). Today, perhaps because the colonialists replaced their physical presence with economic control from a comfortable distance, or possibly because the Jewish minority has become so small as to be irrelevant, the space is no longer divided according to ethno-religious categories. Today, the city is divided into seven bureaucratic districts, including Ain-Diab, which is the most populated. As of the turn of the century, it is estimated that more than half a million residents out of about 4 million of all the city residents lived in this district (the one following it is the Sidi Bernoussi District with about half a million residents). The majority of Jews are concentrated in Ain-Diab, which also includes the wealthy Anfa neighborhood.

The city residents are well aware of the division into districts, since this division was accompanied by many bureaucratic issues. However, focusing on these dividing lines will mislead those who wish to understand the nature of the city. A mere glance at the streets of Casablanca shows that the Moroccan metropolis is not frozen into separate quarters, but is a hectic city, full of life, confusing and somewhat chaotic. In her book *Picturing Casablanca,* the Moroccan anthropologist Susan Ossman vividly describes the endless sights of the city which radiate to all those who are exposed to it. See, for example, the description of the tumultuous and overflowing traffic found in the first chapter, which she appropriately entitles "Urbanity as a Way to Move": "In the street, communication seems fierce, swift, effortless. Talk is rampant, greetings effusive. In fact, though, establishing continued links with other people can be quite difficult. Casablanca is enormous and growing rapidly. Bridging distances requires money, time, or both. . . . Not surprisingly, even poor Casablancans will make enormous sacrifices to purchase cars or motorbikes. Once 'motorized,' one is free to move from place to place, in search of a friend, a newspaper, or an ocean breeze on a humid August evening" (Ossman 1994:21).

Ossman is correct in emphasizing the madness of the city's traffic. One of the first images that strike a person arriving to the city for the first time is the sight of people riding heavily overloaded motorized scooters, zooming down the roads. (When I first returned to Casablanca as an adult, I understood why my parents chose to bring two scooters with them to Israel. These two scooters were for a long time given a respectable place on the little balcony of our house, until my father decided to sell them. In Ashdod of the early sixties there weren't enough roads, transportation was sparse, and the distances were small.) The scooters buzz like bees busy with their never-ending work. The noise and clatter are so loud that you cannot even hear the birds chirping. Only the month of Ramadan offers moments of grace every evening, when people return home for a large meal after another day of fasting. Only then does the peace and quiet come (for just a short time) to the city.

André Adam, in my mind one of the most prominent historians of the city, claimed that Casablanca suffers from a lack of historical depth (Adam 1968). At the time that the imperialistic cities (Fez, Marrakech, Rabat, and Meknes) played significant roles in the history of Morocco, Casablanca was but a small fishing village. Insistence on historical inquiry reveals that Casablanca's roots were planted in the thirteenth century in what is today the Anfa neighborhood; but its shape, size, and character are a pronounced result of French colonial rule. The residents as well see their city as new, without a past. They accept the dictates of colonial history. Possibly, this is because a fairly large bulk of the city's residents only recently arrived; they have lived there for a few decades at most. The feeling of historical shallowness also contributes to the wild population growth. The leaders of the city are unable to control the flow of immigrants. The architectural approach to the city also contributes its part to the feeling of historical weakness: buildings are frequently destroyed and in their place new, more modern ones are erected. This architectural frenzy is unconducive to establishing *lieux de mémoires* which might help anchor the resident's memory into the vast and raging spaces of the city; instead, it generates collective amnesia (Nora 1989).

Casablanca Jews live right in the midst of this urban cauldron. They struggle to organize the tumultuous and dynamic social space and to weave it in such a way that it takes the form of a controlled environment, neither dangerous nor threatening (Douglas 1966). As part of this struggle to organize their surroundings, they stay away from large areas of the city, where "Casablanca is really an Arab town!" Political demarcation of the spatial is reflected in their uncompromising commitment to geographical contraction and indicates the sense of vulnerability the Jews feel. This spatial demarcation also indicates that the more they withdraw from their surroundings the more the self-definition of their own identity is reduced; they are unable to negotiate with the majority population as they did in the past. They no longer have the ability to play between multiple identities (Deshen 1989; Rosen 1984).

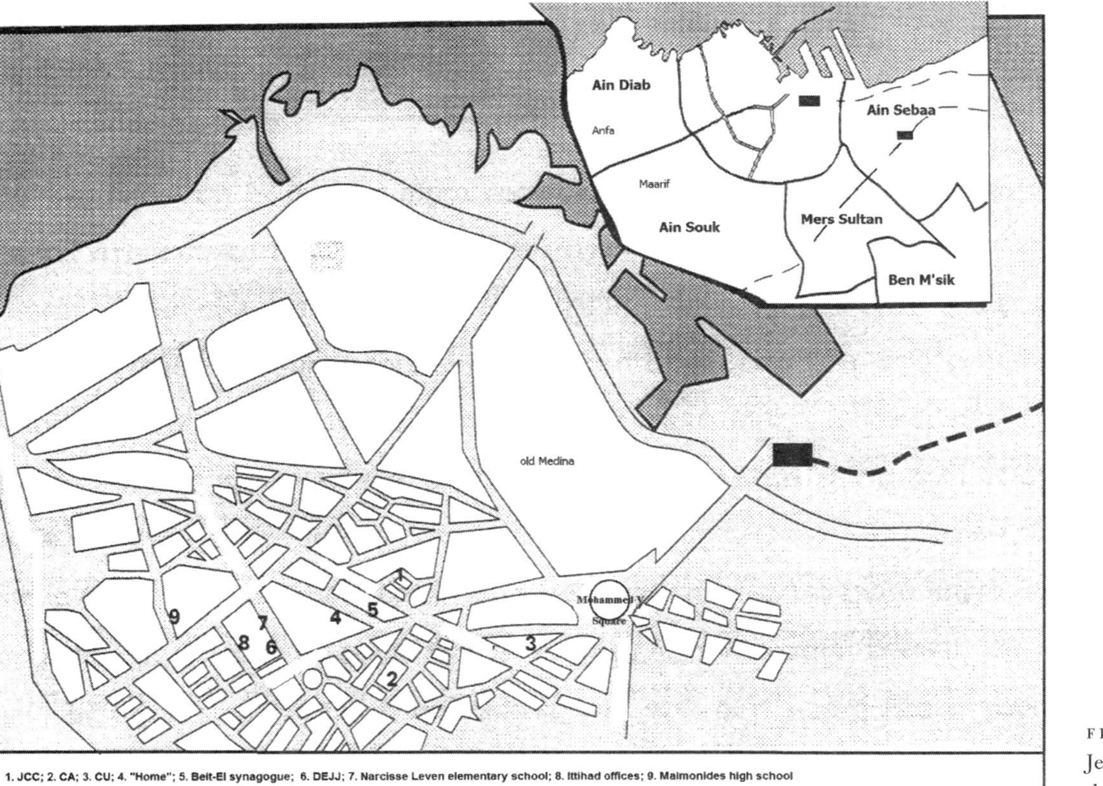

FIGURE 6. Dispersion of Jewish institutions and sites at the center of Casablanca

CONTRACTION: PAST AND PRESENT

Contraction is experienced and generated by Jews both individually and as a group. As individuals, Jews make serious efforts to avoid going to municipal or state institutions or bureaucratic offices. For example, when they need to handle official business they employ Muslim intermediaries whom they know or employ. I often saw the Muslim gatekeeper at the entrance to the CA club being sent to deal with property taxes, water, electricity, or telephone bills and so on for a good tip. Many Jews, as stated, avoided visiting large areas of the city. When driving, they often used set routes. Joël Lallouche, a teacher in his fifties, in the prestigious Jewish high school, described his daily life routine: "I live as if I am in a corridor. Most of the time I am at the [boarding] school, and when I need to go out to the center of the city—I drive in my car, only to get the things I need. I [say that I] live in a corridor because I only know the way from my house to the city center. If someone would divert me right or left—I wouldn't know where I am, I would be totally lost!"

Mr. Lallouche describes a sense of suffocation and claustrophobia in his vast city. Not surprisingly, Jews rarely enjoy touring around Morocco. They feel there is danger in the unmitigated, intimate encounter with Muslims. When I went to the *hillulah* celebrations, which took place an hour away from Casablanca by public transportation, it aroused amazement, bordering on annoyance. There were those who saw it as an unreasonable dedication to my research: "To tell you the truth, even though this is the holy *hillulah*, if I were you I would not have come here today," Joe Elmaliach said. Baber Zaguri immediately added: "I wouldn't make a journey as dangerous as this. To travel alone with Arabs . . . you're simply crazy!"

This self-seclusion gets a boost of encouragement from the Committee policies. In a meeting with one of the senior Committee leaders of the community, he laid out his vision regarding the future of Jews in Morocco. He spoke of the architectural plan that had recently been formulated by the Committee. He spread out engineering plans for a towering building in the city center, onto a large table. This building, he said will house "all the needy Jews, the mentally ill, the elderly and the isolated." He initiated the program because he was not satisfied with the existing situation in which the apartments rented by the Committee were scattered throughout the Ain-Diab District. As such, the spatial contraction policy of the Jews who are dependent upon the mercy of the Committee was conceived in terms of economic efficiency and an ability to assert a measure of control.

Indeed, the Committee and its satellite organizations reap benefits from the Jewish trend of self-seclusion. By fortifying mental dividing walls between Jews and Muslims the Committee gains more of a grasp on its constituency. The Committee, like other Jewish institutions, is involved in many spheres of the daily lives, including financial support of the needy, education, health, social welfare, management of religious life, and even support of recreational and holiday services. The fullness of services deepens individual Jews' dependence on the Committee by making the services into essential needs which are granted on an ethno-religious basis; such that the Jews are even more isolated from the Muslims.

As efficient as these mechanisms may be, they cannot completely cut Jews off from their Muslim surroundings. The process of demographic contraction itself requires Jews to be in contact with Muslims, because they are just too small a group to be able to provide for all their own needs.

SPHERES OF POWER

Jews and Muslims meet in a wide range of social spheres, whether directly (in interactions on the street, at work or on the beach) or indirectly—aware of themselves as a minority among the Muslim majority (such as when watching TV, for example). The prominence of the Jewish or Muslim presence in these domains varies from one context to another. The difference in the extent of prominence of one or another's presence signifies the perceived degree of control which that particular group has in defining the situation of that domain.

Schematically, one may divide the Jewish domains of interaction into private and public arenas. The home, for example, is a private space that envelops intimate and significant interactions between Jews and Muslims. These interactions are usually direct, such as when dealing with a Muslim housekeeper, fleeting encounters with Muslim neighbors in stairwells, or in even more brief exchanges with porters carrying shopping bags home from the *suq* (marketplace). These interactions, as mentioned, may be indirect, as when watching Moroccan television, listening to the radio, or watching original movies or movies dubbed in Arabic. While watching national television, for example, there are those who in a patronizing tone compliment the broadcasters on how they are dressed: "See how European they look," Georgette said to me. "You could get confused between them and us (*les nôtres,* one of ours—meaning Jews)." For Jews, a European appearance has been a clear signifier of "progress," and by implication "the Jewish way." Even if such a signifier may be misleading and thereby obscure one's ability to categorically differentiate between Jew and Muslim, by definition the fact is that the ones who use these criteria of "European" and "progressive" are the Jews.

Despite the Jews being a negligible minority, Jewish power spheres are not limited to private domains; they are also structured in the public sphere. The three major Jewish clubs that operate in Casablanca (the CU, CA, and SOC) and the Youth Educational Club (DEJJ), which is responsible for the organization of numerous youth activities and Jewish schools, the Jewish Public Medical Services (OSE), and so on, all fall under the category of public Jewish power spheres. Although some of the Jewish schools have their own limited degree of control, all of these institutions are spheres of Jewish power due to their legal definition as such. The legal definition grants them a considerable amount of control on the inter-ethnic interactions within their domains.

Most of the interactions between Jews and Muslims take place in "intermediate spheres." By this I refer to a fairly wide range of spheres which are characterized by a relatively ambiguous degree of capacity and control. The range of encounters within these spheres is very broad. At one end are the rather permissive arenas, where relatively unlimited intimate contact between Jews and Muslims transpires, such as at the dance club "La Cage," which is under Jewish ownership. Despite the Jewish ownership, the club does not systematically select clientele on an ethno-religious basis. As far as the young Jews are concerned, the Muslims' strong desire to "come to the club" is an expression of the cultural supremacy of the Jews. "They are dying to be where we are," said Sami Gazizy, one of the more prominent party goers at the club. Some of the more restrained arenas are coffee shops or bars that sell alcohol, where Jews often gather at fairly regular tables. The closed beach "Tahiti," a space where direct encounters are controlled and supervised, represents another type of "intermediate arena." This beach is unofficially divided into Jewish and Muslim areas. This division is relatively flexible because Jews "invade" the Muslim area and vice versa.[40]

Such flexibility is entirely absent in the Muslim spheres of power. These spheres include all places that are beyond the Jewish horizon; that is, most of the areas of Casablanca, large sections of the marketplaces, and a substantial share of coffee shops. In these domains the encounters with Muslims are direct and almost entirely devoid of Jewish control. This is why Jews go out of their way to avoid domains such as these. When they do enter them (accidentally or due to forced circumstances) they tend to curtail their stay there as much as possible. Jews prefer domains where there is an option for an easy retreat in a moment of need, such as marketplaces, streets, or coffee shops (as opposed to Muslims' homes, for example). The main means for control in Muslim spheres is avoidance. As a result, large segments of Casablanca are considered *terra non grata*.

THE UNDERLYING LOGIC OF THE SPHERES

When a young man entered the CA Jewish club and made a big commotion around him, he evoked a chilly comment from Armand: "André, don't look at the way he comes in here, making a lot of noise. Here in our club, all of us, all the Jews you see here, they behave like lions. They act as if they are not afraid of anyone. But if you see them outside . . . in the street, not one of these Jews who you see here would dare to raise his head. Not one would raise his head next to a Muslim! Next to them they are all like sheep, they are all afraid to talk to them!"

Armand's remark reveals a position that emphatically demands behavior that is consistent with the character of different spaces (Jewish or Muslim). It has a sharp and clear understanding of the existence of different venues of meeting. This position is shared by many Jews. An outside observer would find it difficult to understand the logic that classifies the venues of "Muslim" and "Jewish," since the domains are not concretely or even symbolically marked. Sometimes what appears as a priori a domain of a certain type will seem different on a second look, and on a third look will once again change. For example, on one of the nights of Ramadan, Joël Lallouche invited me to join him in "girl watching." Joël, a man of about forty-five at the time, made his living by working about half his time in Casablanca and the rest in Montreal. His wife and five children lived in Canada, and he had a *garçonnière* (bachelor's apartment) that he shared with a flat mate. He and his flat mate would proudly boast of their contacts with Muslim women, who, in return for the gifts showered upon them, spent time in the company of Joël and his friend. It was even their custom to pass these women from one to the other, with recommendations on desired sexual positions with them. I was not comfortable with the invitation, but for reasons that still remain unclear to me, I felt locked into the situation and therefore agreed to the request. We drove in his car on streets that had begun to empty from the city's residents, who rushed from their work places to their homes in order to feast after the end of another day of Ramadan. I was very surprised by the invitation, and even more so from the way Joël drove here and there with no real purpose or direction. I was relieved when I understood that his gesture was empty. But then he surprised me even more, when he asked that I accompany him to a nightclub located on the beach. "It's a Jewish club," he explained and added: "But what you will see there is very interesting, because we are going to see how young Arab men let loose at the end of each fast day."

The club was crowded and noisy. It was full of men, only men, most of them Muslims. Despite the religious taboo, they drank alcohol; some appeared to be drunk, just like the young Jewish men who grouped together, separate from the Muslims. On stage, the "Pinchas" (Cohen) band played. They sang songs in Arabic, songs that got the audience all worked up. Suddenly, and without any preliminary sign, they played a song that sounded familiar, but because of the context I didn't recognize it right away. Only after a few long minutes did I realize that the band, led by Pinchas Cohen, was playing a song that the whole audience enthusiastically sang along with; the song was "What a Country" (*Aizeh Medina*) by Eli Louzon, an Israeli singer. I was very surprised to see that the young Muslims were enjoying celebrating Ramadan with an Israeli song. I was even more surprised by the choice of this particular song, whose words, written by Eli Louzon and Yoni Ro'eh, are a list of complaints about the Israeli government.

> Oh, what a country, what a country
> Oh, what a country, one of a kind
> The government applies a press, the country lives in stress
> Oh, what a country, what a country
>
> People are crying, the prices are rising
> I need to pay the taxes and my health insurance too.
> Ain't got no more work, the cash container's broke.
> Got no bread to live on, the welfare offices are shut.
> They sit there in the Knesset, and cheat us off our butts
> They stole all of our savings, our entire pension too.
> We're all fed up, and then they hit us with another fine
> They even added tax on milk.
> Oh, what a country, what a country . . .
>
> We have ministers, who only want a seat
> They don't do anything, only make promises
> Where's the equality, where is the vision?

Where is the morality, what a disgrace!
What can I sing to you, what can I say,
There are many things we'll have to give up on.
Despite the mess and the shortcomings
You're our country, for all generations to come!

What a country, what a country . . .

The time that I spent with Joël, the different times we wandered around together, showed to me the difficulty in deciphering the underlying logic of the various domains. It wasn't enough, this difficulty to identify in advance the different domains, but even the character of the domains wasn't stable. A space can change its character over time and in different social contexts. I emphasize this fluidity not (only) because I want to demonstrate how difficult it is to organize such a complex life in a coherent fashion. This fluidity may also be the Jew's lot, particularly with regard to these "intermediate" domains, and even the polar domains (Jewish and Muslim) are not stable or permanent. This fluidity constitutes a serious problem for the Jews because they strive to maintain a stable state of domains and to achieve this goal through a variety of means, most of which have a spatial component. In addition to the feelings of security that come from being able to predict interactions with Muslims in particular spheres, the stability also allows for an internal-community-based compartmentalization of information. Thus, when Alice wants to smoke on the Sabbath she goes to "Muslim" coffee shops:

> There I can easily avoid [meeting with] Jews. There, no one will tell my husband that I am smoking on the Sabbath. If I smoked in the [Jewish] club they would tell. Here [in the Muslim coffee shop] you will only find Arabs, and they don't care if I am smoking or not. If by chance a Jew happens to come in here, he won't tell anyone that I am smoking on the Sabbath because he won't feel comfortable saying that he went to an Arab coffee shop, especially on the Sabbath. And besides, if he is coming to an Arab coffee shop that means that he also wants to smoke on the Sabbath without anyone [Jews] seeing him, or gossiping about him, so it's clear that he has no interest in hurting my reputation.

As indicated by Alice, these Muslim enclaves, which provide a thick veil, sometimes even impermeable, are crucial in the context of contraction. They provide a cover from the claustrophobic, controlling Jewish social eye. They provide a place to rest, a place to hide from the inquisitive eyes, both concerned and angry, which follow anyone who violates the social norms of Jews living under the enormous pressures of demographic contraction.

The encounters with Muslims are based on power. Generally, the more the arenas are "Jewish," the power play that exists there will run contrary to the common social order. In these arenas the Jews serve as supervisors and managers; they pay salaries and take part in other activities which emphasize their control over the situation.

It is uncommon for Jews to be in balanced relationships with Muslims or beneath them. This is not a testimony to the Jews' power, but to the fact that Jews will go to extraordinary efforts to avoid situations in which they have no control. I was surprised that I did not come across friendly relationships or casual friendships between Jews and Muslims which did not explicitly and intensely relate to the ethno-religious divide and its implied stratification. Moreover, this stratification comprises an integral part of the rhetoric concerning relations with Muslims. For example, Beber Benizri, who worked for a prestigious international institution in Morocco, enjoyed a respected status among many in the Jewish community because of his "position." He claimed that he had many equal relationships with Muslims at his institution. He even had "brave" friendships, he said, with Muslim colleagues. But, he himself claimed that it is quite unusual to have friendships of this kind with Muslim, just as he was telling me in a rather formal style about his good relations with them: "I meet people [Muslims] with whom I can have a genuine and open conversation. On a political level, for example, [we discuss] the question of Israel, the Palestinian issue, the Middle Eastern issues. We speak very openly, just as I speak with you now. I share my ideas and opinions; and because of this I enjoy their respect, precisely because I am honest and open regarding these matters. Often they are surprised that I speak so directly and freely with them. Then I am appreciated even more."

Even Beber Benizri, who wished to present an idyllic picture of his relationships with his Muslim colleagues, spoke in actuality of the constant tension present in these relationships. His emphasis of the freedom of language he has in dialogues about political questions relating to the Middle East conflict (where he takes a fairly hawkish position) only sharpens the inability to maintain relaxed friendships, defused from the political backdrop.

In all the time that I spent in Morocco, I met but a few cases of intimate or close relationships between Jews and Muslims. These were always complicated, complex, and charged with tensions stemming from the ethno-religious divide. Closer relations between Jews and Muslims used to occur on the night of the Mimouna, which in its past played an important part in the logic and structure of relations between Jews and Muslims. Due to the Jews' desire to avoid, as much as possible, encounters with Muslims, particularly in their own homes, the Mimouna festival was altered. The Mimouna was emptied of Muslims. There is a concrete threat when inviting Muslims to Jewish homes. Some of the Jews spoke of Muslims entering into their homes in terms of a "desecration," not in the religious sense, but as if they were violated. Even so the festival continues in Morocco today. Muslims still supply the wheat and flour, but these are no longer offered as a gift in the form of an exchange, but are sold by those few Muslims who still remember the Jewish customs. It is true that a few of the Muslim neighbors come to visit the Jewish homes on the Mimouna evening, but these are uninvited guests. For the most part, the Jews anxiously await the moment their neighbors will depart. Lively conversations abruptly end as soon as a Muslim neighbor knocks on the door. The tension is felt immediately. The only wanted guests are other Jews, and therefore Jews with fewer social ties to other Jews in the community don't usually do all of the practices and customs of the Mimouna. They are content to make do with some "symbolic," limited gestures, which do not include visits by their Muslim neighbors.

On the night of the Mimouna I visited many homes, true to the tradition of hospitality on this holiday. Each and every family ensured that a family member (usually a younger one) stayed at home while the others visited the homes of family and friends. Thus, there was a wide circle of visits and return visits, where few actually met. Of all the places I visited, the only home which received Muslim friends without any difficulty or reservation was the Vaknin family. The youngest child and only son, George, had exceptional ties with Muslim friends from the vocational school where he studied. George Vaknin studied in a school for *haute couture,* high-fashion design, a profession which suffered from a most negative image amongst Jews and was considered to attest to clear homosexual tendencies. What reinforced this impression was the open fact that George wanted to be a quality *couturier,* a fashion designer, just like his widowed mother. For me, George's flagrant dismissal of the Jewish attitudes attests to an overall approach that ignored community pressures.

Hospitality to Muslims in the Vaknin home on the holiday was relatively tranquil. Yet, even there, elaborate and intricate efforts were made to maintain the separation between different categories of guests inside the house. George, as the only adult male in the family, took responsibility for managing the evening. Just as I arrived at the Vaknin home, George's classmates also arrived. They were invited with due respect to the "French" guest room, while

I was gently referred to the "Muslim" room. Like many middle-class Muslim homes in Casablanca, many Jewish homes have two different guest rooms. The "French" room (sometimes called the "European" room) is laden with "Louis XIV" style furniture—heavy tables and chairs, massive mirrors covering a large wall, chinaware adorned with European motifs such as flowers or swans and the like. In addition, hanging on the walls were embroidered pictures with swans, deer, snowcapped mountains, fox-hunting designs, and so on. In contrast, the "Muslim" room was decorated with simple typical handicrafts—*artisana*—mostly plates, vases, and candlesticks in copper or pottery work. On the floor there were "Rabati" carpets (in the style of the city of Rabat—large and heavy carpets whose dominant color is blood-red, woven in a loose weave but rich in symmetrical pictures).

The large table in the "French" room was full of French-style pastry, nut cookies, soft drinks, and sweet liqueurs. As mentioned, I was led to the Muslim room, which was separate from the French living room, so that I could not exchange curious glances with George's guests. In response to my question about *mofleta* (a quickly fired pastry which is a strong signifier of the holiday), the fish, the peas, the flour, and all the many symbolic foods associated with fertility, abundance, and protection against the evil eye, I was invited by George's mother into the kitchen. She hid these symbolic foods in the corner of the kitchen so all the traditional foods (meaning Moroccan) of the holiday would not be seen from the two guest rooms. Only the "French" foods were visible, mainly to George's guests.

This spatial division of the holiday, and the play with the revealed and the hidden, between the exposed and the concealed, was fascinating; I, the Israeli anthropologist, was concealed from the Muslim eye. I was pushed into a place where George's friends would not be able to see me. Still, I could not clearly make out whether perhaps it was they who were being hidden from me, for after all, hosting them was not a typical event. Jews usually felt extreme discomfort in the presence of Muslims in their homes. I note the presence of Muslims in order to make a distinction between this group and those who remain transparent throughout the year: those same Muslims, who, despite their physical presence among Jews, do not take up any room in the actual social space. An episode in this context is portrayed in a conversation that I held with Danielle, Sami Gazizy's mother. Sami invited me to visit his mother one Saturday night, to witness the Mimouna preparations. At that point I wasn't aware just how much Muslims were absent from the holiday. Danielle Gazizy told me that she zealously refrains from meeting with Muslims. According to her, excepting at her work place, where she is compelled to meet with them, she avoids meeting Muslims socially. Even her housekeeper (Muslim, of course), who has worked for her for over ten years, never "touches the food." Danielle doesn't permit her to cook, "even though she knows the laws of Kashrut." Eating food that has been prepared by a Muslim was too intimate an act, one which she was not able to digest. During the conversation where she described in detail how much she refrains from voluntary encounters with Muslims there was a knock at the door. On the doorstep stood her (Muslim) neighbor; the neighbor blessed Danielle for a "good week" (in Hebrew), and they fell over each other with kisses. Danielle Gazizy hurried to the kitchen and gave her the leftovers from the *shachina* (or *chulent*, a stew made specifically for the Sabbath), a long-standing custom of exchange between Jews and Muslims. The neighbor thanked her, and they parted with kisses on the cheeks. Danielle returned to me to finish our conversation, and without any sign of confusion, finished her line of thought: "I never meet with Muslims."

In distinction from this situation in which Muslims weren't "really Muslims" but "good neighbors," at the Vaknin home they were in a clear and visible category. George had a clear sense of his priorities; his teachers and fellow students were without a doubt more important to him than a curious Israeli anthropologist who came by invitation of George's sister, who was two years his senior. It is important to emphasize that in many of the Jewish homes; the Mimouna celebration would take place in the "French" room and therefore took on a "French" character. In the Vaknin home, characteristics of traditional Mimouna were covered up and hidden in the small kitchen. This tendency toward all things "French" intensified the split, which in the past the holiday sought to bridge. Therefore, if it wasn't enough that the participants were hidden from each other, even the holiday basics themselves were concealed from everyone.

Towards midnight I joined a group of young people who decided to spend the last hours of the Mimouna together. They went to Gilbert's house and sat together around a table laden with typical holiday dishes, sweet cakes, and high-quality alcoholic beverages. I knew all the young people except one who seemed shy, closed and introverted. I was told his name was Nanet and that he wasn't Jewish. "That has become his name," one of the youth explained to me, but "in fact, I don't remember what his name really is. We call him Nanet because he's an Arab, and we fear for him. If it would be known that an Arab is hanging around with Jews he would be beaten to death. He likes being with us, very much, more than he likes being with Arabs. They always take advantage of him. They use him—he's got a lot of money, because he owns a large business. And besides—now he has become a Jew!"

The patronizing attitude toward Nanet did not end with changing his conspicuously Muslim name; while the conversation with him was somewhat dry and sterile with a slight French aroma, it went on to include a series of teasing. The banter and teasing were all about his religion. The cheerful atmosphere of the holiday intensified the legitimacy of this attitude, which was certainly influenced by the quantity of alcohol consumed at this meeting that ran late into the night.

Interactions with Muslims are always defined by stratifying ethno-religious criteria. The many stories I heard about attempted relationships with Muslims teach to what extent these discursive foundations, focusing on the underlying differences between Jews and Muslims, evoke their failure. Even in relationships between neighbors, where the encounters are frequent and are in many respects on an equal basis (such as a socioeconomic one), there is still a hierarchical emphasis. Sol Suissa, a woman of about sixty-five who lives with her husband in an apartment building that has known better days (and was once considered prestigious), spoke to me about her loneliness; she said that in the past, the building was populated mostly by Jews, but today they are the only Jews who remain. She, so she said, relies on her Muslim neighbors to ease her loneliness, because her husband continues to work, even though he has reached retirement age:

> Once, the whole building was full of Jews. They were all doctors, lawyers, engineers and there were also bankers. . . . Today, they have all left Morocco. There are no more Jewish neighbors. I am the only Jew here; I have nobody to talk to. I live here with my husband. He works from seven in the morning to five in the afternoon. I have no one to talk to, I am alone. I live on the fifth floor and we don't have an elevator. It is difficult at my age to go all the way downstairs, so I go to the neighbor across the hall. She is not *les nôtres* (one of us). But, to tell you the truth, they are not really Arabs either! And they are so helpful! For example when the electricity went out in my house her son came and fixed it for us. He is such a nice man, so charming! They are not really Arabs, that son of hers, he's a doctor. We don't have any contact with real Arabs. Only with neighbors, and they are O.K., all of their children were born here in this building. They are like Jews really, and they have been living in this building even longer than we have.

Sol found she was dependent on people whom she considered a priori inferior. However, she was caught in a situation where she was unable, due to health reasons and the location of her building, to maintain ongoing contact with Jews. In order to overcome this difficulty that she found herself in, and to explain the generosity of her Muslim neighbors, Sol denies their Arabism. By "raising" their level to that of "just like Jews," she explains to herself and to me her relationship with her neighbors, thereby diminishing the feelings of humiliation from her dependency on those who are not *les nôtres,* "one of us." Calling them "Jews" was possible because of their generosity, the assistance they provided, and their children's academic degrees and because they were veterans in the building and so belonged to the period in which "the whole building was full of Jews."

PUBLIC SPHERES—NUDITY AND EXPOSURE IN THE *HAMAM*

Public venues are of course the most challenging for the Jew; for how can one turn a public sphere, which is already bustling with Muslims, who constitute the vast majority of the city's residents, into a place that can be controlled? I will discuss this in the next chapter, where I will analyze up close and in great detail the dynamics of card games between Jews and Muslims on the Casablanca beach. I will mention here only one central tactic of managing this situation: an ongoing effort to enlist unique characteristics of public arenas, such that at certain times a strong Jewish presence gives a sense of control. For instance: the hamam (Turkish bath). Since Friday is a holy day for Muslims, the Jews take advantage of the Muslims' sparse presence in the hamam in the afternoon, and they come to the hamam in groups. "Now I have some quiet here," Mr. Avitan whispered to me in Hebrew, alluding to the absence of Muslims. "I come here every Friday, there is no one here [he is referring to Muslims]. They know our hours and we know their hours. It is like having days for men and days for women at the hamam. I arrive a few hours before going to synagogue for Shabbat eve prayer, get cleaned up well, shave—the bristles get so soft I don't even need shaving cream—I go home wrapped in a towel [he means a bathrobe], get dressed, and go to synagogue."

The slight presence of Muslim bathers does not, of course, conceal them entirely. However, it is clear that Jews try to maintain a respectable distance from them. This distance, together with the condensed vapors from the water bath, obscures the vision and reduces visibility, allowing the threatening presence of Muslims to be blurred as well. A slightly greater difficulty could be seen in coping with the Muslim boys who ran around in loose underwear, giving any who asked a deep muscle massage or a vigorous rubdown on the skin. In my first visits to the hamam, it appeared to me that the contact would be too close for the Jews. However, the boys were almost without bodily presence or identity; they were invisible. The Jews called them all "Ahmed" (the use of a generic name frequently employed for housekeepers: Fatima).[41] Even the gesture of giving a tip for the physical treatment transmitted a message of absolute absence of presence. Thus, the convenient choice of times, combined with the recruitment of physical and socioeconomic aspects allowed for the creation of a Jewish space for a limited time.

The bathhouse space could remain "Jewish" as long as the basic, unwritten rules of behavior were not violated. For example, the topics of conversation that the Jews spoke of out loud never dealt with issues that would define them as Jews. That is, they never spoke about the upcoming Sabbath, of news about relatives in Israel, and so on. The louder conversations were always about work issues, economics, or sports. Conversations identifying them as Jews were always whispered. In all the times that I went to the bathhouse, I never came across a violation of these rules of conduct.

Another potential violation, less discussed, was the possibility of homosexual relations between Jews and Muslims. My impression throughout the entire period I was in Morocco was that the attitude of Jews to homosexuality was less strict and less severe from what I was familiar with at home. In other words, homosexuality was not a serious issue, even though such male behavior was still considered perverse. Homosexual Jews I met in Morocco did not declare their homosexuality although it might be known to all and although some of them did not make any effort to hide it. It was not spoken. The only rule was that they shouldn't reveal the known secret, an approach somewhat reminiscent of the U.S. military's "Don't Ask, Don't Tell" policy. The requirement that in the bathhouse men should cover their loins seemed reasonable to the Jews, mainly for fear that sexual relations might develop between Jews and Muslims. The main fear was that any semi-public sexual relations might trigger immense Muslim rage toward the Jews.

PRIVATE ARENAS—TRANSPARENCY IN THE HOME

Despite the utopian *imaginaire* of Morocco absent of Muslims, Jews were forced to meet them in a variety of venues, even those which were clearly and thoroughly "Jewish". What made these domains "Jewish" was not the absence of Muslims, but the Jews' ability to establish in advance an unchallenged framework of control and, with this ability, to ignore the presence of Muslims in their midst. However, despite the efforts to maintain an organized system of divided domains, social lives are too fluid, even in those places that seem the most able to be controlled, such as—the home. Routine actions, like dramatic events, challenge the realistic construction of clear domains. Cultural sentinels are unable to provide protective armor that is perpetually secure from these occasions. It happens that individuals lose control over information that is meant to be confined to certain venues. Just before I completed my main fieldwork, I decided to give a souvenir from Israel to some of my friends. On these souvenirs the inscription "Jerusalem" was engraved. A few days after I gave this gift to one of my friends I went to visit him. He hadn't hung it up in his home. Only after my third or fourth visit did I see it hanging on the wall. He hung it at the end of a long and narrow corridor, out of sight. A stranger knocking at the door would not be able to see it. Only those permitted to enter the more private areas of the house might catch a glimpse of the souvenir. I encountered a similar approach in the Subahi family's house. Mr. Subahi invited me into his teenage son's room. He wanted to show me something. On one of the walls hung a huge flag of the United States; it covered the entire wall. When I entered the room, Subahi immediately commented: "I wanted to put up a flag of Israel, but I was afraid. Arab neighbors often come into the house, so I must be very discreet!"

The most routine, frequent, and intimate meetings in Jewish domains take place in the Jews' homes, mainly in interactions with the housekeepers. The majority of Jewish homes employ at least one housekeeper. The work conditions of these Muslim housekeepers and the nature of their work varies among the different homes, with the conditions being dependent mainly on the economic capabilities of the Jewish employers. Generally, the employment consisted of a daily cleaning of the home. It should be noted that cleaning the house is considered one of the lowliest tasks among the Jews, even to the point that the homes financed by the Committee Council are cleaned not by their inhabitants, but by housekeepers employed by the Committee. Households that enjoy higher incomes also employ housekeepers to do laundry, care for the children, do the shopping in the market, and prepare daily meals. In the more established homes, the housekeepers are responsible for all these tasks and stay overnight at their employer's home throughout the week (except for one day of rest).

Contact with neighbors is more controllable, of course, than contact with housekeepers. In any case, exposure to them is more limited as to time. The Muslim neighbors are not welcome guests except for at specific events (such as the Mimouna), and for a very limited time. Regulating their entry into the home helps to reduce anxiety toward them, anxiety that arises when Jews meet Muslims, and found mainly in the framework of intimate and revealing venues such as those in the house.

Not only do Jews avoid physical encounters with Muslims, but they also manage to ignore their presence. Remember the story of Mrs. Sol Suissa, who defined her neighbors as "like Jews" in order to cope with her frequent meetings with them? This form of ignoring reality was not rare, since it provided the Jews with the possibility to employ Muslim housekeepers without being overly concerned by this on a daily basis.

One day I was invited to dinner at the home of one of the more prominent personalities of the Jewish community. The house was very impressive and full of assorted items that gave it a very elegant, "oriental" look: expensive paintings by Moroccan artists hung on the walls, enormous copper jugs made in the best of Moroccan traditions stood in different corners of the guest room, large and heavy pieces of "woven" furniture (various types of furniture made from the juniper tree which grows in the area of Essawira, from its spectacularly twisted roots), and other kinds of "artisan" items (handmade works of art) were scattered throughout the house.

Various dignitaries from the community leadership were invited to dinner. The great efforts invested in preparing dinner were evident and integrated a delicate and fine balance between Moroccan and French cuisine. It was apparent that much trouble had been taken to make a positive impression. Therefore, when I watched the housekeepers serve the food I was very surprised. They seemed to be a perfect contrast to the prestigious look the household attempted to convey; their clothes were simple, with many large grease stains and tears. One of the younger women wore a faded t-shirt. The t-shirt had a deep tear at the neck exposing her breasts every time she served a dish to the table. Later, when I asked one of the guests about this huge gap between the wealth and the appearance of the help, and especially about this young woman, he claimed that he didn't even notice. That may be the case, and on that level the young woman, like the other helpers, was completely transparent. But even if he chose not to address my question, the mere fact that the hosts permitted such a sight, or disregarded it, points to a mechanism of ignoring that which is present, something that I would like to clarify.[42]

As part of the mechanism of ignoring that which is there, Jews do not know even basic information about their housekeeper's lives, and make no effort to do so. When I asked Daniel Elgarbali, a widower for over thirty years, details about his housekeeper, who had worked in his household from the time his wife was still alive, he could not say much. Although he treated her with great kindness, he didn't even know if the housekeeper, Rabiha, was single, married, divorced, or widowed. Only after I asked him did he return to me with the simplest details about her. Only after I asked about her did he think that maybe he could take an interest in Rabiha's life after she had spent over three decades caring for him on a daily basis.

This practice of ignoring makes room for the Muslim presence in intimate quarters. By definition, their transparency transforms these same Muslims into "non-Muslims." This transparency greatly reduces the anxiety that would seemingly flourish in private domains in the presence of Muslims. Moreover, the working condition of the housekeepers reverses the power structure. The inferior image of cleaning work further reinforces the feelings of reversed roles. This mechanism is not unknown to the Jews; they are fully aware of it. During a conversation about the benefits of living in Morocco, Lissette Gazizy declared, "Only in Morocco can you find an Arab who will clean a Jew's home for a trivial sum of Dirham [the Moroccan currency] in an Arab country!"

This reversal of roles is especially complex and intricate when it involves housekeepers. During a conversation that took place among Jewish women about the cost of a housekeeper, one woman asked to demonstrate just how dangerous life is in Morocco by saying, "Yes, it's true that life is easy [thanks to the low cost of housekeepers]. But, one day some Abed,[43] who carries baskets from the market place for five Dirham [a little over 0.1 USD] will come to you and say: 'Now you pick up my baskets for two Dirham!' And there will be nothing anybody can do!"

This statement, like the frequent comparisons to the situation of eastern European Jews before World War Two—and even more so on the eve of the Holocaust—demonstrate the Jewish awareness of the possibility that the borders that separate the different domains are flexible and alterable. But, as stated, Jews routinely tend to ignore the presence of the housekeeper in their homes by making them transparent. Overlooking household help personnel who enter the home is not of course, a unique characteristic to Jews in the present Moroccan context. This is a phenomenon that is found mostly in encounters between people from opposing social classes. However, ignoring the housekeeper is not always possible. In some households disputes between the housekeepers and their Jewish employers arise quite frequently (women are responsible for the employment of the housekeepers). In these same households (usually a small but steady number), the quarrels relate to the employer's criticism and dissatisfaction with the quality of the housekeeper's work, her seriousness and diligence. But this can be a mixed blessing: while the criticism makes the housekeeper's presence more felt in the Jews' home, reinforcing the dissatisfaction with her performance perpetuates a vicious cycle which almost always ends with the dismissal of the housekeeper. In these same households one will encounter the repeating motif of employing a housekeeper, criticism (that is, awareness of their presence), dismissal, and over again.

Part of the mechanism instrumental in causing changes in the borders relates to the fact that the definition of domains as Jewish is under attack. Poor Jews who live in small homes rented by the Committee experience this attack more so, precisely because of their low economic status. These Jews don't enjoy economic supremacy while facing their housekeepers, a supremacy that allows for the positioning of a relatively firm border. The interaction between the poor and their housekeepers is one that is on a fairly equal basis. It appears that for this reason these Jews will turn to the Committee for help to recruit a powerful person who can represent them from a position of superiority opposite their housekeeper.[44]

In addition to the violation of the ethno-status border in a situation where there is equal status, there are other situations that break the balance and allow the borders to be damaged. One such example is due to political reasons. During the First Gulf War there was a rumor among the Jews of Casablanca, a rumor that later proved to be correct, that an old Jewish woman who lived all by herself in Maarif (an area with almost no Jews), was murdered by her housekeeper. Since the old woman didn't live in close proximity to other Jews, as many Jews explained to themselves, her body was only discovered a few days later. There was no one to check on what happened to her, as Jews usually do. This difficult incident demonstrated to the Jews just how much transparency, as a reasonable code of social behavior, was not stable; housekeepers could suddenly become a presence. The exposure of housekeepers to the Jewish eye—that is, Jewish awareness of the existence of Muslims in their own homes—means a disturbing shift of utopian borders. "Outside" events penetrate (in this case—the war against Iraq) and shatter the already fragile routine, and along with it the illusion of a comforting peace.

A BRIEF SUMMARY

Common knowledge assumes that weak minorities are located in marginal areas (Shields 1991). However, as I have demonstrated in this chapter, there are (diasporic) minorities that are situated in the economic centers of the metropolis, testifying to their survival ability and their surprising ability to act. This location does not necessarily indicate a remarkable political ability, and at times there may be a significant economic capacity, but one that lacks essential political backing. Since the location in the economic center does not always improve one's political ability, groups may establish spatial distinctions between areas that are suitable to live in and those that are not. An existence such as this, which wavers between economic ability and political weakness, simultaneously generates claims of superiority and expressions of fear and anxiety, which in turn encourage trends of isolation and a hardening of one's identity. The question that remains and that lies before us is: what are the everyday characteristics involved in the construction of limitations in these two contradictory processes of distancing. Moreover, does the minority indeed have the ability to impose upon itself such strict self-isolation? The answer is self-evident: no. Then what are the mechanisms that allow for encounters in such a charged context as this? The next chapter will discuss these topics, while focusing on the dynamics of the daily routine.

CHAPTER 5

Contraction and Control: Jews, Muslims, and Card Games in Casablanca

"If it weren't for our exclusive clubs . . . if we didn't have our *Israelite* [Jewish] enclaves, we would not survive here, we would not last a single day in Morocco!" declared Joe Elmakias in despair during a card game in the CA club (Cercle de l'Alliance Israélite) in Casablanca. Those present, all Jewish residents of the city, wearily nodded their agreement to what was an obvious statement. During the course of the game, this taken-for-granted statement was meant to bring up once again the central existential experience of the Jews: the decline of Jewish spheres of activity. As mentioned in the two previous chapters, contraction is the process of decrease and convening; that is, in the gradual process of the dwindling of life's elements, a gathering inwards from the world around.

The preceding chapter presented a panoramic discussion of the various spatial spheres in and among which the Jews of Morocco moved. In contrast, in this chapter, I will focus on one specific spatial activity: card games on a beach. I will offer a fairly detailed interpretation of the card game scene, while relating to it both as a "game" and as "play," in order to gain an intimate and hopefully even deeper understanding of the relationships between Jews and Muslims in Morocco. I would like to show that, as a game, card playing provides a framework of structural, ritual behavior, disciplined, regulated, and predictable, with its own control and feedback systems, and in Morocco allowed a protective ground for Jews to meet Muslims on the beach. But as play—namely, as a "nonserious" and yet subversive activity—it poses many provocative and even undermining questions about the social order by proposing an anarchic bricolage of the normative existence. Card games destabilize the social fabric between the two groups and stand at odds with the persistent desire of Jews to conduct peaceful and controlled relations with Muslims.

Another way to look at the tension that games provoke relates to the question of the relevance of the context surrounding them, because even though card games are bound by rules, they are not isolated from their surrounding sociopolitical and cultural contexts. In the words of anthropologist Michael Herzfeld, games are a "medium for rich, metaphorical discourse that plays out some of the most essential themes of a society" (Herzfeld 1985:152). However, unlike Herzfeld's ethnographic tales, in which the Glendiot people's adherence to the rules is "of relatively little interest in the uncertain idiom of Glendiot life" (Herzfeld 1985:152), for Moroccan Jews there is crucial importance to following the rules. As I will show later, adhering to the rules serves the Jews with one of their most fundamental issues, allowing them to separate their own complexities from those of Muslims.

I offer here an interpretation for the Jews' motives in conducting meetings with Muslims under such complicated conditions. This interpretation will serve as a further step in deepening the understanding of the intricate and complex relationship with Muslims. Card games that take place on one of the private beaches of Casablanca are of immense ethnographic interest because they provide the only stable and consistent social framework for voluntary encounters between Jews and Muslims. It is important to note that, outside of the beach area, very few Jews play cards with Muslims. I myself never witnessed any of these games (although I know they existed from various reports of a few isolated events). These clubs were off limits for me, as they were for most Moroccan Jews. In the same vein, Jewish clubs did not welcome Muslim presence; in fact, I witnessed only a handful of events in which Muslims entered Jewish clubs as visitors (and not as employees). Only once a year did Jews allow Muslims to enter their clubs and play cards. Not surprisingly, it was on the Purim holiday, full of symbolic reversal. This carnival-holiday encourages Jews to drink wine to the point of not being able to differentiate between ("cursed is") Haman and ("blessed is") Mordechai; that is, to the point where the person celebrating will no longer notice the boundary lines distinguishing between Jews and non-Jews. So, within this formal yet playful framework, which temporarily suspends ethnic-religious borders, Muslims were allowed to enter the socio-cultural Jewish enclaves.

Games such as these took place in Maghreb in the past as well. Jews and Muslims played different types of soccer (Bahloul 1992:81–83; Herr 1982), or violent versions of "tag" (Bilu and Levy 1996:296–297; Pascon and Schroeter 1982). Not surprisingly, these games were organized around ethnic boundaries, as such, they were also perceived that way by the participants. In anthropologist Joël Bahloul's words, "Jews established their identities in this hostile world. In the street, boys' games acted out these interethnic antagonisms" (Bahloul 1996:72). Hence, as political tensions grew stronger, such as after the end of the Qaramanli regime in Libya, so too violent incidents became more frequent during the interethnic games. David Ha-Cohen, for instance, maintains that because of "incidents the games were curtailed by the Turkish authorities in 1845 . . . and were completely eliminated in 1850" (in Goldberg 1990:34). As such, for these researchers, games served as a yardstick for examining the relations with Muslims. Likewise, in the days following the colonial period, there were those who saw (and still see today) the very existence of interethnic games as a suitable prism through which to examine the political situation in general and the nature of the relationship between Jews and Muslims in particular. Thus, various Jewish organizations point at the existence of interethnic games as a measure of political calm (Laskier 1990).[45]

SET ONE: RULES OF THE GAME

Despite the somewhat moralistic stance which rejects them entirely, card games are without a doubt one of the most common leisure activities among Jews in Morocco. Many men and women play cards on a daily basis in a variety of clubs. So much so that I, too, joined these card games in the clubs. Nevertheless, to maintain stress-free relations with the club members, I did not participate in the actual gambling. However, my hesitations "to get wet," as professional player would call it, did not prevent me from participating in games that involved gambling. In the games where the stakes were for insignificant amounts of money, I was invited to join as a "Jockey,": that is to say, I was invited as a player that didn't have to gamble.[46] My partner ("the owner") gambled for both of us; if he won—he got the money. In time, I enjoyed the image of a gifted, successful, and fine player and was even given the title of "Professor." As such, when there was "heavy" playing going on, I played the role of "outside spectator," and when the gambling involved small amounts of money I was a "participant." As an observer I was able to closely follow the dynamics between the players themselves and between them and the "kibbitzers" (playful spectators). These conditions were favorable to me, because it was impossible (at least for me) to split my attention between playing the game and observing it; I was unable to carefully follow the complex and subtle dynamics between the players during the game if I was involved as an active player. I have experienced card games as a total, sweeping activity and, to some degree, both seductive and addictive.

"Rummy Couples" was the most popular card game, both in the clubs and on the beach. On the surface it appears to be a simple game with fixed and well-defined rules: participants include two pairs of players. Each player has fourteen cards and in turn picks a card and discards an unwanted card with the goal of organizing the cards in his hand into series. The cards are taken from the deck or from a player who had previously discarded an unwanted card onto the table. A player plays a series on the table that was arranged during the set. A couple wins a set when one of the pair succeeds in organizing all of his fourteen cards into series. In order to accomplish this he can play out his own series or integrate his cards with card sets that have already been laid out on the table. At the conclusion of the set, the number of the opponents' points retained in their hands is counted and scored as a negative value (according to the value of the cards that were not placed on the table). As the game proceeds there is constant tension between the desire to lay down a card series on the table and the desire to prevent the opponent from having the opportunity to integrate his remaining cards into the series on the table. In other words, it is not always a good idea to play your series, for the more cards that are exposed, the more the opponent's chances of using them to organize his hand are increased. The game is over when a couple reaches the number of negative points agreed upon in advance, and only then is the value of the bet paid.

The basic rules of the Rummy game are quite clear, simple, and binding. Like soccer or basketball, card games are rule-bound activities, with the rules being strict and not negotiable or given to interpretation, just as traffic signs, for example, are not meant to be ambiguous. It is therefore no wonder that when Michael Kruyat, accepted among the professional players (namely, among those who played for large sums of money) and considered a refined and sophisticated (*"fin"*) player, doubted a certain rule of a "Blote" game, he encountered the strong and outraged opposition of Sam Buhatseira. The latter, who was also counted among the exclusive club of the most sophisticated players, said that this rule contested by Kruyat appears in black and white in *The Book of Belote*, published by the Belote organization in Paris. Michael first denied the existence of such a book, claiming these were outrageous rumors. But when he came up against a brick wall of agreement from everyone present in the debate, he opposed the interpretation of the controversial rule, claiming to Sam Buhatseira that "anybody can write a book. If they say this is the rule then you can tear apart this book." All those witnessing this argument were shocked by his blasphemy. Game rules are not to be contested. Agreement with the rules is critical, precisely because unlike games such as soccer or basketball, there is no referee who decides at every moment what the appropriate behavior is. But, like any other game, the agreement to accede to the rules is a prerequisite and unwavering.

Even if the basic rules of Rummy Couples are few and fairly simple, players establish a large number of unwritten regulations, including endless subrules and tactics (like the question of when to expose your hand) aimed at reducing the effect of random distribution of cards. These unwritten regulations are mostly concerned with the ways in which players track their rivals' and partners' course of play. What distinguishes a good player (sophisticated, cunning, and usually successful) from a bad one (unskilled, simplistic, and usually losing) is the mastery over the different tactics. An unskilled player relies solely on the random distribution of cards and hopes for the best. A good player is one who is considered knowledgable in overcoming the randomness of card distribution; he knows how to follow developing situations from clues exposed during the set (for example: which cards did his opponent or partner dispose of). A good player knows how to evaluate and analyze the other players' situations and knows which cards he needs to complete his series. Likewise, good players will make every effort to keep cards that are vital to their opponent in their own hands (if these are in their possession), even if they don't need them and even if holding onto them means the possibility of "breaking" one's own hand. A good player should know when to hide the set of cards in his hand and to conceal his situation from his opponent; it is especially important not to reveal the type of series he is holding. He also knows the correct timing for disposing of part of the card series he holds and placing them on the table, thereby allowing his partner to integrate his extra cards into these series (and at the same time to ensure that this act of exposure will not make it too easy for his opponent to end the game) and the set. In short, there are a multitude of aspects to take into consideration, all of which relate to the need to follow the actions of others and to be attentive to both the partner and the rivals.

Players and kibitzers alike are supposed to remain quiet while playing. This rule is considered even more sacred in "serious" games. However, when I was present, at the end of each turn conversations would suddenly erupt, usually with people trying to explain their crafty actions, their sophisticated ideas, and their knowledge and mastery of the game. Losers did this with greater enthusiasm since they had to prove that it was only bad luck that prevented them from winning. Winners would stress how they used their abilities to exploit the weakness of their rival's reasoning in order to overcome the weak cards they were dealt. Partners analyzed their hands and the complex moves they made, while boasting their profound understanding of their partner's situation when they won the game and blaming each other when they lost. This rhetorical action following each set clarified the intentions of each of the teams. During these lively discussions partners sought to both praise themselves on their ingenuity and to coordinate expectations for the continuation of the game, while making an effort to better understand their partner's intentions.

Even so, despite the games' being regulated by very clear rules, their nature and dynamics were also shaped by their context. One of the most relevant contexts of the games was the club in which they were held. The more polite games took place at the CU club. As already mentioned, this was the most prestigious and exclusive establishment of the Jewish community. It had clear, tough, and undisputed rules of membership criteria, with most of its members counted among the middle-class or well-off of the Jewish community. There card games were not defined by simple gender boundaries. Men and women played together or separately, and the games were conducted in complete silence. Many members played bridge, which was considered an elitist game in the club, even if they preferred the more popular French card games such as Belote. Gambling, even on large sums of money, was not regarded as violating the dignified atmosphere of the club, such that even in games considered "refined" or sophisticated, there was gambling.

The CU club stood in almost complete contrast to another Jewish club, the CA. In the past the CA had served as the club for Alliance graduates; despite this, its admission criteria had become quite lenient. It was rare that someone was expelled from the CA club (even if there were temporary removals). Club members did not display the same level of restraint as in the CU. Card games were quite noisy, and club members talked between them, laughing, joking, and loudly teasing one another. At times, the storminess of the games even led to an exchange of blows. Arguments and quarrels arose every now and again, mainly alongside accusations of cheating at cards. It is important to note at this time that despite the inclusive nature of the club, the games were exclusive. They were single-sex: informally but systematically prohibited to women.[47]

The connection I make between the exchanging of blows and the exclusion of women is not accidental. According to the opinion shared by both men and women in the CA club, it is inappropriate for women to witness—let alone participate in—such dubious incidents. Therefore, card games were held on the top floor of the club, where there were no women or children. The latter came for the most part at their mother's command, who asked them to remind the father that it was time to go home. "We are not like the CU, where women participate in card games," said Sam Buhatseira, one of the more prominent people at the CA club told me, and he added: "They have many problems there [at the CU]. Since married couples play together there, they find it hard to close the club at reasonable hours. Husbands do not have any limits—since their wives are with them, they can stay for long hours. It's also not polite that women witness all the aggression and the scandalous cheating."

Despite these words, which seemed to summarize the main opposition to women's participation in card games, there was another unspoken reason, although obvious to everyone: the games were replete with sexual rhetoric and bodily gestures. For example, always when a player integrated his card into his opponent's exposed series he used movements metaphoric of sexual intercourse: he would spread open (the opponent's cards) and insert (his card). In many cases, at the end of each set, there were outbursts of sexual gestures whose meaning was "I screwed you," "I fucked you," "I fixed you," "I got you by the balls," and so on. Sexual use of the cards themselves was varied: poking it into the groin (of the player) or to the butt (of the opponent, the Muslim waiter that passed by, the player himself), use of the card symbols to convey messages ("my prince screwed you"), or even in reverse ("my queen screwed your king"). All these expressions were strongly conveyed and loudly spoken.

The more I watched these games, the more I thought I understood them: or understood their meaning. I thought I understood the picture of passionate, vibrant, and enthusiastic card games within the protective patronage of Jewish clubs. But with the arrival of summer all at once the cards were reshuffled (I must use this metaphor!) because then, Muslims joined the games.

EXPOSURE AT THE BEACH: SET TWO

Toward the start of my second summer in Casablanca I noticed that the CA club, which was full of life throughout the winter, was now emptying. Attendance dwindled rapidly. Following a brief inquiry, I found that club members favored spending time at the beach. When I arrived there, I was very surprised at what I saw: not only did Jews attend a beach that was largely populated by Muslims, but they were intensively involved in card games with them. At first glance it seemed that the ease and calm I saw, which characterized leisure time on the beach, could not sit well with the tremendous sense of threat that Jews feel in the face of such proximity and intimacy with Muslims. If I had not witnessed this myself, I would have bet that Jews would tend to avoid attending such revealing settings. It was not only the closeness to the Muslims, but also that the whole interaction transpired on a site that exposed to all the diminishing numbers of the Jewish community. After all, everyone could see for themselves the growing decrease each summer.

"Just like our clubs," lamented Momo Elmaliach, in rich poetic French, of the situation of the Jews, "such is the beach: It is a place of refuge and not a site for relaxation. I go there only because it is a place where other Jews also come to be together. In this way we create a Ghetto. It is our own doing!" But Momo revealed only a partial truth. After all, most Jews enjoyed going to the beach, even though it was accompanied by a faint—almost inexplicit or indiscernible—feeling of distress and anxiety.

In a nutshell, the attenuating tension in the presence of Muslims on the beach is the result of socio-cultural mechanisms that provide a sense of control in the relations with Muslims. Apparently, the relaxation that results from recreational activity (E. Cohen 1979), symbolically expressed by the removal of clothing, and the removal of signs of cultural distinction, simultaneously produces borders and rigid socio-cultural limits as to rules of conduct on the beach. As anthropologist Victor Turner taught us, it is precisely the situations of permitted social loosening that become the most socially controlled (Turner 1967). Or, in the words of sociologist Erving Goffman upon relating to the naked body: "When bodies are naked, glances are clothed" (Goffman 1971:46). The societal "clothing" of the intrusive stare restrains the anarchic potential of the metaphoric nakedness.

There were many guidelines involved in moderating fears resulting from exposure in the presence of Muslims. The most fundamental rule Jews maintained was the strict observance of the boundary portraying ethnic differences. The Jews were particularly careful about making that border apparent to all. They persisted in maintaining outward manifestations, for the most pressing threat that lay at the doorstep of the Jews on the beach stemmed both concretely and metaphorically from the exposure of the body. They did not want to be standing stark naked before the Muslims, for nudity might endanger the stability of relations and, even worse, might openly expose their weakness. Control over relations with Muslims at the beach (or at very least their peaceful management) was achieved by employing various codes of behavior on the beach to their advantage.

CONTROL AND SPATIAL ORGANIZATION–THIRD SET

For many Jews (and not only those who frequented the clubs) the summer marked the beginning of regular visits to the beach. The majority chose "Tahiti," a beach situated among other private beaches, whose names are likewise mostly borrowed from resorts in the Pacific. Like the other closed beaches, Tahiti's space was bordered, small, and crowded.

The vacationers let the beating sun burn their skin for long hours, indifferent to the dangers of ultraviolet rays. On weekdays, men usually spent time during their long afternoon breaks on the beach. Toward evening, after work hours, they would return for another few hours. Frequently their wives would join them in the afternoon, and together they would have a light lunch of roast beef sandwiches. The beach was more populated on weekends (Saturday and Sunday), when many would arrive in the early morning and stay to relax until the late evening hours.

Playing into the Jews' hands, in their desire to maintain control of their relationships with the Muslims on the closed beach, were two "gatekeepers." In using this term, I am referring to the same socio-cultural and economic barriers that define the profile of the people who visit the beach. One of these mechanisms, economic ability, is not at all unique to the Moroccan context: only those who could afford the relatively high cost of an admission fee (whether annual or daily) were able to enter. Presumably, the structure of the unequal distribution of wealth compartmentalized the majority of the Muslim population as well as a small portion of the Jewish population. The second gatekeeper is a unique variety in the Moroccan context; it acts on the principle of self-restraint for those who are not welcome at the beach, and it is they themselves who choose to keep their distance from it. In other words, only those willing to expose their bodies publicly, both men and women, will come to the beach. Therefore orthodox Jews and Muslims did not attend the beach. The Jews and Muslims who did frequent the beach belonged to a socioeconomic and culturally defined class that was characterized by its commitment to what they perceived as "European culture," or, to be more precise, "French culture." It soon became clear that this socio-cultural characteristic manifested itself in the relatively common use of French on the beach (even if Muslims tended to use colloquial Arabic on the beach). Moreover, relative to what took place in other public spaces in Morocco, women were not subject to the threatening male stares and were not afraid to walk on public beaches without a male escort, even while wearing minimal clothing (even though almost no women came by themselves).

On the beach there was a concrete pathway connecting several areas: this path became a fashion runway where men and women walked together in an intriguing colorful parade. Those participating in the procession wore the fanciest bathing suits from top European designers. Bikinis and beach clothes were changed frequently, both in response to the dictates of fashion and in the desire to tan more body parts. The parade was a colorful and lively event in which people enjoyed both watching and being watched. Up-to-date fashion, partial nakedness, and suntans joined together in blurring any signs that still remained visible after the unifying actions of the "gatekeepers." Indeed, an outside eye would find it difficult to distinguish the differences between the groups on the beach, since two weeks after the swimming season opened, all were equally dark-skinned. The entire scene looked like a Moroccan version of French middle-class culture, blurring ethno-religious differences for the good of the general republican codes of conduct.

The "gatekeepers," in what seemed like a unifying process, undermined the Jews' goal of establishing a visible and clear boundary distinguishing themselves from the Muslims. However, a closer look revealed the socio-cultural differences among the seemingly uniform, human mass of sunbathers. These partitions were particularly apparent in the distinct relationships that existed between various areas on the beach.

Bungalow Rooms

On the southern part of the beach there were two levels of bungalows. The lowest was populated almost entirely by Jews, while the Muslims usually occupied most of the upper level. In terms of prestige, upper and lower are reversed: the upper bungalows were considered to be inferior (at least to the Jews) because they were too close to the outside fence and therefore subject to the wistful-annoying and embarrassing gaze of the passerby, who looked longingly from the sidewalk outside, to see what was happening at the beach. In addition, this level was far from the bustling activity below, on the beach itself. The choosing of the bungalow rooms according to a criterion of belonging to a particular group was not accidental; it was deliberately created by the Jews. Every year, a Jewish community employee took the effort to arrange collective purchasing of annual rental tickets for Jews. Thus, the collective rental of rooms prevented a situation where Jews would find themselves in too close proximity to a bungalow room of Muslims. Typically, the women managed the bungalows, in which domain they fulfilled their traditional tasks as housewives; they prepared sandwiches and cold drinks for the house members and drop-in guests, they watched the children and chatted with neighboring Jews. They rarely interacted with Muslim neighbors, men or women. The small yard in front of the bungalow served as a sunbathing area, half private, half public. Women were not restricted in their movements in these areas, only because they were always under the careful watch of the men. I, for example, was

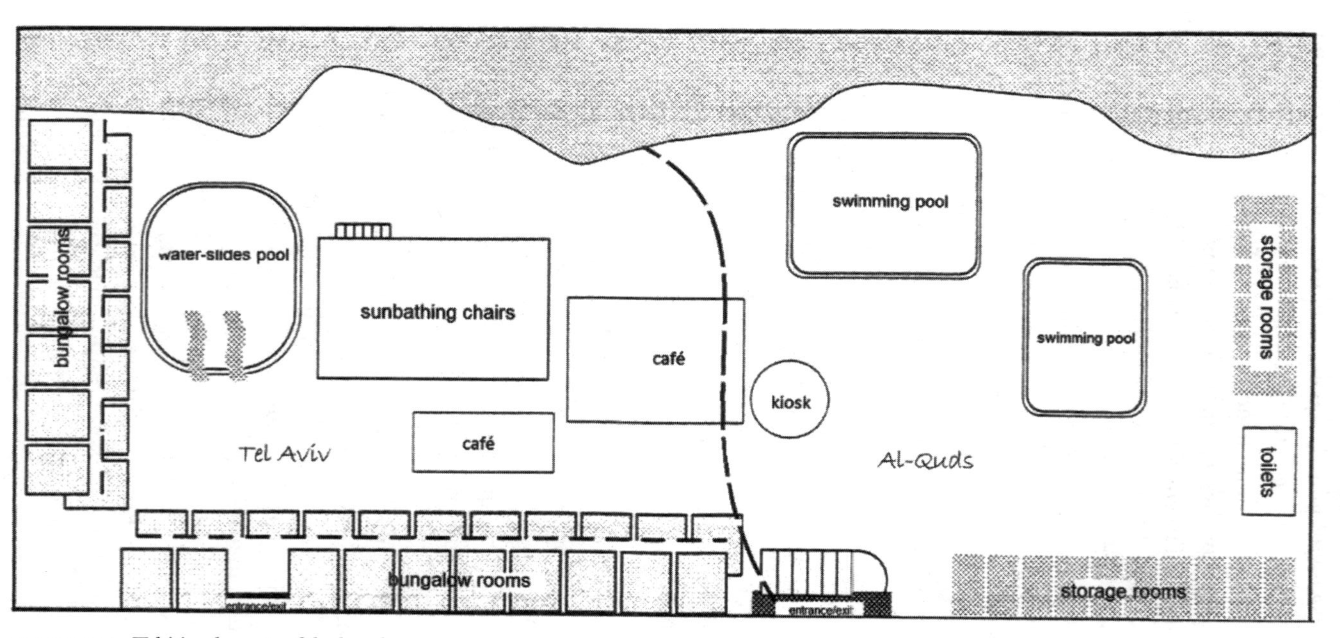

FIGURE 7. Tahiti: schemata of the beach

never able to hold a private conversation with a woman on the beach without a man—a spouse, relative, or friend—suddenly appearing. Muslim women were even more limited then Jewish women. It was rare to see them moving about by themselves for more than a brief moment.

Changing/Storage Rooms

To the north of the bungalow area, and directly opposite them, were two rows of small rooms used for changing and stowing clothes. Only a few Jews (usually the young singles or the less affluent) rented these cabins. The symbolic socioeconomic division between the storage cabins and the bungalows were an unmarked, yet well conceptualized, boundary between the Muslim and Jewish areas of the beach. The distinction between the north and south areas of the beach not only related to the minority presence of Jews in the cabin area, but mainly, to the degree of control. The spatial division was not a figment of my commentator imagination; it was conceptualized in the nicknames that both Jews and Muslims ascribed to each of these spaces: "Tel-Aviv" and "Al-Quds" (Arabic: Jerusalem). The symbolic division of the beach did not only carry a political message, but also a message of socioeconomic hierarchy. The northern area included the storage and changing rooms and bathrooms. Thus, the Muslim area becomes the backyard of the Jews. The spatial hierarchical distinction of an area this small allowed Jews to send a double message: first, it reflected the Jewish insistence in emphasizing the boundaries between them and the Muslims. Second, the hierarchical division allowed for the definition of Muslim areas as inferior.

Playground

In accordance with the socioeconomic division, most of the recreational facilities (such as the water slides or the large swimming pools) were within the "Tel Aviv" boundaries. Muslims who wished to enjoy these recreational facilities had to cross the unmarked, but very real, border and go to "Tel Aviv." When Jewish children found themselves alone in the playground without a Jewish friend nearby, they preferred to play by themselves and ignore the Muslim children of their age. Jewish mothers immediately intervened when there seemed to be a possibility of interaction between Jewish and Muslim children. The most common method to stop the unnamed, unwelcomed meeting was by calling the child to the bungalow to come and have something to eat. Thus mothers fulfilled the visible and expected role well, of nourishing their children, as well as the hidden one of overseeing their children's encounters with Muslim peers. This act of prevention was due, among other things, to the fact that children were considered to be divulgers of information that should not be expressed in the presence of Muslims. Parents frequently told half-frightening, half-amusing stories of embarrassing incidents when children repeated offensive and insulting jokes that made fun of Muslims, jokes which they had heard from their parents.

Sunbathing Chairs

Those who could not afford the seasonal rental of a bungalow rented lounge chairs for a day of sunbathing on the beach. The area allocated for this was in the border area between "Al Quds" and "Tel Aviv": in the middle, neither here nor there. The space was quite small and only a limited number of chairs could be spread out there. The sense of a zero-sum game due to the limit of chairs created a fierce competition and dictated efforts to take control over the limited space. Throughout the day a constant and intricate dynamic evolved between Jews and Muslims sprawled on the chairs, while the ethnic barrier between them had not been specified in advance. The changing spatial boundary in this small area was the result of its location between the territories and from the fact that physically one may expand or contract the space; chairs were rented to individuals—not to the collective. Thus, the vacationers who could not establish previously determined ethnic borders (relatively, of course) would initially place their chairs in open areas. Indeed, Jews could not create preset Jewish enclaves, but they attempted to arrive in small groups and over time take spaces that were vacated and create small islands that constantly grew as the day passed. Sometimes Jews found themselves "isolated"–alone among large groups of Muslims. In that case, they signaled their desire to be alone, disengaged, and avoided interaction. They used clear, simple codes such as wearing large hats that covered their face or putting on dark glasses to avoid eye contact, by listening to music with earphones, by scattering bags, towels, t-shirts, and other belongings around their chair to mark the border and increase their private space. Sometimes they simply fell asleep.

Up to this point I have made an effort to describe the successful creation of boundaries that, with the help of structural mechanisms, separate and mollify, despite the symbolic and real exposure. However, observing only the structural components is liable to oversimplify the interpretation of events, as it accentuates even more intensely the ability of Jews to establish a hierarchical relationship with Muslims and ignores the inherent challenge that exists in almost every interaction that takes place between the two groups.

The actual interactions, nevertheless, constantly challenge the boundaries, if only because Muslims evidently do not accept Jewish definitions of reality (Rosen 1984). A structural-mechanical view such as this on the spatial organization gives rise to limited interpretation that emphasizes the dynamic nature of human beings. As an example of this, I offer the observation of the dynamic interaction among Jewish and Muslim card players which takes place around the coffeehouse tables of "Tel Aviv."

CARDPLAYERS ON THE BEACH: PLAYING, AT LAST

Both men and women played cards on the beach, although the latter were not involved in "serious" games. Jewish women played cards among themselves and sometimes with their male counterparts within the borders of the bungalow rooms. I never saw them play with Muslim women, and certainly never with Muslim men. Games that were not serious ("for respect" or "just to kill time") were played for soft drinks, or even for nothing. "Mixed" games (games in which Jews and Muslims played together) usually entailed bets of large sums of money.[48] The most popular game on the beach was Rummy Couples.

Rummy Couples is a game for pairs, and it requires close coordination between the partners in the game. The necessity of following one's partner and rivals during the game, as well as the interpretation of the rhetoric that takes place at the end of each set, demands a great deal of sensitivity to each other, whether a Jew or a Muslim. What especially complicates the need to be attentive to the other is an unwritten, undeclared, but extremely rigid rule, strictly adhered to when Jews and Muslims play together in pairs: a Jewish couple never plays against a Muslim one. As if without noticing, Jews and Muslims form mixed couples: A Jew and Muslim against a Jew and Muslim, two Jews against a Jew and Muslim, and rarely two Muslims against a Muslim and Jew. This configuration is not accidental. Even if not publicly stated, it is an intentional and conscious construction of the way the game is played. One summer day, when Roger Adas gave me a ride home from the beach he called my attention to this principle: "Did you notice that Jews never play against Muslims? We do it on purpose. We don't want them to think that we are double-dealing them. Who needs that trouble?!" The Jews were eager to avoid allegations and accusations that ran along ethnic lines and therefore the game was seemingly not organized around ethnic borders. Indeed, in contrast to what I saw at games at the CA (which were only conducted among Jews), I never witnessed a breach of mixed games, even if there was a valid suspicion of fraud in the game. The game framework was always maintained. This mechanism ensured a calm management of relations with Muslims.

A controlled management of relations with Muslims was attained by maintaining regular playing partners, who had known each other for a long period of time. Consistency ensured predictability, moderating the fact that the game by definition was unexpected, due to the innumerable combinations of cards distributed. Time allowed for a chance to become familiar with the quirks and folly of one's partner. Even when Jews were not satisfied with the skills or temperament of their Muslim partner, they tended not to replace him. This preference is explained by the Jews' lack of desire to restart the process of building mutual understanding with a new partner, while also not wanting to change their luck. It seems to me that this preference is also indicative of an effort to maintain predictable and stable relations with Muslims.

Seemingly, the configuration of mixed couples, like the need to follow the "Other," breaks the iron rule of strict separation between Jews and Muslims. But, as it may be deduced from Roger Adas's words, this was not the Jews' intention. As far as they were concerned, the mixing of couples *within the game* was not indicative of an integrative ethnic trend; on the contrary, it was an indication of deep social division *outside* of the game.

The relevance of an ethnic dichotomy between card players appears already in the act of pairing the players, but it is also an essential part of the game dynamics itself. Provoking and teasing relationships based on ethnic-religious division, for example, occur frequently in the course of the games. For example, when David Cohen bragged after winning a game, his Muslim rival, Sa'id al-Kaslasi, immediately responded in a bitter but moderate tone: "you—*ya Shrif*—you don't 'play it' right!" By that al-Kaslasi declared that David was fibbing in the game and therefore his victory was not kosher. Interestingly enough, however, was the nickname he used for David, "Shrif," that is, a descendant of a holy Muslim family.[49] Like Muslims who are linked to the Prophet Muhammad's family (Shrif), David also belongs to a category of priestly Jewish descendants (Cohen). Thus although Sa'id used an Islamic term in order to express the notion of holy Jewish genealogy, he also used this term in order to tease and even criticize the Jew: he accused David of playing an "un-kosher" game. Not only was David playing a "secular" game, but he was also cheating. His participation in a game that was all frivolity (not to mention the context of partial nudity on the beach) intensified the criticism embedded in Sa'id's words. Needless to say that a game played for money, on the Sabbath, sharpened even more strongly the criticism of David.[50]

Teasing and provoking were not only the Muslims' dominion, with Jews sitting quietly on the side. Sami Gazizy, for example, tended to use clowning tactics in hierarchical relationships, whether toward Muslims or toward Jews in places of power. Sami—who was nicknamed by his acquaintances "Spinning Top" due to his stormy temperament, quick thinking, and impulsivity—mocked his Muslim rival, Mahmid ben-Tulila, who lost lots of money in a game: "Why are you crying so much about the money you lost? You can cover your losses immediately, by selling ten grams of gold to some Jewish suckers!" Another Jew, who wanted to take Mahmid's place at the table, continued after him, in the hope that Mahmid would leave the game: "Go to work! You need to open your jewelry store! Many Jews are waiting in line for your gold!" Mahmid, one of the regular couple players on the beach, responded immediately, "What are you talking about??!! It's Shabbat; no Jew will buy from me today." In the Maghrebi context, this teasing also had bound into it a reversed symbolic historical memory; in the past, it was the Jews who were responsible for the craft of jewelry making, since observant Muslim men are not allowed to wear gold jewelry, and in the above interaction the jeweler was in fact, a Muslim.

The mixing of couples doesn't always succeed in attaining the goal of reducing ethnic tensions. Sometimes the mixing works in the opposite direction and may cause tensions to deepen and sharpen the division on an ethnic basis. The game may create pressures that stem from the inherent tension in couples' games, between the need to act as an individual (a virtuoso player) and the crucial need to cooperate with the partner and be attentive to his moves. At times, this cooperation and attentiveness may require acknowledging that the partner's hand is better than your own. As such, a player would be expected to work toward improving his partner's hand, or to promote his chances of winning the set, by purposely sabotaging the arrangement of his own cards. By implication this is a recognition that one is, even if only momentarily, inferior to one's partner and submitting to his needs. Therefore, this obliges the player to withdraw from his notions and to give up his honor for the sake of the partner, who in most cases is also his "Other."

Jews frequently talked about their problematic need to concede and give in to the Muslim partner. They did not recognize this as an inherent problem for couple games, but chose to blame "the Muslim character," which because of its preoccupation with honor did not know how to concede and give in (to the Jewish partner!). "A Muslim partner is usually very stubborn," said George Levy when he wished to praise his partner's excellent manner of play by way of contrast. According to George, his partner, 'Abdallah Agbariya, had repeatedly agreed to reveal his hand, giving George more room to get rid of the cards he held which did not match his series. Thanks to his exceptional partner, they had won many times, he explained.

Most of the tensions between Jews and Muslims touched on accusations of acts of cheating. Public and open accusations were almost always a Muslim privilege. It was rare for Jews to publicly challenge Muslims. In fact, in the hundreds of games that I watched, never did a situation occur, not even once, where a Jew publicly accused a Muslim of cheating. It seems that the Jewish silence on the issue of Muslim deception was associated with the inherent fear of Jews for Muslims.

The kibitzers have always been an active part of the game circle. These same observers, Muslims and Jews, that surrounded the players and followed the game, were an integral part of the game itself, even though they refrained from "getting their hands dirty." In principle they were meant to be the passive part of the game, which was usually the way things were. They were permitted to let their voices be heard only at the point following each hand, when the players were reviewing the set. But there were occasions when they became more active, when they signaled the adversary's situation to their friends that were playing. Muslim kibitzers did not shy away from exposing cheating during the game. Jewish kibitzers always remained silent, even when they clearly witnessed Muslim kibitzers assisting in cheating. Even if their friends lost considerable amounts of money, Jews only intervened if an accusation was directed against Jews.

Suspicions about cheating did not only arise in connection to kibitzers or the opponents. A player might accuse his partner of being a collaborator with his rivals. It was not uncommon to hear accusations that a partner deliberately caused a game to be lost and would later secretly divide up the spoils with the opponents. These suspicions, it must be explained, were not the result of baseless paranoia associated with the great ambiguity of the game. Just as in the acts of cheating in which kibitzers were involved, whenever there were suspicions, the accusations of Jews were directed only at other Jews or by Muslims against Jews. Jews were always careful not to publicly defame Muslims. In general, public accusations against Muslims were something Jews were very careful about.

The only public accusations that were made were directed against players who did not pay their debts immediately after the game (and there were many). Since payment was not always made on the spot, there were many players in debt. Some Muslims were known by the Jews to be chronically in debt and tended never to return what they owed. Like other accusations, these were never made in public. This issue of failure to pay debts was raised again and again mainly surrounding the name of Aziz Balakhsin. All Jewish cardplayers agreed that Aziz belongs to the category of chronic debtors that it was best to avoid playing against. Gey Malcha went on to say in one of our discussions: "He also always teases us (Jews), but we can't retaliate." Those present nodded silently in agreement.

Aziz Balakhsin was the subject of another conversation that began when Albert Ohayon, one of the more devoted Jewish beach players, asked to demonstrate just how dangerous open confrontation was between Jews and Muslims. "A number of years ago," related Albert, "Richard Balili came to the beach following his father's death. Richard was still very sensitive about it," explained Albert; "he had just gotten up from the "*shiva,*" the mourning period. But Aziz, who had lost a lot that day, as usual, cursed Richard's father. Aziz did not know about the death of Richard's father, and Richard almost beat him to death, punching him in his face until Aziz fell to the ground!" Moshe Cohen interrupted, confirming Albert's version, and added that "on the next day Aziz was beaten once again, this time because he deliberately cursed Richard's father, but," Cohen concluded, "the third day Richard had to run away from the beach. Many Arabs . . . on the beach were furious that a Jew kept on beating an Arab, one of their brothers. He couldn't come to the beach for several months. Later, when he came, Richard said to Aziz 'Hi,' and thus the story ended."

Albert, who had carefully listened to the story, added his own conclusion: "Yes, one should know that it's better to behave correctly with Arabs! They speak nicely to Jews, but if they have to choose a side, they'll always support their brothers."

The rhetoric used to bring up the story of Richard highlighted its anomaly. It did not attempt to teach a rule. This rhetoric framed the story as an exception; there were clear circumstances that justified the deviation from the norm. It was not incidental that the fact that Richard was still mourning his father's death was inserted into a story of an exchanging of blows between Richard Balili and Aziz Balakhsin. In fact, the grief following the death served as a rhetoric justification of a rare violent outburst against a Muslim. For Jews, the danger of such conflict stemmed from the fact that Muslims would never see them as conflicts between cardplayers, but rather as conflicts between ethnic categories. In the story about Richard Balili, Albert's conclusion reaffirmed the Jews' widely accepted wisdom of self-restraint; it was pointless, foolish, and even dangerous to be involved in a situation in which there was danger of losing control of one's emotions in front of Muslims.

The fear of losing control explained the absence of women in mixed card games. It seems that in mixed games there was a taboo that resembled that of incestuous relations, as if women were too close to get involved. These unspoken rules indicate a shared view of Jews and Muslims about the dangers that could break out due to the uncontrolled emotions of women (Goldberg 1978, 1993:166–67; Mernissi 1975). Women are seen as dangerous and capricious creatures and as such are liable to endanger the delicate fabric of relations between Jews and Muslims and the ethnic boundaries that distinguish them. Moreover, because women are perceived as controlled by their sexuality and unrestrained, they might ignite tensions and provoke undesirable strife. Therefore, women should be symbolically held in confined areas and should not be exposed to the fiery and scorching card games, which, as was already mentioned, were laden with sexual expressions (compare to Herzfeld 1985:157–59).

*

"Even playing," Fatima Mernissi's mother cautions her young daughter, ". . . is a kind of war" (Mernissi 1995:3–4).

*

EXCITING ENCOUNTERS WITHIN BOUNDED SETTINGS: INSTEAD OF AN ENDGAME

During times preceding the independence of modern Morocco, interactions between Muslims and Jews were both woven into the daily routine and part of intricate and patterned relations that took place by means of rituals and games. Following the great emigration of Jews from Morocco many of these relations and patterns of interaction became unraveled, and all that remained were the games (Levy 1994). Moreover, unlike other games (such as soccer tournaments), card games were the only arena in which continual voluntary and routine relationships between Jews and Muslims were conducted. Therefore, despite the frivolity attributed to card games, it would be wise to view them seriously, since their uniqueness implies that they concealed deeper meanings than was readily apparent. However, when I told my friends in Morocco that I was writing a paper on card games they raised their eyebrows. Each and every one were of the opinion that this wasn't a serious event, worth investing thought into, beyond the statement, in itself correct, that it was a "*pour décontracter,*" emotionally relaxing activity. When I pointed out the unique character of these meetings, they expressed complete surprise and no longer negated the fact that these events were special and worthy of generating interest.

On the surface, the encounter between Jews and Muslims, precisely in a competitive environment, is surprising, because, unlike social rituals that work to connect and unite, "the game seems to divide: in the end it institutionalizes the differences between individuals or groups of players where originally there was no sign of inequality" (Levi-Strauss 1962:46).

Not only do competitive games produce schisms where none previously existed (or which weren't visible), as Levi-Strauss says, but in this case competitive games have the potential to deepen and widen schisms that already existed between Jews and Muslims. Participation in these games is particularly surprising in light of their somewhat chronic aspiration to maintain predictable, controlled, and calm relationships with Muslims. If this is the case, given that card games involve fierce rivalry, the question begs to be asked, why do Jews voluntarily choose to meet Muslims on such shaky and risky ground? It seems to me that the frivolous nature of the beach setting complicates the riddle, but also suggests possible answers to Jewish involvement in the games.

First and foremost, I note that the games are less threatening than they are portrayed from the universalist perspective of Levi-Strauss. There are three immediate regulating circles that moderate these encounters: the beach, the card games, and the primary message which maintains that the games are a source of amusement. In the first circle, the beach, its structure and organization and its rules of conduct are all enlisted to achieve some measure of control in relationships with Muslims; there, the Jews succeed in marking boundaries even within this restricted area. In concrete terms, the beach therefore is the most protected circle in which card games with Muslims take place.

The card games themselves are the second inner circle of interaction with Muslims. It appears that because card games are rule-bound activities, they offer a convenient security net for Jews. Within the relatively strict framework of the game, Jews can establish safe and controlled relations with Muslims. This goal is achieved by the pre-acceptance of a "higher authority," the strict and universal nature of the rules of the game, whatever they may be; that is, entry into the game is conditional on the acceptance of the fact that the rules are not specific to one situation or another, nor are they negotiable. Here the principle of universal social consensus of an a priori acceptance of the rules takes place; a quasi "pre-contract" in Durkheim's terms (Durkheim 1964). Included in this, then, are universal dimensions of compliance to rules. However, this type of compliance is culturally-historically specific; that is, because the players are participants in a game that they perceive as French-European, both groups take upon themselves the existence of French "outside" rules. These rules stabilize the ground on which the two groups meet. The impression of uncontestable rules, which symbolically are offered precisely by the former colonizer, allows for a dialogue between Jews and Muslims.

The third and innermost circle that moderates the threat in encounters between Jews and Muslims is connected to the meta-message concerning the nonserious nature of the *game* as characterized by *play*. Anthropologist Gregory Bateson has already emphasized this idea, when referring to the meta-message of "this is just for fun" that hovers over every game. This epistemological framing (through this meta-message) guides the awareness of the participants and establishes a line demarcating the boundary between nonplay and play (Bateson 1956, 1972). Frequently, statements such as "It's only a game [in the sense of 'fun']" that were regularly heard during games at which I was present reminded players of this boundary. Through these kinds of statements players were able to momentarily step out of the game and state seriously that this was a nonserious event. In this way, players diffused tensions that according to Levi-Strauss were inherent in the game (compare: Handelman 1977). Additional messages, played on yet a different level, were more culturally specific. When players wished to relieve tensions at certain times, they invoked the well-established cultural code of "honor" and "shame" (Gilmore 1987). Rhetorical expressions such as "It's only money," or "I play for the fun, not for the money" (and other similar statements) prevented potential outbreaks and moderated the possibility of humiliating the losers. It is important to note that such statements indicated a rhetorical partnership of Jews and Muslims involving mutual cultural idioms associated with honor and shame. Another parallel of shared idioms was expressed in the attitude toward the status of women in the games. Women, after all, possess the dangerous ability to harm honor and bring shame. Therefore, respectable women should not be exposed to the cunning and aggressive behavior (during games) of men. They should also not be witness to their disgrace when they lose.

Even deeper alliance between Jews and Muslims involves agreement on the question of fairness, cheating, and the thin border distinguishing between nonlegitimate fraud and legitimate cunning. The ability to be crafty as well as the real possibility to agree on accepted definitions of "cheating" attests a thousand times over to the existence of a "common reasoning" to all participants. "It is not *tricherie* [cheating]," explained Dede Ben-Baruch in French, "but rather '*tricotage*' [knitting]" when he wished to clarify the thin and elusive distinction between cheating and gently, cleverly bending the rules of the game. The phonetic similarity of the terms in French indicates that there is only a hair's breadth separating the two. Successfully "knitting" a situation in one's favor demands not only quick hands but also–perhaps most importantly–rhetoric ability, smooth speech, and a high level of articulateness, all of which must be accepted by both Jews and Muslims. It demands a cultural "virtuosity" that will be credible to Jews and Muslims alike (Compare: Herzfeld 1985).

What I have presented so far in my summary explains how the environmental framework is mobilized for maintaining stability in relationships. However, I have not explained why Jews are interested in participating in this interaction in the first place.

Primarily, I think that Jews cannot permit themselves to entirely ignore Muslims in such a small and crowded space as the beach. Avoiding an encounter can itself be violent if it's done in a too blatant manner, and its damage may be more than its benefit. In addition, the framework offers an opportunity for the individual to convey messages, in statements like "it's (only) a game." This statement establishes a well-defined border between the "world outside" and the "world inside." It marks a clear border between the sphere of the game and the ordinary world. Within the game's sphere, players can permit themselves, and should allow others, conduct that in the outside world would be considered threatening, improper, or insulting (like the teasing relationships that convey messages regarding the identities of both groups). However, because the Jews continually strive to prevent reciprocity in their routine relationships, in the game they can convey frugal and focused messages, using simple language based on superficial-stereotypical images (such as "greedy Jew," "sly Muslim," etc.). Jews can enter into ritualized social exchanges with Muslims under this protective umbrella. Moreover, the arbitrary distribution of cards and the sly and clever character needed to play the game lay the groundwork for successful competition with Muslims at a relatively low price. The game offers a fairly equal opportunity to defeat the opponent, while protecting the winner with the message of "triviality." The cards after all, are randomly distributed. Jews seek to enter into exciting and emotional interactions such as these to convey messages that are dangerous outside of the game and, in a more existential way, to look at the Muslim world while being protected by the framework of the game. The opportunity to look into a world that sometime ago became closed to them is priceless. This is an exceptional opportunity to get very close to the Muslims without taking unnecessary risks, while peeking into an exciting and emotional world.

Besides these three circles relating to the game itself, there are also broader contexts that are relevant to giving meaning to the games. One context relates to the process of decline and its inherent tension for Jews. Just as the gradual process of disintegration of the community involves a tightening of social control (especially the intensive activity of its institutions), so too in the card games at the beach there is an inherent tension between social disintegration (recreation or, as my friend put it, *pour décontracter*) and strict rules for upholding codes of proper behavior. Within the limited space of the coffee tables at the beach, Jews embody and condense their contradictory life experiences of overcontrol and disintegration.

I have described here three converging circles of "nonserious" interactive frameworks. These circles, of course, do not constitute a real threat to Muslims, because the Jews are but a tiny minority in Morocco and because they allow the Jews to convey messages of criticism under the cloak of nonseriousness. As court jesters or clowns, Jews are not harmful. They may comment on the social structure, but will not make any changes or even give it a slight shake-up. For Jews, on the other hand, limiting the meetings to nonserious frameworks allows for the construction of boundaries between them and the Muslims. From another angle: I have already mentioned the fact that there is no economic significance to the card games. To expand on this, I would like to argue that the games do not change anything in the relationship between Jews and Muslims. The game cycles repeatedly open dynamics that have no final purpose or end goal. They begin, end, and begin over again (for comparison see: Geertz 1973b). Jews and Muslims build and destroy their tower of cards at regular intervals; like children playing at the beach, together they build sand castles, and the waves of the sea come again and again and ruin them. In and of themselves, the sand castles have absolutely no value and the children know that when they build a sand castle, it will not last forever. The surrounding ocean obstinately destroys all that they build. But the very sharing in the construction of these transient sand castles has paramount importance to them.

*

The microscopic examination of the relationships between Jews and Muslims through a prism of card games may create the impression that the whole purpose of Jewish existence can be summarized in relations with Muslims in Morocco. This is not so. Occasionally throughout this chapter, I scattered hints, sometimes more obvious, other times less, as to the importance of other life cycles in Jewish life in Morocco. For example, when I pointed out that meetings on the beach became more comfortable the more they could be categorized as "European" (that is to say French). This is also the case in relation to other countries and certainly with regard to Israel. Just as in the question of the Jews' relationships with Muslims, so too the place of these national categories is complex and full of contradictions. In the next chapter I will discuss these issues emphasizing the ambivalent place Israel takes in the lives of Moroccan Jews.

CHAPTER 6

To Be a Community That Is Both Homeland and Diaspora

During one of my visits to the Jewish old-age home (Asile de Vieillards), known by the Jews in Morocco as "*le* Home," Miriam Tamsut, upon noticing that I did not fit in, turned to me and asked in Darija, "Where are you living in France?" I, who was not prepared for her unexpected question, responded that I was from Israel. Once again she asked me exactly the same question, making sure that I heard her correctly and that I understood Darija. I told her that I understood her, and yes, I lived in Israel, permanently. She then added, making sure to clarify if I had at least planned my strategy wisely and had come to Morocco in order to "arrange my papers," that is, obtaining a Moroccan passport that would ease my way to having a French one. Miriam knew what she was talking about; many Moroccan-born Israelis did so. To this day, they come to Morocco to receive a Moroccan ID card and passport as a necessary step to acquiring the longed-for French passport. Much to my embarrassment, I had to disappoint her once again. Astonished, she asked if I intended to return to Israel upon finishing my business in Morocco. When I responded positively to this question also, she shook her head and with a mixture of despair, rebuke, and sobriety said: "That is not a good thing . . . a man should live in Morocco, and die and be buried in Israel!"

From the many issues that arose from this short exchange between Miriam and me, I will address only a few. In concrete terms, two issues that I will touch upon relate to how Jews in Morocco perceive the higher quality of life they prefer in their country (as opposed to Israel) and the sacred status of the Land of Israel (compared to Morocco). Miriam Tamsut's remarks as well as her conclusions, accurately expressed the tension that exists between the mythical and utopian vision of the homeland on the one hand (a place to be buried in), and on the other, the realization in day-to-day terms of the homeland as a disappointment as a socio-cultural, economic, and political reality. To put it slightly differently, I will address the difference between a state and a land. From the perspective of those who live in the homeland, Miriam Tamsut's statement illustrates the difficulty of the rhetoric of the nation-state, which, on a moral basis, emphatically demands from those living abroad that they "come home" (see, for example, Pattie 1994). Furthermore, her statement points to difficulties encountered by the rhetoric for those living abroad to recognize the symbolic centrality of the nation-state as their homeland. In addition, the very rhetoric calling them to "come home" erodes the country's efforts to establish itself symbolically as the homeland, and therefore it acts as a self-defeating mechanism. Even more so, the danger that waits at the doorstep of that same rhetoric (from the bureaucrat's perspective, who speaks on behalf of countries that crown themselves as homelands) is that this erosion will challenge their uniqueness as a moral center.

These two issues, intertwined and dependent on one another, raise important questions both on the theoretical development and on the public-political discourse of a model, which I call the "solar system model," that describes relations between homeland and diaspora. Since it is either a descriptive or interpretive model (theoretically at least), I will argue that it reveals an ideological-nationalist view regarding the anticipated moral and desirable relations between the homeland and diaspora. The term "solar system model" indicates the way researchers, as well as officials who invoke the name of the nation-state homeland, construct the diaspora communities as satellites; lacking a spirit of their own, their entire existence is dependent on the nurturing radiation of the homeland. In this chapter, using the Jews of Morocco (remaining after the great migration) as a reference point, I will point to the many questions emerging from this ideological-nationalistic perspective, which is based on modern political reality. This chapter therefore shifts the view from the internal dynamics in Morocco itself to the relations existing between Moroccan Jews after the great migration to Israel and other Jewish communities ("diasporas").

DIASPORAS AND HOMELANDS

One of the images of diaspora communities described in research depicts them as societies filled with nostalgia toward their symbolic center, their homeland. The center is perceived as the cradle of their existence and their geographical origins before they were scattered everywhere, while at the same time, diaspora communities are described as nurturing and nourishing values, suckled from their (only) homeland. Therefore, these communities are described as satellites surrounding the "sun" (their nation-state, their homeland), which nourishes them and sustains them through a history of many years. One of the prominent manifestations of the relationship between the homeland and the diaspora is that the diaspora communities arrange their historiography according to the "dream of return." For researchers who perceive these relations as such (for simplicity I will refer to them as "state-oriented") their characteristics represent the basic elements that define the diaspora (R. Cohen 1997; Safran 1991).

To be sure, state bureaucracy confirms and fortifies the image of the state as Homeland to its nation. For instance, in December 1992 King Hassan II allowed the "return" of the bones and other remains from the ship *Egoz* that sank in January 1961 with forty-four Jews who had emigrated illegally from Morocco to Israel. The twenty-two recovered bodies that were buried in Al Hociema were brought to Mt. Herzl in Jerusalem for final burial. Such an action of Israeli state bureaucrats seems to support the notion of the nation-state as a homeland.

Basic assumptions of "state-oriented" researchers and thinkers have been subject to sharp criticism over the years. This chapter joins that criticism. For example, the brothers Jonathan and Daniel Boyarin challenge, among other things, the manner in which Zionism denies the legitimacy of a diaspora existence (Boyarin and Boyarin 1993, 2002). According to them, the Zionist nation-state cannot, or is not worthy of, offering a moral model from which diaspora Jewry should draw its values. Sander Gilman presents a similar argument when he criticizes Israel for placing itself as the imagined center that defines me as someone who lives in the periphery. He continues by stating that in his opinion this model today does not seem appropriate to describe Jewish history, not even the history of Israel (Gilman 1999:1). Like the Boyarin brothers, Gilman refutes the moral and political status of Israel as a symbolic center. Unlike them, he acknowledges that his effort did not succeed.

These criticisms, which rest on postcolonial reasoning (and partially on postmodern thought), provide important tools not only for discussion about questions of diasporas but also to clarify the category of a "nation-state," particularly with regard to its role as a symbolic center. This line of thought opposes accepting the "facts" constituted by the hegemonic discourse of bureaucrats speaking on behalf of the homeland. I would like to continue this

FIGURE 8. Reburying *Egoz* voyagers

critical line by describing the ambivalent relationship between Morocco and Israel, claiming that the model is unidirectional and simplistic. I will demonstrate how the model is challenged by the very ambivalent approach of Moroccan Jews both toward that which is supposedly their homeland (Israel) and toward their alleged diaspora. We will realize that these Jews see their community in Morocco not only as part of the general Jewish diaspora but also as a homeland which itself has numerous Moroccan diasporas. In order that I may clarify this line of thought, I will systematically review the discussion on the issue of diasporas and homelands.

Many of the "state-oriented" researchers discuss the relationships between homeland and diaspora as historically fixed and symbolically unidirectional relationships between two poles: at one pole is the center, the object of longing, identification, and aspiration. At the other pole are various scattered groups, who maintain contact—at times stronger, and at times weaker—both with the same symbolic center and with other groups that identify themselves as belonging to the same center and therefore to the same nation (Safran 1991). According to them, the existence of the diaspora as distinct cultural groups depends on the continuous cultivation of intercommunity relationships. The dichotomous structure of the "solar system model" ("here" is the focus, and "there" is the periphery) characterizes the symbolic center, the homeland, by using categories such as "eternity," "sacred," "myth," and "home," while the periphery is described in terminology such as "temporary," "profane," "ephemeral," "estranged," and "guest."

Not only is this dichotomy proposed by the state-oriented researchers limited and itself limiting by virtue of its being based on a comparative relationship that ignores the political role of the nation-state in establishing and maintaining its image, but the comparison they propose assumes continuity and stability in these relationships over an extended period of time. According to this, the stability and permanency of relationships are preserved by attributing characteristics from the mythological and religious sphere to the nation-state. Myths about indigenous sanctity that construct a natural identity between a nation and a place are characteristic of every modern nation-state. Indeed Hobsbawm and Ranger best expressed their criticism of this identification of a nation-state with the mythological sphere; they argued that: "modern nations with their abundance of accessories, usually claim to be completely opposite to the new, that is to say, to be deeply rooted in the most distant antiquities, and to be the opposite of the structure, namely for their acceptance to be so 'natural' that there is no need for any further definition of self" (Hobsbawm and Ranger 1983:14).

The discourse that rests on the mythological sphere is particularly evident when it comes to the study of "traditional" diasporas, such as the Jewish (compare: Gurevitch and Aran 1994) or Armenian diaspora (Pattie 1997). In the Jewish case, for example, the spaces of the homeland merited the status of holiness in this discourse, of a sacred entity from which the nation was cut off in one thrust due to an original sin and an immoral behavior ("*because of our sins we were exiled from our land*"). This symbolic sacred space, which is carefully distinguished from the everyday and mundane, radiates a sense of stability and permanence because the homeland, the indigenous source, is seen as eternal. I argue that the dichotomous distinction between the sacred and secular spaces itself reflects socio-cultural and political construction, which accordingly permits people to be either "within" or "outside" of their space. This construction, created by the nation-state discourse, undermines the possibility of belonging to the space occupied by those who "abandoned" the Homeland. Life in exile means life in limbo, 'living out of a suitcase."

In the dichotomous division between those "within" and those on the "outside" there is an implicit but unambiguous assumption that the symbolic authority and the creation of significant symbols are exclusively in the hands of the "center." This is, after all, the fundamental political meaning of the center as a category. During the heydays of the modern nation-state, when it was complacently unaware of the approaching dangers on its premises, this dichotomy embodied and even demonstrated the triumph of the homelands discourse. This discourse encouraged and promoted the idea of exclusivity in belonging to a place and a nation, and it blurred any possibility of complex, irregular relationships between different socio-cultural groups that dwell in other places. This dichotomous division also reduced the possibility of simultaneously belonging to more than one place.

In recent decades, the status of the nation-state as a natural and omnipotent phenomenon has weakened, and concurrently it has come under theoretical and political-economic attack. Publications declaring the diaspora as the preferred place to live are quickly accumulating and positioning themselves at the forefront of this criticism (see Levy 2005). For example, Tölölyan emphasizes (Tölölyan 1996) the contribution of intellectuals to the growth of the critical diaspora discourse, an outcome of the global nature of their profession. A few years earlier, anthropologist James Clifford called to shift the analytical focus from questions about fixation in space to issues relating to mobility (Clifford 1997). The mobility of people, commodities, and ideas is closely related to the establishment of the diaspora as a significant research site, because it demonstrates and embodies unsolvable tension between mobility and permanence. People leave their birthplace and root themselves elsewhere as distinct cultural groups. By this act of movement and attachment to another place they challenge the appearance of very comfortable immovability to a discourse on the nation-state, which ties people to one territory.

As mentioned, the "state-oriented' research emphasizes that among diasporic groups, feelings of nostalgic connection toward the land left behind are widespread. Paraphrasing Arjun Appadurai—diasporas always leave a trail of collective memory about another place and time and create new maps of desire and of attachment (Appadurai and Breckenbridge 1989). The study also emphasizes that diasporas encourage feelings of nostalgia for landscapes, smells, and sounds as a part of people establishing themselves as a unique and special identity group. Indeed, diaspora rhetoric increasingly serves people who have been detached from their locality and who feel a connection with their previous home (Clifford 1997). The sense of "diaspora" is both creatively and politically inspired.

The mechanism that produces these feelings is not unique to the diaspora, nor is it surprising that it is similar in its logic and action to the nation-state discourse. Benedict Anderson, a highly quoted intellectual on issues relating to the nation-state, reminds us that one of the characteristics *common* to all nations is their efforts of self-decoration of their unique heroic past that *distinguishes* them from other nations (Anderson 1983). Part of this mechanism is the cultivation of the unique past enlisted for the needs of the present. Indeed, the diaspora, like nationalism, is not bound to "real" historiography, because its survival is tied to its ability to plant and enhance identification with "traditional" values, which are used to address the needs of the present. The similarity between the discourse on nationalism and that of diaspora is not surprising, because the latter is in need of its "real" nation-state and an acceptance of its reasoning in order to be defined as a diaspora. Simply put, without a state you cannot establish a diaspora.

Therefore, in this chapter, I present events and attitudes of the Jews of Casablanca that touch upon their ambivalent relationship toward Israel. Equipped with their perspectives, I will question modernist assumptions about the success of the Israeli nation-state to hold the crown of a symbolic center versus an alleged marginal diaspora. I would like to consider the limitations of nation-states (such as Israel) in their efforts to establish an unchallenged discourse, one that is complete, undivided, and taken for granted. I will demonstrate how the relationship between diaspora and homeland, or better, how the dichotomous division that is expressed by actually creating the relationship between two poles of the "solar system model," may be dissolvable, historically conditional, and multidirectional. That I will establish, as said, while drawing a picture of the space that simultaneously exists both as a diaspora and as a homeland. These are large-scale questions that are reliant on listening to the quiet and minor, though still defiant, voices that come from people who live in spaces perceived as diasporic. I will address the reluctance of these people to be seen as marginal in relation to the homeland.

Despite the criticism that can be gleaned from the position that rejects the simplistic division between homeland and diaspora, the quiet voices that I bring here do not doubt the very "binary system" itself (Foucault 1978), a system that makes it difficult to overcome the bipolar construction of the "homeland" against the "diaspora." In this sense, it seems to me that Gilman preaches more of a moral position instead of sketching political-cultural trends (Gilman 1999). In other words, even if Moroccan Jews are critical toward Zionist Israel, which demands exclusivity in belonging, they are not criticizing the foundation of the "solar system model"; they accept the organization of the world into pairs of nation-states and diasporas. This fundamental acceptance moderates, as I would like to show, the effectiveness of their undermining attitudes toward Israel, as the ultimate center for Jews.

A DIASPORIC COMMUNITY

The decline of the Moroccan Jewish community has changed the Moroccan Jews from a unique ethnic-religious group in a Muslim context to a diaspora. The complex processes of contraction described in the pages of this book, with their institutional expressions, mark a harsh, isolating line distinguishing between the Jews and the country in which they live—Morocco. Moroccan Jews of the late twentieth and early twenty-first century have become foreigners in their own country. They are foreigners among the general population, foreigners in Moroccan politics, and to some extent they are also foreigners to the architecture of "Moroccan culture."

Unfortunately, Morocco as a political entity which redefined itself as a nation-state following its liberation from the yoke of colonialism did not assist in transforming its Jews into an ethnic group. Even though the Jews saw themselves as an integral part of the renewed state despite their ethno-religious uniqueness, the unfolding of Moroccan nationalism did not allow a place for the definition of Jews as a cultural group. In light of the national commitment to "Islam" and "Arabism," the leaders and bureaucrats of Morocco were not capable or failed to offer protection from the influences of Zionism in general, and particularly from the harsh consequences of the bloody conflict between Israel and the surrounding Arab countries. Guy Levy, a man of about forty-five at the time, who was a familiar figure in the Jewish community mainly because of his informal involvement in the decision-making circles of the community, told me one day how he learned to treat Muslim workers in his factory:

> I was in Israel, on a kibbutz, and met a senior army officer. It was in the seventies. He told me about the Six Day War. He was an officer then and they had captured many prisoners. Do you remember . . . how the Egyptian soldiers left everything, took off their shoes and ran away to the desert . . . ? So, they are sitting there, the captured soldiers are sitting on the floor, without shoes, their heads between their legs, miserable. There were a few Israeli soldiers surrounding them so they wouldn't run away. There was one who sat upright. The officer, who told me this story (which was an important life lesson for me), was responsible for guarding the prisoners. Suddenly the prisoner who had sat upright stood up and began to run away. One of the soldiers raised his rifle to shoot him. But the officer said to him: "Don't shoot!" he gave him an order. "Why?" I asked him. "That's what my soldiers asked me!" He said. "I explained to them that if he has the dignity to pick himself up and run away—we should let him run away!" This, André, is my life lesson. If I give respect to my

workers, not like most of the Jews here who have factories . . . if I give them respect—they will be excellent workers!

Guy Levy, who lived all his life with Muslims in Morocco, needed the advice of an Israeli soldier in order to learn how to behave toward his workers. Israel, with its militaristic character, turned into a role model for a man who lived with Muslims his entire life. This is a testimony which appears at face value to point to Israel's great strength as a symbolic center for diaspora Jewry. Israel, as she appears in this story, stands as a partition between the Jews of Morocco and their majority Muslim surroundings.

It seems, then, that the process of geopolitical change in Morocco caused surprising multifaceted processes amongst the Jews: even to the point that with their decline into a diaspora community which made them into foreigners in their land, they needed to turn toward Israel as a role model. However, as we shall see, these processes also turned Morocco into a metaphorical place for Jews, a place that contains and produces powerful symbolic images for them, which in fact, have turned it into a symbolic center, into a "homeland."

In order to clarify my general arguments and to give them a foundation, I will focus on daily, prosaic events of this complex process in which Morocco is both a diaspora and a homeland. I will introduce interpretations of short ethnographic scenes that demonstrate the complex dynamics that move between these two constructed polarities: homeland-diaspora. The first scene will focus on a brief description of three cases of death and burial, as this concretely, symbolically, and quite impressively demonstrates the complexity of feelings of belonging to Morocco; these events involve the very planting of the body into the place, the land. The next scene will discuss a murder case of a Jewish employer by Muslim employees. I will present different interpretations, diametrically opposed, of the same event by deciphering the narrative describing the murder. These interpretations will change the picture of the dynamics, which I have already pointed out, into an even more complex and ambivalent picture. Through the interpretation of these stories I will underline the diasporic aspect of Jewish existence in Morocco and raise some questions stemming from this perception. The third scene will briefly focus on another aspect of belonging to a place: the attitude toward emigration from Morocco. This is to say, that if death and burial relate to the permanence of the space, then the third scene will emphasize in particular the movement away from it. In the last section I will also present the final scene that raises polemical attitudes of Jews in Morocco toward the Hebrew language. Here I will focus on disputes as to the meaning and character of the Hebrew language, which will serve as a prism through which one may examine attitudes toward Israel, and especially the possibility that Israel is not necessarily the ultimate center that controls the holy language. Differences of opinion about the Hebrew language are an example of just how complex, fluid, and multifaceted the relations between the categories "diaspora" and "homeland" are. I will show that these categories are not limited to physical spaces (like a burial place) alone, but that they too touch upon conceptual and ideological issues (such as language).

DEATH, BURIAL, AND THE ABSENCE OF A SELF-EVIDENT SPACE

Death, research literature says, is deeply absorbed in the discourse that connects people to their land (Malkki 1995). Death, with its abundance of ceremonial components, reveals the way in which different communities, such as diaspora communities, express in a sophisticated manner their ties to the land and toward their imagined homeland. Indeed, Moroccan Jews express their views and attitudes of belonging to Morocco and Israel through the rhetoric of death and burial. For example, Michael Elhadad often reflected with me whether it was desirable for him to transfer his father's bones, which were already interred in the new cemetery of Casablanca, to Israel. Michael even told me that he consulted with one of therabbis in Casablanca, who firmly ruled that it was not fitting to move his father's bones and that he should leave his father in his resting place until the arrival of the Messiah.[51] Michael Elhadad, as Miriam Tamsut, an elderly woman I quoted at the beginning of this chapter, hoped to establish a metonymic relationship between himself (as an extension of his late father) and the Holy Land. Michael hoped that his father's burial place would "represent" him in Israel as a symbolic substitute for his missing presence, and that Israel would exist in him, through his father's body, buried in its lumps of earth. It is important to note here that the rabbinic-orthodox decision that is not based on Zionist beliefs rejects this relationship until the end of days.

During my main period of study (July 1990 to September 1991) I was direct witness to three occasions of death.[52] As unexpected deaths often are, the first case I witnessed was tragic: a young woman burned to death in a terrible car accident while she was with her spouse on a working trip in Montreal, Canada. Her parents brought her body for burial to Casablanca. The young Casablanca woman's father was a man of great influence in the Jewish community. The funeral was massive. There were even those who made special and exceptional efforts and came from distant cities. It seemed as though a third or half of the members of the Jewish community in Morocco were there to offer their condolences and share in the family's deep sorrow. In addition, even senior representatives of the Muslim government, mainly from the municipality, came to the Jewish cemetery.

The second case of death I came directly in contact with was that of a woman who died of old age. She was buried in Casablanca. Her funeral was attended by only a few, and her son, Monsieur Joël Elkayim, a single man in his early sixties who was one of the few Jewish lawyers, was left childless and alone in Casablanca. Joël had lived with his mother until her death. He now felt that he had reached a significant crossroads in his life and that he was left alone in Morocco, without any close relatives nearby. He wanted to talk with me about this. He shared his hidden thoughts and especially wanted to talk about his desire to leave everything, including his moderately successful business and beautiful office, and immigrate to Israel. He asked many questions about the benefits of "making Aliyah." He wanted to know all about the social benefits he would be entitled to, what the social conditions were for a person like himself, what the cost of living was there, and answers to additional questions, and clarifications. A month or two after his mother's burial he returned to himself; he calmed down and stopped interrogating me about life in Israel. He remained in Morocco until his death in the summer of 2004.

The third episode of death was that of Joe Cohen, a man in his mid-forties. It seemed to me that for a long time he suffered from clinical depression. Whenever I met him he seemed depressed, melancholy, and absent. It also turned out that he was sick with a variety of diseases. Mostly, Joe suffered from lung infections—resulting from health complications following a suicide attempt. I was told that due to unrequited love, he attempted to jump to his death from a high window. He survived the jump, but was left with broken ribs and punctured lungs. He died in the winter of 1991 after a severe complication of pneumonia. His family, who were well known in Casablanca, held a short ceremony at the Jewish cemetery in Casablanca, with many people in attendance. Immediately following the ceremony the body was flown to Israel for burial.

These telegraphic descriptions of three deaths will serve me for the moment to present a somewhat limited claim; three circumstances of death seemed to pose existential questions relating to the connection to [physical] spaces in diaspora life. What connects the three events is the necessity to consciously and explicitly confront the question of where to bury the dead. In the last case for example, Joe's elderly parents decided to bury their son in Israel. Their decision was not based on the tradition of burying their son's body in the holy soil of the Mount of Olives in Jerusalem. In fact, his parents chose as the burial site a smaller town in northern Israel where they planned to immigrate in the future. So the decision as to where their son's burial place should be was determined by the issue of their future plans in Morocco. It is important to emphasize that, despite that, over a decade has passed since the son's death and his elderly parents are still living in Casablanca. Up until my last visit to Morocco in the summer of 2014, they seemed to show no intention of immigrating. Also in the first event, where it was clear to the parents that they wished to bring their child's body from Canada to burial in Casablanca, there was a need for a decision and immediate action to bring the remains of their child's charred body to Morocco. Some of the participants at the funeral questioned the wisdom of the parents, for they assumed that quite certainly the parents would immigrate to Canada in the foreseeable future. For after all, the daughter had gone on this visit in order to locate financial opportunities for their future in Canada.

Belonging to a place, as it seems from these descriptions, does not sit easily with the existential diaspora experience. The reality of Israel's existence, as an actual place, as a national-political entity, undermines the obvious feelings of belonging to any other place. Israel's actual presence as a realistic option for migration (even if un-actualized) demands constant attention as an alternative. Thus, the death of a dear one raises questions about the place of burial. In the case before us, the realistic possibility of burial in a place other than "here" is a source of undermining the accepted belonging to the place where one lives. For the moment, such observations about the question of belonging teach us that the "solar system model" works well and fits the prevailing attitude toward the diaspora-homeland relationship. However, as we shall see later, the erosion of the sense of belonging raises alternative interpretations, and even competing ones, about life in the diaspora and the question of the "center's" uniqueness as the exclusive symbolic source of cultural and moral legitimacy.

ONE MURDER: TWO STORIES

Robert and Raphael Alankwa were two young cousins who were deeply attached to each other. A death occurred in their family, and each of them, independently of the other, told me his account of this death. Robert was the first who told me his story; he described to me his father's murder at the hands of his (father's) Muslim workers. A few weeks later, I heard a different version, this time from Raphael. The differences between the two versions illustrate a connection between death and territory, and death and belonging, which will then make the solar system model even more problematic.

The conversation with Robert, the son, was conducted mainly in Hebrew. He, like his cousin after him, insisted on talking to me in Hebrew. Robert's words were halting and difficult to understand; he spoke as if he had pebbles in his mouth. Speaking about his father's murder was extremely difficult for him. Despite the hardship of speaking about the tragedy, however, he insisted on talking with me. At this point, I will present short parts of a long, fragmented, and tormented conversation. According to Robert, his father had a thriving pesticides factory:

ROBERT—They killed him because of jealousy, not because of the business.

ANDRÉ (Me)—Who was it, Muslims? Where did it happen?

R—At his business . . . fifteen years ago (in 1985) . . . because . . . you know . . . here everyone (the Muslims) is jealous. It's a fact. Everyone knows. Because a Jew . . . a Jew . . . when you say "the Jews" you mean "the rich." When they talk amongst themselves, one says to the other; "What—are you Jewish?" when he wants to say "Are you rich?" Do you know what I mean? . . . They had a plan. They planned it.

A—How did the Jews here respond?

R—They were afraid. Everyone came to the *shiva* [mourning period] and they . . . when they realized that we wanted to leave Morocco and go to Israel . . . well . . . the Jews of the community (the leaders) understood that we were saying that it was not good to live in Morocco. Do you understand that?

A—Do you mean that because you were leaving Morocco that means that you don't like the lifestyle here?

R—As a Jew you dominate. You control the people, and they (the leadership) are rich like us . . . and they [the Muslims] killed a Jew . . . a very rich one. Someone came and shot him on the spot.

A—I understand what you are trying to say. You are saying that by leaving, you were criticizing the Jews.

R—It's a criticism, but we did not intend for it to be that way. We just wanted to leave.

According to Robert, the murder happened for one reason only, and there was no real need to elaborate or expand on it. He was to the point, and all my attempts to glean additional information failed. The information was meager: employees who worked in his father's modest factory planned the murder.

Motivation for the murder had typical anti-Semitic roots—jealousy of the wealth and success of the Jew. This, then, is a rather stereotypical story.

Raphael, the cousin, offered a different story, richer in detail. Like Robert, Raphael was young, about twenty-five at the time. He unraveled the story to me during a stay at a summer camp for Jewish youth in Imouzzer, a pleasant resort village in the Middle Atlas Mountains, around thirty-five kilometers in a straight line from the big city of Fez. We were together in a room—Raphael, Robert, Lisa (Robert's girlfriend, a Jewish American volunteer) and I—and were talking about this and that, but the moment Robert left the room with Lisa, Raphael began the story:

RAPHAEL—His father was a miser, May G-d have mercy! That's why they killed him. He didn't want to give his worker money to buy a sheep for their "*la fête de mouton*" (festival of the sacrifice). He didn't want to give them a sheep.

A—Why did they think he should give them a sheep?

R—The Jews here always give a sheep as a gift for the Muslim holiday. It's a gift for their festival. The Arab asked him to at least lend him money and promised to return it, requesting that it be deducted in parts from his monthly salary after the holiday period. Robert's father agreed, but took out two hundred Dirham every month. The Arab got angry at him. His (Robert's) father was really stingy, may G-d help him; he would ride on a moped to his factory! He didn't buy himself a car and wouldn't even take a *petit taxi,* a city taxi. Also, every day he would eat a baguette with cheese so as not to waste time by going home to eat a good meal. He also never took off time to eat at a restaurant, so as not to lose money. Even poor Robert, didn't get a *centime* (penny) from him when he was a kid. I remember giving him money . . . lending it to him.

A—How did they kill him?

R—Look, Jews never—well not exactly never . . . but most of the time—never lend their workers money for the holiday. They give them money to buy a sheep. And he, not only did he not want to give the sheep as a gift, he took off two hundred Dirham each month from his salary, which is an awful lot for a simple worker in Morocco. So, you know what they did? His father always sat at his work desk, which had a lot of barrels of toxic matter on a shelf above it. So . . . his workers placed more and more barrels of this substance on the shelf. Until one day it all fell on his head. He died on the spot. Now people from our community often say to Robert that his father died because of a sheep.

Besides the idiosyncratic differences, which certainly affects the style of each of the cousins' story, differences which of course also relate to the extent of the involvement in the story and the different temperaments of the two (Raphael was outgoing and Robert introverted), the contrast in the stories and the meaning that these opposing views gives to the events are clearly evident. These differences relate, among other things, to the way each of them formulates their understanding of homeland and diaspora. Robert, the son of the murdered man, focused on the Muslims' responsibility for the murder, which was motivated by pure anti-Semitism. Raphael, however, almost openly accused his uncle, who was driven by miserliness. These two stereotypical perspectives place the responsibility for the murder at opposing ends. As a starting point, it should be mentioned that Robert and his family, as it appears from the conversation with him, left Morocco and migrated to Israel.

Despite his emigration, Robert often returns to Morocco "to settle the family's businesses" as he says. The conversation about his father's murder took place during one of these visits.[53] In contrast, Raphael and his family did not intend to emigrate. He himself serves today as a tour guide and travel agent, working to rehabilitate the synagogues and Jewish cemeteries in order to encourage Jewish tourism, mainly from the United States. The way in which Raphael explained the murder hinted at explanations that justified his remaining in Morocco. In this respect, he stood opposed to his cousin and family, who decided to emigrate. His explanation did not place blame for the murder on the ultimate "Other"—the Muslims. Accusing a Muslim implies an undermining or shattering of a sense of control for your personal safety. Such an event is likely to undermine those feelings of control, especially when discussing such a close and threatening incident as the murder of a relative. In contrast, Robert wove the event into a somewhat simplistic style of a classic Zionist rhetoric; it is not good for Jews to be in exile.

Raphael constructed a story that supported his sense of control and personal determination for the future of his fate. He fashioned a story that calls for behavior according to local standards, and for sensitivity to the local cultural rules of the game ("In Morocco be a Moroccan"). In this story he expressed recognition for the necessity of cultural understanding and integration. This understanding provides control over personal security and prevents unexpected and difficult situations. In a sense, his criticism of his uncle encourages the anti-Semitic discourse about the Jew as the Other, the outcast.

Robert, in contrast to his cousin, suggested a story diametrically opposite in terms of its conclusions and analogy. Stylistically too, as noted, it is different.

Unlike Raphael he was brief and laconic. He didn't offer an elaborate or detailed explanation. He stuck to a very general explanation, making it appear as if there was no personal story. I was not able to hear very much from him about his father. As any constitutive classical myth, there were no coordinates of time and place in his story. He reconstructed a typical Jewish, almost mythical story, told for centuries (and especially since the eighteenth century in eastern Europe and England). In his story, Robert introduced us to an almost helpless man, a figure opposite to that which Raphael painted—a harsh, almost tyrant-like father. Even if Raphael did not actually say it, one may understand from his words that the father was to blame for bringing about his own death ("His father was a miser, may G-d have mercy! That is why they killed him"). He is responsible for his own death, due to his inappropriate behavior. The event, therefore, occurred as a result of a Jew's actions.

As mentioned, the different versions of this story are connected, among other things, to the roles attributed to diaspora and homeland. The two cousins understand their lives within this context. The same way the three short opening stories about death and burial required a decision from all those involved (as stories taking place in the diaspora) about the place or the meaningful space, here too we are speaking about a diaspora story. When using the term "diaspora story" I mean that explicit questions of belonging to a place as opposed to transience are intricately intertwined. As such, because this is a diaspora story, the different positions of the cousins do not indicate disagreement; rather they question the nature of life in the diaspora and the lessons one must learn about life in the diaspora. Consequently, it is clear why the family's decision to migrate to Israel wasn't fundamentally challenged by Raphael. For both of them Israel was a long-awaited place, a symbolic center, and the ultimate place for every Jew. As already stated, the disagreements were about the nature of life in the diaspora; Raphael wished to emphasize that a Jew may live in comfort "beneath his vine and under his fig tree" also in the diaspora, as long as he behaves according to the rules of the place. What separates the cousins' interpretations from the incidents of death that I presented earlier is that the earlier incidents show a measure of disagreement about the intrinsic significance of the place, while Robert and Raphael do not differ on the significant role of Israel.

The three cases of death and, even more so, the two murder stories largely substantiate the "solar system model." This model can properly explain the attitude toward Israel, even if at times the homeland is met by challenges. For example, the quick burial, free of misgivings, of Monsieur Joël Elkayim's elderly mother points to this type of challenge;so to does Raphael's approach to his uncle's murder. These underminings become even more evident the more we discuss questions that combine cultural and human movement.

IMMIGRATION AND SYMBOLIC CENTRALITY

The ambiguous position of Moroccan Jews toward Israel as a homeland is even more prominent in relation to migration. I have already pointed out conflicting approaches to migration to Israel in the different versions of the two murder stories. I am not just discussing two different approaches to migration to Israel (both cousins see this as a value), but rather the ongoing and continual migration of Robert. The opposition of different community leaders to migration, indicated by Robert, is not surprising. Moroccan Jews' attitude toward Israel is ambivalent because despite the fact that ideationally the majority see Israel as their homeland, migration endangers the very existence of the framework of their Jewish community in a very real, concrete, and immediate way. Moreover, Moroccan Jews prefer other places, as opposed to Israel, as their migration destinations (especially France). Israel is a place to die in, not to live in. However, here I will specifically refer to migration to Israel, because it poses a meaningful existential and symbolic challenge for Jews in Morocco. After all, they cannot avoid the gap between their very own rhetoric surrounding longing for Israel and the Zionist ideology and their daily struggles to sustain a normal life in Morocco.

The process that took place following the great migration from Morocco does not necessarily follow common sense; instead of being emptied of its symbolic meaning with its demographic demise, Morocco has turned into a symbolic center, precisely as a competitor to Israel. Morocco has become a place of memory, and in the words of Pierre Nora, a place that has turned the Jewish Moroccan community into a center in their own eyes and its land into a homeland. The process in which Morocco dried up is that which produced for the Jewish community there its own Jewish diaspora communities throughout the world. In their own eyes, they did not become a minor ethnic group in their country, but they established diaspora communities for themselves all around the globe, using symbolic processes that nurture nostalgic feelings toward Morocco. It is important to emphasize, that this construction of a reality (like any other construction of reality) is supported by a long series of external evidence that appear real.

The north African Jewish communities that scattered in all directions confirm and nurture a collective-mythical memory about the Maghreb. For example, anthropologist Joëlle Bahloul in her book *La maison de mémoire* tells of a family that emigrated from Algeria to France and relates their memories about Dar Refayil, the residence they left. Another example is the documentary film by French director Charlotte Szlovak entitled *Retour à Oujda* (Return to Oujda), which presents the story of Jewish tourists journeying from France to visit their childhood provinces in Oujda, in northern Morocco. Israel also serves as a base or starting point from which many go to Morocco, as a symbolic focus. These trips, which combine tourism and pilgrimages, nourish the sense Moroccan Jews have of Morocco as the center of admiration and longing (see next chapter).

Strengthening the perception of their land as a homeland in the eyes of Moroccan Jews is the phenomenon, though limited in scope, but profound with symbolic implications, of Israelis returning to settle in Morocco. It is my estimate that in the last three decades about one hundred Israelis, at most, migrated to Morocco. Some would argue that even that is an exaggeration. These Israelis return bit by bit to Morocco to find better living opportunities than those in Israel. Sometimes they return to Morocco because of difficult life circumstances in Israel, such as those escaping from the hands of Israeli law for murder, smuggling drugs, or the like. The absence of an extradition treaty between Morocco and Israel makes Morocco a convenient destination for Moroccan-born Israelis. Few remain permanently in Morocco. At times an attempt is made to improve one's economic situation, such as a former Israeli who established a factory for stonewashing jeans. There were those who returned to Morocco in order to manage their parent's inheritance. An example of this was Mr. Sabach, an active member in the right-wing Likud party in Ashdod, who after his father's death in Marrakech learned of a large plant that the father had owned. In order to take over his father's business, Mr. Sabach chose to settle in Morocco on a permanent basis. From the Jews' perspective the circumstances around settling in Morocco do not add or detract. The very fact that Israelis choose Morocco as a country to settle in strengthens the feeling which Jews have that Morocco is an appropriate and valuable symbolic center.

There seems to be a paradox of sorts in the historical process that has turned Morocco from a diaspora that nicely fits the "solar system model" to a diaspora that is likewise a homeland. The solution to the paradox is concealed in the fact that the process that turned Morocco into a symbolic center resulted precisely from the demographic weakening of the Jewish community. In other words, the emigration from Morocco, which caused the community to become a dying diaspora, is the very same one which established Moroccan communities elsewhere. Thus additional hubs of Moroccan diasporas were created outside of Morocco. These new diaspora communities nourished the nostalgic rhetoric toward Morocco as well as the romantic attitudes toward it as a new homeland (compare: Bilu and Levy 1996; Bahloul 1996).

The demographic process that threatens to diminish the Moroccan community to a point of elimination presents a critical situation to the Jews, mainly in face of the existence of the Moroccan diasporas in Israel, France, and Canada. Their demographic marginality does not sit easily with their self-perception as a symbolic center and frequently raises new tensions. This, for example, is what happened following the publication of the critical book by the French journalist Gilles Perrault *Notre ami le Roi*, which reviewed the actions of King Hassan II during the years of his rule. The book emphasized the king's cruel behavior toward his political opponents. With its publication, Morocco's public circles were in turmoil. The enormous exposure the book received caused severe political tension between Morocco and France. The then French president's wife, Mrs. Mitterrand, was seen as the main person responsible for stirring up tension by starting an independent campaign of criticism against the Moroccan monarchy. In reaction, Moroccan National Television countered with a sharp and intensive advertising campaign. Morocco stopped broadcasting channel TV5, the French television channel, which broadcasts to all of the Mediterranean Basin. Daily, television broadcasters read hundreds of letters written by "concerned citizens" disturbed by the "colonialist behavior of France, interfering with the internal affairs of Morocco." The Jews were concerned by the extensive television coverage and were most troubled by the frequent appearances of the king on their screens. They understood from the frequency of his appearances that the campaign was being conducted from above, and in his repeated appearances was a clear indication of the government's precarious position. Nevertheless, many Jews were relieved and even proud when a national television broadcaster read letters of support written by community leaders from their diaspora community. For example, a letter arrived from Israel from Rabbi Mashash, who had years earlier served as chief rabbi of Morocco. The broadcasters read his letter in its entirety. In his letter the rabbi noted the very tolerant behavior of the Moroccan regime toward Jews and mentioned the positive attitude of Muhammed V, the present king's father, during World War ll, when he protected Jews that the Nazis attempted to harm. He also praised Muhammad's successor—his son Hassan II. Despite the absence of open diplomatic relations between the countries, the television people made no attempt to hide the fact that the letter was sent from Israel. The Moroccan Jewish leadership in France also sent letters of support for the king. To the disappointment of many, the Moroccan Jewish community in Montreal did not send a similar letter: "We are no longer of any importance to the Jews there," complained one of the Jews briefly. He, like many Jews in a club in Casablanca, was disappointed by their unimportance on the agenda of their diaspora community in Canada. The sense of dependency of the center on the support of the periphery was distressing in the eyes of many.

The Jews do not ignore, of course, the undeniable consequences resulting from the fact that their community is negligible in its size compared to Moroccan Jewish communities abroad. Moreover, they are aware that their minimal size is shrinking every year, and that this reduction process is enormously visible in their day-to-day lives. Their painful, anxiety-ridden awareness of the declining process has a substantial influence on their epistemology, in shaping their daily lives. For example, in one of the Jewish high schools an argument broke out following the irresponsible behavior of one of the teachers. The assistant principal acted in a manner very unlike him when he got involved vigorously, silencing the debate in a decisive and even violent manner. The argument ended immediately. Around an hour later, I found him restlessly walking back and forth in the school yard. Seeming embarrassed by his outburst, he tried justifying his behavior to me by saying that he was pretty troubled these days because he was thinking of leaving Morocco. He told me that he had received an interesting offer:

> I received an offer to be a principal in a Jewish school in Black Africa. I was promised a lot of money. There is no future here. I don't understand why they are arguing about the problems they have with this teacher. How much time do we have left here? What does it matter how she behaves? We don't have a future here. How much time is left already, so why this whole mess? We don't have much ammunition left to fire. We only have a few bullets left in our guns, so why bother with a future that is over?

Despite the disappointment and the sense of marginality that accompanies it, it is worthwhile noting that the disappointment in itself testifies to the expectations of Jews from the Moroccan homeland for their diaspora communities. Both the expectations as well as the disappointment indicate an unsolvable existential paradox: the source of demographic decline, the emigration from Morocco, is in itself the cause that establishes Morocco as a homeland and its communities of migrants as diasporas.

The short ethnographic images surrounding the issue of emigration and its impact on the Moroccan Jewish community specifically emphasize the weakness of the Moroccan homeland against its diaspora: a weakness that is, as mentioned, a result of the large-scale emigration from Morocco. However, this is not a common or dominant experience among the Jews. Many expressions of high self-esteem, especially in comparison to Israel, can be seen in the daily lives of Jews in Morocco. Many emphatic-patronizing expressions, such as "Israel has developed so much!" or "Things are finally becoming beautiful in Israel," were repeated by those visiting Israel as tourists. One of the main expressions I was exposed to in the context of the centrality of the Moroccan Jewish community arose surrounding the attitude toward Hebrew, the holy language used in daily life in Israel.

THE SYMBOLIC PLACE OF LANGUAGE

When I arrived in Morocco for my PhD fieldwork, I requested to work in one of the schools as a Hebrew teacher. I did this in order to support myself, as my research grant was limited relative to the cost of living in Casablanca, as well as to maintain good connections with teachers and students. To my surprise, I had to overcome some unexpected obstacles. The directors of the Hebrew teaching program had requirements that to my naïveté were unexpected for teaching Hebrew. According to them, Hebrew is a holy language and therefore not to be taught separately from its historical and cultural contexts. I had thought of the language in terms of vocabulary and grammar, but they thought differently. Thus, the cultural context of the Hebrew language that had been transparent to me at the beginning was now becoming visible in its full force. Moreover, the Hebrew teachers in Morocco questioned the cultural wealth of which I had assumed I had control. In order to teach Hebrew, so they claimed, the teacher must know religious laws, Midrashim, religious interpretations, rituals, customs, holidays, and so on. They wanted to ensure that I was familiar with all these—that I could teach Hebrew not only in the "narrow sense," as they expressed it. Eventually I was hired as a Hebrew teacher, but only after they were assured that I could indeed contribute "to Hebrew studies in the broader meaning." However, the directors were extra careful and sent me to teach the weaker children for whom the teachers didn't have much hope from the start.

The approach to the general status of Hebrew, and the significance of teaching Hebrew in particular, were clearly articulated in a conversation that took place (in Hebrew, of course) between a French inspector of Hebrew language and some teachers at the prestigious Jewish high school ENH (École Normale Hébraïque). Maurice Levy, one of the most prominent Hebrew teachers at this boarding school, claimed that the best way to teach Hebrew was as follows:

"Male teachers, in contrast to women, have a broad knowledge of religious studies. Teaching Hebrew is not like teaching any other languages . . . as we teach French, for example. Hebrew has great cultural depth. One must know a lot. The women teachers, at least in Morocco, do not have this training. Because of this they cannot serve as Hebrew teachers on the more advanced levels. We cannot limit the instruction of Hebrew to simply analyzing syntax, for example. Hebrew is not something external or foreign for us. We are in fact, melded in it.

André Ovadiya (another teacher): "I totally agree. Tell me, André (addressing me), how do teachers teach Hebrew in Israel? Like any other language in the world? Yes?"

The French inspector, Moïse Nahon, intervenes: "Yes, that's the way it is in Israel, and I believe that is the way it should be. We need to teach its structure, its syntax, like other languages. See—in France we also teach the Bible this way. We treat it like any other text, with historical facts, but with greater caution and more questions. We apply analytical tools to the Bible . . . as we would to Chekhov's or Balzac's texts. There are teachers who are believers, religious, and they have a tendency to refer to the text as you mentioned, but they must inform the students and parents in advance that they believe the Bible is holy. Therefore it is clear to everyone that their teaching will be deeply connected to faith."

Of course, every language has its own cultural levels. In this conversation, the local-cultural depth of the Hebrew language was becoming clear. Moreover, Moroccan Jewish teachers are aware of the cultural project in which they are involved, and they mobilize themselves fully. But they are also aware of the existence of other styles of Hebrew instruction, even if they do not accept them.

The conflict between different versions of Hebrew instruction openly exploded in a pointed and stormy debate that arose between two Hebrew matriculation examiners and between teachers in the (aforementioned) prestigious high school. The examiners themselves came from France in order to examine the verbal ability of the students. Since the students of the institute were going to matriculate in the high-status French matriculation exam (*baccalauréat*), it was necessary that the test be under the supervision of the French Education Ministry. The Hebrew teacher complained against the French inspectors that they were adversely affected by the way the inspectors give an exam for spoken language in Israel and by the preference given to the verbal language, which is also characteristic of those who live using it. The inspectors, it is important to emphasize, were former Israelis. The critical argument of the ENH teachers was partially based on this knowledge. The teachers claimed that the inspectors were undiscerningly adopting the assumption that the supreme test of verbal language control is the ability of Jewish students to communicate with an Israeli. "Not only do I disagree with that," Moïse Levy passionately argued to me, "but Israelis do not even speak correct Hebrew. Incorporated in their language are many mistakes. Therefore they cannot serve as a yardstick for verbal knowledge of the language!" In another context, I heard an interesting observation that is connected to this argument: "In Israel they don't speak Hebrew; they speak Israeli!"

These arguments outright reject the enforcement of Israel as a homeland and its position as a symbolic center to shape one of the central components of cultural characteristics: language. The activities of the homeland to preserve its legitimacy to serve as the "Keeper of the Seals" of the language is being challenged by those who should be passive satellites in its system. As do the anti-Zionists Ultra-Orthodox Neturei Karta—a Jewish group that categorically rejects Zionism and calls for an abolishment of the State of Israel until such time as the Jewish Messiah arrives—Jews in Morocco clearly distinguish between the Land of Israel and the State of Israel and reject the homology between them which the Zionists sought to establish. They seek to clearly distinguish between what Gurevitch and Aran called the "great place" and the "small place" (Gurevitch and Aran 1994).

However, let us not overstate the potency behind this criticism, since after all, this is a struggle whose end is well known. By way of example, I will state that even though I was not found to have a special command of religious law and customs, I, although Israeli, was eventually taken as a teacher. Moreover, formally, the French inspectors had the final word on the accepted criteria for knowledge of the Hebrew language because they had the backing of the French Education Ministry. It is worth noting that within their capacity, the inspectors themselves embody a two-stage process: for them Israel, where they were educated, is the determining criteria. They move to France, which is currently one of the largest Jewish diasporas, and in France they receive approval to judge the Hebrew of the members of a smaller diaspora—Morocco. Symbolically, this path is a reversal of the historical process that the Jewish-Zionist homeland demands (from Morocco, to France, to Israel).

By virtue of their position representing the hegemony of the language of Israel as a standard for Hebrew, the inspectors' opinion was that, from their viewpoint, it is appropriate to characterize spoken Hebrew in Morocco as "archaic." "A student of yours would not be able to buy milk in the grocery store with the language you teach!" asserted one of the inspectors passionately. And so, this course of events indicates a kind of Israeli cultural colonialism mediated by the former colonialist: France. Cultural colonialism continues its activities in Morocco. However, the Hebrew teachers did not hesitate to express their displeasure and to compete, from a position of equals amongst equals, against the colonialism of the infiltrating language via the center's messengers. Even if in the end they had to surrender to the requirements of the French Education Ministry, the protest itself made a crack in the transparency of its hegemonic existence. It eroded the center's legitimacy in serving as a "guardian of the language" by the very awareness of Israel's dominance, by the criticism of its style, and by offering an alternative to it.

The criticism and various objections (for example, concerning the exercising of appropriate language criteria) reveal an additional facet to the relationship between diaspora and homeland. The realization of "the dream of return" by immigrating to the homeland, as well as the rhetoric surrounding political renewal ("the Third Temple") do not guarantee turning the homeland into a symbolic unchallenged center. Thus, the political-national realization of the idea of a homeland may carry within it seeds of critique and perhaps its failure to serve as a unique center. So, for example, the decision to bring the young woman's charred body from Canada to burial in Morocco testifies to a decision based on clear intention to bury their beloved daughter in a place where they intend to stay. As long as "the dream of return" is in the scope of a linear wish without concrete political expression, so it is that this decision does not serve as a threat to the status of the homeland as a symbolic center. However, when this dream comes true and becomes a concrete-national political project, there are actions that will take place in the diaspora that may be seen as declarations toward a commitment to stand by the diaspora. This implied commitment challenges the symbolic center. These activities are especially challenging from the perspective of the homeland when they come from small and marginal communities such as the Jewish community in Morocco.

CENTERS, DIASPORAS, DEATH, AND LANGUAGE

At the same time that the realization of the dream of return may carry within it seeds of destruction, so too it undermines life outside its realization, in the diaspora. It is therefore not especially surprising that all of the decisions made about the burial sites were not taken for granted by all participants of the burial ceremonies. The decision by the lawyer Monsieur Joël Elkayim to stay in Morocco after all, following a long reflection process that began after his mother's death, testifies to the very need to choose, a choosing which undermines the community's existence in Morocco. His hesitancy places him somewhere midway between two polar positions. The parents who chose to bury their daughter in Morocco mark one pole (of implied defiance and criticism), while the parents who decided to bury their son Joe in Israel mark the other pole (of accepting the centrality of the homeland). The selective choice of the latter (who did not bury their son in the Mount of Olives, as is traditional) teaches that this option is always available—a comforting idea for the Jews of Morocco. However, Joe's parents had still not left Morocco a decade later. They behaved as the old woman whom I mentioned at the beginning: it is fitting that a man should live in Morocco and be laid to rest in Israel.

Decisions regarding burial places touch upon two interrelated issues: the lack of an obvious place, on one hand, and the variety of options that exist for Jews, on the other. These two issues generate disturbance in the rhetoric of each of the poles (or in each of the twin categories): homeland and diaspora. Symbolically, the double impact on each of these extremes goes against the basic situation of the daily life experiences of Moroccan Jews; a situation in which they are simultaneously a homeland and also a diaspora; a center as well as a periphery.

The simultaneous presence of a territory that is both a homeland and a diaspora is associated with the rise of modern nation-states as multipowered political phenomena. In this case, the majority of Jews living in Morocco feel alienated and foreign to the political Morocco, while at the same time feeling nostalgic for "Morocco" as a concept. In a somewhat parallel manner, they yearn for the "Land of Israel," while criticizing the State of Israel. In other words—both Morocco and Israel pay a price for the realization of the vision of the nation-state. In both cases, the Jews escape into nostalgia. They abandon the State in favor of the Land. They reject the demands of the nation-state for sole loyalty, which harms the flexibility of belonging, of which they are in need, and adopt multivoiced associations to the different parts of their lives. The narrow confines of the national project are rejected by many of them. The nostalgia for "Morocco" is alive and well in their midst, even if they never left its land. As mentioned, this complex attitude does not undermine the very binary system of the homeland versus the diaspora because in the end it employs a nation-state discourse. However, this position offers an alternative to both extremes of the binary system simultaneously, and as a result slightly jolts the structuring of the binary categories.

A FEW WORDS OF SUMMARY

At first glance it seems that the "solar system model" describes the existence of the Jews of Casablanca well: they perceive the Land of Israel as their holy homeland, from which their forefathers were expelled and to which they or their descendants will return in the end. However, it appears that in their very existence these Jews are contradicting the utopian agenda that was outlined, by the Boyarin brothers for example, by calling for an ongoing moral diaspora; and they contradict Gilman's criticism against the simplistic model of the center-periphery. As I have argued, most of them talk about going back to Zion without any significant challenge to the secular Zionist interpretation. Morally, they are rejecting the existence of the diaspora and see it as a tragic consequence of the sins of our ancestors. Casablanca's Jews, for the most part, accept the punishing tone found in the Books of Prophets, and they endorse the requirement to "return to Israel" in order to correct the unhealthy existence of the diaspora.

But as we have seen with help from various ethnographic scenes, even if in the initial observation it seems that the existence of Moroccan Jews fits the solar system model like a glove, a closer look at the details of daily life reveals informative and surprising elements that are incompatible with the coarse generalization of this model. Morocco, as a conceptual category, has become a homeland. Yesterday's place of exile has today become a symbolic center. Concurrent to this development, Israel has become host to the diaspora of the Moroccan center. Moroccan-born Israelis are perceived as a diaspora community to Jews in Morocco. In a slightly different wording, Morocco has become a place of longing and nostalgia even for Jews living there.

This symbolic reversal integrates dialectically with the paradoxical change in *imaginaire* of "Morocco" and "Israel." Morocco ceased to be a home taken for granted because it turned into a place that "hosts." As long as the Jews perceived Morocco as their unquestionable or undeniable home (when there were no other options on the horizon), their country was a place of exile and Israel as a land was a utopian place. But this picture changed dramatically in the years following the establishment of the State of Israel, which in their eyes appeared to appropriate the Land of Israel. At the same time, Jews became like foreigners in their country of birth when it was liberated from the yoke of French colonialism and Morocco likewise became a nation-state. The Moroccan State, which in time was connected to the "Arab Issue," became a place of hosting, and at the same time the imagined Land of Morocco became a desirable homeland. Nostalgia for places "that were" and are no longer allow for the rejection, or at least for the avoidance, of demands of exclusivity of belonging, inherent in the nation-state. In the case of Morocco, this matter is particularly fascinating because the Jews became nostalgic toward Morocco without ever leaving its soil. An epistemological barrier was established between them and the place of their birth.

Not only is this development astonishing and intriguing, but it indicates the complexity inherent in the relationship between the categories of "homeland" and "diaspora." I have brought many questions which counter the inflexible and rough architecture of the "solar system model." This inflexibility is connected, among other things, to the appearance of a powerful debate on the nation-state. A nation-state discourse, like its sister discourse, the diaspora, assumes a "natural" belonging for the majority of the nation's citizens to the state and its territory, and it demands an exclusivity of belonging. In short, contrary to the moral aim of the Boyarin brothers, it seems to me that a diaspora discourse stems from the discourse of the nation-state and is not disconnected from it. Even if the diaspora doesn't eliminate the ability of the nation-state to impose a binary system of "homeland" and "diaspora," as well as its demand for exclusivity of belonging, the diaspora can offer a refuge that provides an ability to escape from the nation-state's demands of exclusivity and, to a limited extent, to whittle away at this powerful coercive binary system. These very dialectic relationships between homeland and diasporas will be examined yet again in the next chapter, but it will be seen through the perspective of the alleged homeland—Israel.

CHAPTER 7

Searching for Roots in the Diaspora: Nationalism and State in Israelis' Journey to Morocco

The bus moved slowly away from the burning heat of the city into the shaded valleys. The heat of Marrakech was unbearable and everyone was pleased to be going toward the cooler Atlas Mountains. It was almost enough just to see the faraway snowcapped peaks from this year's lingering winter in order to cool the soul. The bus began to slow down as we entered Ourika Valley, whose green bends and twists begin at the foot of the towering mountains. The driver maintained a slow ascent up the mountains, allowing us to enjoy the breathtaking beauty of the deep canyon which gradually climbs almost to the peak of the Oukaimeden, the location of one of Morocco's ski resorts. Small streams still thawing from the plentiful winter rains trickled into a river and glittered in the dazzling sun. The soil was blood red and perfectly complemented the surrounding lush green. "This explains the colors of the Moroccan flag," I thought to myself. The passengers, all Moroccan-born Israelis, were excitedly glued to the wide bus windows, wanting to take in every detail of the sights.

Simi, one of the passengers, caught my attention. Until that day she had sat quietly withdrawn in the back of the bus, not letting anyone, except for her youngest daughter, who was accompanying her on the trip, get close to her. This time she chose to sit in the center of the bus; she looked excited, just as she would be a few days later when we would visit her hometown, Sefrou, and even more so when we would visit her former home, which she had left upon immigrating to Israel. Simi's gestures were nervous, her back was taut, her neck upright, and her eyes darted back and forth excitedly. Suddenly, she became talkative. I could see in her eyes that she wanted me to sit beside her.

Willingly and curiously, I accepted. She opened in a noncharacteristic monologue, mixing Hebrew, French, and Darija:

> Look how beautiful everything is here! Apple trees, apricots . . . and look at the size of the pears! What a wonderful place! I can't control my excitement . . . do you understand? We are approaching the *tsaddiq* (Righteous Man)'s gravesite, Rabbi Shlomo Bel-Khans (lit.: of the snake). He is marvelous . . . he saved me once when I was a young woman. I had just gotten married and I had a nervous breakdown disease. I was unable to keep control of my body, it shook all the time. I kept shaking and trembling. My husband took me to rabbis, but to no avail. They wrote notes with instructions for me to drink the juice of all sorts of things, but nothing helped. It was very difficult for me. One day we went to the *hilulah* (annual celebration in memory) of Rabbi Shlomo Bel-Khans, May His Merits Protect Us, Amen! There were a lot of people there. They placed me right onto his grave. As soon as I was placed on the grave, I immediately fainted. I don't know what happened after that. Suddenly I woke up, and lots of people picked me up and held me high up. Since then the disease has never come back!
>
> I am overwhelmed . . . this is so exciting! Look at how beautiful this is! Look at what a beautiful place the *tsaddiq* chose. No wonder he wanted to be buried right here.

Suddenly without warning, Simi became silent. Her face became yellow; her eyes slowly closed. Sighing, she explained later when she recovered: "You know, André, it's very strange . . . I don't remember looking at the view when I was a young girl and we lived in Morocco and I would walk to the ziyarah [pilgrimage, visit to holy grave sites]. . . . I was young and never paid attention to the scenery."

Simi's insight was painfully difficult. With uncompromising harshness it shattered a sweet illusion. All at once she understood that the burial site of this tsaddiq is not part of the familiar and commonplace setting; it had become a piece of the scenery. The split that suddenly and cruelly appeared and as a sharp brandished sword abruptly disrupted her unshakable safety in memories of the most intimate places and hurt her very deeply. Her assumptions that she could return to her childhood districts and experience that same intimate and direct connection with those places was shattered in a single moment. It was a very disconcerting self-discovery.

Armand (another traveler) expressed a similar understanding, except that he conveyed it in an amusing and sharply ironic way. When I met him after the trip he said that when he first emerged from the bus and treaded the ground of Morocco he burst out unrestrainedly, "There are so many Arabs here in Morocco!" Then composing himself he muttered under his breath "What did I think I was going to find here—Chinese?"

There are no Jews in Morocco! I thought to myself, there is a distant landscape and even more distant are Muslims. Both of these have become too visible. We, of course, were responsible for this, because we (or our mothers and fathers) chose to leave Morocco and by doing so left in it a great void. Now, this emptiness has grown and has developed an uncompromising and disappointing presence. I too was disappointed by the trip, whose prosaic shape was formed by my failure to find in the place where I spent my childhood, evidence that I hoped would awaken memories of that period. False expectations.

I was a beginning anthropologist on this trip and I participated in the journey as part of the final paper for my master's degree. I was an anthropologist of a most curious species; I thought that I was equipped with "the point of view of a native" and connected wholeheartedly to the ethnographic reality I was trying to understand. There was a lot of truth in that assumption, and even had I wanted to, I could not avoid the tangled connection between my intense, very intimate longings toward Morocco and my intellectual curiosities about her. Morocco's presence has accompanied me from my very first memories—my entire life in Israel. As is clear from the beginning of this book, this has had an undeniable, profound effect on me. The Morocco of my imagination influenced the course of my life and likewise my academic career. Morocco captured my imagination and shaped parts of me long before I had the opportunity to visit it as an adult on this very same journey with Simi and other travelers. My choice of Moroccan Jewry as my main research interest demonstrates, more than anything else, my longing. Regrettably, my choice to connect to the country through research is proof of the continual distance that I am unable to fill, because distance is at the heart of research. As such, I am firmly rooted in the plot that I have shared about Israeli Moroccan Jews in their travels to Morocco, and I intimately share the insight that Simi expressed.

The more I thought about the failed attempt to jump over the hurdle of time and connect to Morocco by closing the spatial gap through a trip there "in search of roots," it occurred to me that the gap that has been created is not just a personal issue. It is not only a divide between individuals and private places from their intimate past. With the passing of time, I understood that crossing the border, which is at the heart of a trip to one's roots, is accompanied by an important player, a shadow, contributing to the unbridgeable gap between the past and the present; I am referring to the nation-state.

The desire to return to the past through the use of the concrete and poetic language of space is not limited to a journey in search of one's roots. The language of space serves anyone seeking, through a variety of means, to secure their elusive past. They attempt to connect to physical spaces from their past in order to recall their personal (or communal) memories of their long gone past (Nora 1989; Bahloul 1992). People are able to reconstruct spaces as though they are the embodiment of genuine memories by relating to them as unchanging and as though they are engraved in solid rock (compare: Herzfeld 1997). For the rock is the same rock, the mountain the same mountain, and the wall the same wall. The memories of events that took place there are deeply rooted within them. The poetic act of situating the past into a seemingly everlasting physical place makes them almost eternal and bestows the past with stable and lasting qualities. These activities uncompromisingly emphasize the continuity of places, spaces, and sites. Thus the sweet illusion of the past being molded and carried through these places into the present, with nothing being added or subtracted, is established.

Despite efforts to embed space into the past and thus to stabilize it, these efforts are unfortunately destined to countless failures. As I have already indicated, Simi's harsh failure to acquire the past in the spaces of Morocco was not hers alone. In fact, on the trips to Morocco that I was part of, all of the travelers had parallel experiences. Seemingly, it would appear that such a jarring experience would support claims by sociologist Alfred Schuetz about the inability to connect to the past (Schuetz 1945). Schuetz states that attempts to attain the past by those who he calls "homecomers" are, by definition, doomed to fail. After all, the social fabric, like a river, perhaps keeps its shape but is constantly in motion. One may not dip his finger in the same place twice; human beings do not have the possibility to return to their former social past. In my opinion Schuetz's understanding is somewhat limited. Careful attention to participants in the trip to Morocco and, even more so, skeptical thinking with the help of their insights will reveal a more complex truth. Schuetz is satisfied with focusing on individuals who are seen as autonomous-psychological subjects, driven to connect to their past for a variety of (unaccounted for) reasons. I suggest adding to this interpretation broader contexts beyond the individual; I am referring to ideological, social, and political contexts. These contribute in a substantial way to the failure of efforts to connect to the past. As I will portray in this chapter, nationalism and the varied bureaucratic institutions of the nation-state all play a part in the journey to Morocco.

As implied in the previous chapter, it appears that the same logic that stands as the basis of a nation-state as a structured entity likewise contributes to the construction of an unequivocal dichotomy that distinguishes, among other things, between "us and them," "holy and profane," 'homeland and diaspora," "Israel and abroad." The nation-state "achieves" this through people who define themselves as its "leaders," "messengers," "ambassadors," or simply its officials. Through their various activities these same advocates align the citizens of the nation-state on one side of the dichotomy while finalizing their relationship with those not included (Ferguson and Gupta 2002). As a result, the primordial status, the ontological essence, of the state is approved and re-approved again in the way people imprint within themselves the exclusivity and uniqueness of belonging to it (Levy 2000, 2001). This exclusivity creates substantial impediments for those seeking a sense of longing and belonging to more than one place.

In this chapter I will examine successes and failures planted deep within the national discourse and in the rhetoric uttered on behalf of the state. I will bring anecdotes and stories of minor events interwoven in the experiences of the travelers to Morocco in order to clarify and refine my main claim, that the efforts to connect to the common past found over the border empower the national discourse. Furthermore, both the failures and the (few) successes are formulated from within that same framework of discourse. I will show how this discourse works as a double-edged sword, which, on one hand, motivates, nourishes, and supports efforts to connect to the past and, on the other hand, works to confirm the realization that this effort is doomed to failure.

MOROCCO, ISRAEL, AND WHAT LIES BETWEEN THEM

Before presenting the story of the journey to search for one's roots in Morocco it is important to remind the reader of some of the circumstances that led these seekers to Israel in the first place. As a general rule, it may be said that competing discourses of belonging to different nation-states (Morocco, Israel, and France) were involved in enhancing and deepening the weakening sense of belonging to Morocco, by fanning the flames, whether intentionally or not, of Moroccan Jews' existential fears and anxieties from the end of the nineteenth century. This so critically damaged their expectation for a "routine" daily life that the majority of Jews chose to leave Morocco, thus ending a historical process of a hundred years. They left the diaspora (Morocco) and settled on their portion of the homeland (Israel).

After two thousand years in which Jews were a part of the spaces of north African cultural identity (its ethnoscape), about a thousand of which were prior to the arrival of Arabs and Islam (Hirschberg 1974), the Jews left

Morocco. If during the last millennium ties between Jews and Muslims were ambivalent, a result of Jews first being a separate and inferior religious group (as expressed in the political and symbolic expression *dhimmi*) and second being still inseparable from the cultural landscape and from Moroccan history. Modern historical processes, whose roots were in Europe, arrived in Morocco and created an irreversible disruption (in the daily life of the community) that led to the migration of the Jews. This development was created in stages: first and foremost, from the Jews' point of view, was the changes in the dhimmi status, even though it wasn't abolished *de jure*, it ceased to be relevant *de facto*. This change was accompanied by a demographic process in which initially Jews moved around within Morocco; they left their villages and moved to the larger cities, situated mainly on the coast, with the intention to join the colonial project manifesting itself as inclusive and cosmopolitan (Adam 1950; Flamand 1959; Ossman 1994). The Muslim majority saw this desire to join the colonial project as a betrayal of Moroccan nationalism. When this was formulated into a resistance movement—and later into an old-new nation-state—Moroccan nationalism began shaping its collective identity as Arab (Entelis 1989) and Muslim (Combs-Shilling 1989; Suleiman 1989). Most of the Jews saw this move as an act of rejection (Tessler 1978). Zionist activity also contributed to the Jews' disengagement from Morocco and to an even greater undermining of their sense of belonging, as Zionist activists encouraged Jews to emigrate (Segev 1984). Israel's chronic involvement in bloody conflicts with the Arab world also had its share of the effect on this outcome. All these elements joined together into one radiating force. In the second half of the twentieth century the emigration of Jews seemed inevitable.

Many of the migrants turned hopefully toward Israel but met a harsh reality. The state's lack of material resources increased the many difficulties that were already part of the migration process. Many of the immigrants found they were forced into lower-class positions and sent to settle in economically weak communities on the Israeli periphery without adequate housing, employment, and education and health facilities. On top of all of this, additional difficulties amassed. The already burdened immigrants were targeted for exploitation by Israeli society, including even the settlement institutions whose positions were mostly filled by secular Ashkenazim. The Zionist ideology also contributed its part to the immigrants' difficulties. In the name of the idea of the "melting pot," incorporated within the Zionist enterprise, a cultural-ideological regime was implemented exerting tremendous pressure on the immigrants to give up their traditions in order to become "Israelis." This regime, which sought to negate the "scars" of the diaspora (Almog 2000), caused great pain and a deep sense of bitterness among the immigrants. Adding insult to injury, the Moroccan immigrants suffered from an especially negative stigma; they were viewed as hot-blooded and primitive and considered the most problematic of all the immigrants. These components, consisting of difficult living conditions, racist and discriminatory treatment, and an offensive image, created a process of alienation from the hegemonic Israeli discourse. These pressures had direct consequences; the policy of population dispersal, which was part of this rationale, dismantled communities that had lived together in Morocco. Relatives found themselves in different parts of Israel, isolated and alienated. My family, for example, was spread throughout the entire country, from Dimona in the south to Maalot-Tarshiha in the north (with relatives living in between in Tel Mond, Kfar Saba, Herzliya, Ashdod . . .). It is important to remember that in the nineteen-fifties these distances were great, the majority of the immigrants did not own private cars, and public transportation was simple and meager. Thus, within a brief and engineered historical process, grass-roots and intimate communities became imaginary communities. Over the years, and with the slow progress of some Moroccans attaining key positions in the socioeconomic structure, a cautious sense of belonging began to reformulate, even among those who were condemned to settle in development towns (Ben-Ari and Bilu 1987). Parallel to this slow process, an explicit and unconcealed discourse of nostalgia for the past began to develop, which found expression through various channels (such as in the public status the Mimouna celebrations began to receive). The trips to Morocco combining a return to childhood neighborhoods as well as to holy sites may be seen as a significant part of this trend.

PRELIMINARY COMMENTS ON THE POLITICS OF PILGRIMAGE IN ISRAEL

In its attempt to realize, even if by force, the Zionist idea of "settling the land" (Weingrod 1966) the settlement policy of sending immigrants to live in peripheral communities produced an unintended outcome; it gave residents of the periphery the opportunity to creatively express longings for past traditions, far from the controlling eye of the center. One of the central idioms to which creative new elements were molded into earlier traditions was that of the *tsaddiq*: the "holy" or "righteous" man (compare: Ben-Ari and Bilu 1987). In the Moroccan past, the tsaddiq was a charismatic figure, widely known for his scholarship, piety, and abstinence from mundane pleasures of this world. His uniqueness from other men was in the hidden, out of the world, or supernatural forces attributed to him, abilities that considerably remind one of the Muslim-Maghrebi "Baraka" (Jamous 1981). But in contrast to the Muslim righteous man, the *Marabout*, whose supernatural abilities ideally had no limits, tsaddiqim revealed their forces mostly after their death. Without going into detail of the idiosyncratic differences between the many tsaddiqim, I will only mention that that their burial place was a regular site for pilgrimage (*ziyarra*) throughout the year, and on the day of their death (either authentic or attributed) a celebration was held in their honor (*hilulah*). The virtuosity and creativity surrounding the righteous men, which Yitzhak Ben Yais Halevi—our hero from the beginning of this book—negatively points out, was expressed in the ability to revive traditions associated with their distant grave sites. After all, the tsaddiqim's grave sites were left behind during the great migration from Morocco and could no longer be visited due to the geopolitical situation between Israel and the Arab countries. Thus many forces worked together which led to the same result; the physical separation, the Zionist ideology which negated any expression of diaspora life, and the secular Zionist ethos, all contributed to the disappearance of the tsaddiq from the immigrant's public arena. Tsaddiqim were not forgotten yet; the day of the tsaddiq's death was discreetly commemorated in small communities, in neighborhood synagogues, or behind closed doors in private homes.

The 1970s and, even more so, the 1980s were witness to an enormous growth of the phenomenon of the revival of tsaddiqim veneration (Ben-Ari and Bilu 1987). These years saw a public development of a new, highly local Israeli creation that leaned on past traditions (Bilu 1987), but was also very much based on Zionist soil. Yoram Bilu, one of the most prolific researchers of the veneration of the tsaddiqim phenomenon in Israel, explains just how deep the parallels are between the Zionist ideology, which sought to hold onto the land (re the idea of "redeeming the land"), and the way in which righteous personalities from the biblical past are revealed in a dream and dispossess traditional Muslim legends from certain sites (such as the grave "site of Nebi Rubin, venerated by Muslims, that became the site of Reuven Ben Yaakov (one of the twelve sons of biblical Jacob), or another grave near the Shimshon Junction that became the grave site of Dan Ben Yaakov). The connection between the Zionist idea and the "modus operandi" of saint veneration becomes even more concrete when the graves of the "redeemers of the land" Joshua Nachamkin and his wife become holy sites and are visited as part of the holy sites tours to Amuka and Meron (Bilu 1998).

According to Bilu, there are quite a few innovative paths designed to compensate for the loss of direct contact with the grave sites of saints left behind in Morocco (Bilu 1984). The fastest way is the process of "Moroccoization" of existing sites, such as the grave site of Rabbi Shimon Bar Yochai in Meron. Already in the 1960s this site was the target for veneration of tens of thousands of Moroccan Israelis. Another way, though slower, is the genealogic continuity of saints from Morocco in Israel. After the death of Rabbi Yisrael Abuhatzeira, his grave site in Netivot became a site which is visited by over a hundred thousand people a year, and he is not the only one. There are the grave sites of Rabbi Moshe Pinto in Ashdod (Levy 1991) and Rabbi Haim Houri in Beer Sheva (Weingrod 1990). Another path continuing certain traditions, which Ben Yais Halevi unsympathetically called "the righteous of dreams," is the reestablishment of holy sites that had been in Morocco. The most outstanding example that Bilu studied is the site of Rabbi David u-Moshe in Tzfat. This was the grave site of a tsaddiq in a small village in southern Morocco called Aguim. A Moroccan-born Israeli dreamed that this tsaddiq requested that a site be established for him specifically in this man's home. Although the source for this was in the intimacy of a dream, the site has now become one of the more popular stops on trips of this nature to Amuka and Meiron (Bilu 1987). An additional path, similar to the "righteous of dreams" model but more concrete, is that instead of reviving traditions surrounding tsaddiqim left behind in the migration, the remains of some tsaddiqim, dubbed by Bilu as "saint impresarios" (Bilu 2010), were brought to Israel [for reburial]; an example of this is the collective grave site for a number of tsaddiqim in a small southern town called Kiryat Malachi (see also Rosen 2002).

Despite the compensation received from these creative opportunities, as it turns out, they are not sufficient. The desire to tangibly encounter the grave sites of past saints has not vanished. Thus one may understand part of the motivating factors of Moroccan-born Israelis to visit the country they left. This is the source of excitement for Simi, our heroine.

A MOROCCAN VOYAGE

Beginning in the mid-1980s and up until the years of the (second) Intifada (October 2000), there was a more or less steady stream of about two to three thousand Moroccan-born Israelis who took organized tours to visit their native country.[54] These same *part*-pilgrims *part*-tourists took advantage of the opportunity created by King Hassan II, who, following his meeting in Ifran with then Prime Minister Shimon Peres (July 1986), opened his country's borders to visits from native Moroccans. This opportunity served as a significant milestone for Moroccan-born Israelis, who until that time assumed that they would never be able to return to visit Morocco. It is important to note that even prior to this point, visits of this type had already begun to take place, but they were of a somewhat secretive nature.

With the opening of the borders, a relatively stable and regular pattern of organized tours to Morocco took shape. A trip of this type was usually three weeks long and included visits to the major Moroccan cities (the "Imperial Cities": Fez, Marrakech, Meknes, and Rabat, and also Casablanca [which is not included in this exclusive category]), visits to burial sites of saints and deceased family members, and the opportunity to visit former family homes from earlier lifetimes. The trips included conventional tourist attractions such as visits to the local markets or relaxing at the beach. It is important to emphasize that the pilgrimage aspect of these trips was of paramount importance to the travelers, and they were often organized to coincide with Lag Ba'omer, the day commemorating the passing of Rashbi (acronym for: Rabbi Shimon bar Yohai), the archetypal saint. In addition to the many sites of righteous ones visited by the group on these trips (such as Rabbi Amram Ben Diwan near the town of Ouezzane, the righteous woman Lalla Solika, whose burial site is in the cemetery of Fez, Rabbi Raphael Anqawa in the town of Salah adjacent to Rabat, Rabbi Raphael Ha-Cohen in Marrakech, Rabbi Shlomo Bel Hans in Wadi Ourika, Rabbi Haim Pinto in Essawira, and Rabbi Avraham Mul Nes in the coastal city Azzemour), private initiatives were also formed on "free days," during which many of the travelers visited their own (family's) righteous saints before they returned to Israel.

The range of visitors' ages was quite wide: from those in their thirties to travelers in their eighties. While the majority of travelers did not know each other prior to the trip, there were some small groups of two or three friends or relatives who had registered together. Despite the lack of acquaintance beforehand, however, they all shared a similar experience in their biographies: they emigrated from Morocco to Israel as children or youth.

The travelers shared an additional common denominator—their economic status; they were all mostly lower middle class, and it was evident that they had saved considerably in order to finance this trip. Clearly, this was not a simple holiday trip, but one that much thought had gone into. In Israeli terms, most participants were from medium-size cities (such as Ashkelon, Beer Sheva, or Eilat) and from development towns. The incentive for the trip was also shared by the travelers: to visit family graves, make a pilgrimage to the grave site of an unforgotten saint, meet with relatives left behind in Morocco (mostly in Casablanca), and visit their old homes with the hope of meeting old Muslim acquaintances or neighbors. These motives were not explicitly articulated by

FIGURE 9. Reuniting with family graves: my mother at her mother's grave

the participants, but were expressed through a variety of gestures and actions throughout their voyage. For the travelers the reasoning was very straightforward; they went because they wanted to go.

In April 1986, I joined for my first visit, a group of approximately forty people on a trip to Morocco. As some of the other passengers, I too traveled with family members: my older sister and my mother. Almost all of us wanted to find evidence that would confirm our memories of another time and place. The travelers longed to smell the smells of the past which they remembered, to see familiar sites, to hear long gone sounds, and to feel those same feelings that were imprinted in Morocco. In retrospect, Michel, one of the younger passengers, said to me: "I wanted to go back in time to where I had grown up . . . to wander in my old neighborhood, to feel young once again. I wanted to see if I could do things the same way as before." Indeed, for most of the travelers, finding "things as they had been" served as a confirmation that the travel experience allowed for direct contact with their past.

Despite notable similarities to others' trips in the effort to find things as they had been, Michel's was quite distinct in the way he planned every detail toward his encounter with these things. For example, he didn't want any witnesses present at the scene, so that he could maintain the intimacy of the event:

> You know, I began to wonder if I would succeed in finding my mother's burial plot in the cemetery . . . without any help, alone. I made it my mission. I said to myself: If I fail in this mission, it is not a good thing. It means that I deluded myself throughout my entire life. It's . . . I don't know if you will understand this, but I wanted to go there alone, like I used to when I was a kid, when I would go to my mother's grave with my father. Sometimes he would take me there at four o'clock in the morning.
>
> "You will remember the way" [I told myself]. I pretended I was a kid again. I tried once more to be a fifteen-year-old [his age when his mother died], to see myself walking there alone, turning towards the grave. And when I got there I actually exploded. Then I saw my mother-in-law and was ashamed of how I burst out. I said to her: Get out of here! I wanted to be alone. I stayed there by myself for about forty-five minutes.

Michel understood that he must encounter his past alone, that others "could not enter my memories, and understand what I was feeling walking on the streets of Morocco. A small shop can mean a lot to me . . . but for the others that are with me it is just another . . . street, another shop, another merchant selling butter. What they don't realize is that then, as a child of eight, I would come here to buy butter."

It was not surprising to me that Michel's attempt to find his mother's grave on his own was a self-applied test to confirm the credibility of his memories. Since spaces hold an aura of stability, Michel, like the other sojourners, examined his memories mainly through the encounters with spaces with which he assumed he was intimately familiar. After all, this intimacy was the raison d'être for the journey itself. The encounter with The Place was what it was all about. Thus, when we first arrived in Morocco, there were those who knelt and kissed the soil of the land.

However, as the journey proceeded the gap between the past and the present widened. This revelation was not what the travelers desired; the opposite is true. The majority sought a powerful emotional experience, a direct uncompromising encounter with their past. This is what Armand experienced during the first few days of the trip:

> My breaking point was in Ouezzane, at the site of [the righteous man] Rabbi Amram Ben Diwan. I really lost control, and began crying like a little boy. Not because of the saint . . . but because at that moment when I went into the site, how many people were there? Just two busfuls I think. One was ours and another; I don't know who they were. And . . . well, we went in to see . . . the grave site and the whole thing. There was someone in the synagogue [beside the grave], they were chanting some prayer, and there was one who had a very strong voice! He was the one leading the [*Kedusha*] prayer "We will sanctify and revere you" . . . and I turned around, and [in my imagination] I remembered Ouezzane, and how we would go to the celebrations, there were thousands of tents, and people were slaughtering sheep! And the orchestras! [but now] I see that there were only two buses . . . and that is what killed me! And that one, the *chazan* in the background singing, I didn't know who this person was, he had such a sweet voice, I think he was a cantor, he led the prayers out loud, and . . . and I turned, and I saw this picture—and wow . . . [I cried.] I dropped my camera, I couldn't find it. . . . I didn't know where I was! In the end I went to a corner. . . . I was sitting under a tree, and I couldn't control myself! I tried!! And I was crying, and crying . . . then Margo came [a family friend who was also on the trip] and she took me, and gave me water. She was worried about me! But that was my breaking point on the trip . . .
>
> . . . then I started thinking—why did this happen to me? So I analyzed it, and told myself that I guess it is because of how I remembered what it was like then . . . in contrast to what it is now.

Armand's intense experience in the early days of the trip did not protect him from the slowly widening rift between the past and the present. While this was a very intimate experience, it was so disturbing to Armand that when he calmed down and returned to the bus he felt the need to "analyze" what happened. This need to reflect is one of the expressions of the rift.

The burning expectation of intimacy with the Moroccan ethnoscape was frequently challenged by the Moroccans with whom the participants met throughout the journey. For example, when they tried to negotiate prices like hagglers in the market, as though they had never left Morocco, they discovered how unsuccessful they were at this. Even in the rare event when they succeeded to accurately reenact gestures from their Maghrebi past, the merchants treated them like tourists. Ironically, their clumsy efforts to get local prices meant that they usually bought merchandise at exploitive prices, because for the merchants they remained tourists.

These examples, like many others that could be presented, point to the inability to bridge the multidimensional distance to the past. In order to understand the enormous efforts invested in this encounter, it is essential to include in the framework the broader—ideological, social, and political—frameworks constructed on behalf of the "nation-state." As I will show, nationalism itself, in all its varied garments, contributes to the rift from the past by its vital role in motivating both the efforts and their failures. Note that I do not claim that nationalism is the only social-political player in denying the possibility of returning to the past. There is more than a grain of truth in Schuetz's arguments regarding the psychological/individual inability to return to the social past. There were many examples of this throughout the trip. One example of this was the loss of fluency in Darija which in varying degrees was the experience of all the travelers. The lack of language flexibility, a result of its only partial use in Israel, caused them to feel, clearly and always, their estrangement from their past. While the experience of distance stemming from language was felt daily and therefore may have lost some of its impact, there were different episodes throughout the trip that repeatedly emphasized the distance.

When we arrived at the Jewish cemetery in Essawira, the city of Yitzhak Ben Yais Halevi, our hero from the beginning of this book, we were met by an old beggar. He introduced himself as one of the only Jews left in the city. He told us that he was appointed by the Casablanca Committee Council to serve as the caretaker of the cemetery. He was asked to whitewash the gravestones, to weed, and to sell candles and other objects for visitors who occasionally came to visit the grave sites of relatives or the grave of the righteous man Rabbi Haim Pinto. He told us wonderful stories about the righteous man and almost inaudibly mumbled a familiar blessing when the name of the saint was mentioned. The travelers were very excited to meet the beggar. He was one of the first Jews they met in Morocco during the trip. He stood as a living testimony for the distant and memorable beautiful past. The beggar was also the first one to tell them at length about Jewish life in Morocco today and he was happy to answer questions. He was very patient and answered questions in great detail. He spoke of the living and of the dead. It was evident that he could sense the participant's thirst to hear about the past and the present. He reported on the situation of the remaining Jews left in the city and added sadly that almost all of the Jews who had lived in Essawira had immigrated to France or Canada or else moved to the big city—Casablanca. Others, he whispered nervously, went "there" (referring to Israel). Before the passengers boarded the bus to continue on their journey, they gave the beggar generous donations. Just before they got on the bus, one of the passengers asked him to say the *Kaddish* prayer for the dead. The beggar mumbled something and it was obvious that he was confused and embarrassed. Suddenly the picture became clear. The beggar was a Muslim pretending to be a Jew, in order to get donations from travelers. After their initial shock, the travelers talked mostly of their embarrassment. No real complaints were raised about the beggar deceiving them. What they were most troubled by was their loss of skills in differentiating between a Jew and a Muslim. In the Maghrebi context the absence of such a basic cultural skill was another reminder of their being foreigners in Morocco.

Despite the fascination that can come from considering alienation of this type, I will focus on the question of the place that national discourse has in preventing someone from attaining intimacy with the past. To do this, it is necessary to turn the spotlight onto Israel for a moment, in order to see how nationalism played a role on the trip.

A HOME, A NATIONAL HOME, AND A FOREIGN EXPANSE—THE NATIONALIST ROLE OF THE STATE

The state educational system serves as the central mechanism for transforming a state into a powerful and tangible entity (Bourdieu 1999). Israeli schools engage their students, when they reach the age of thirteen, in questions about their "roots." Students are requested to investigate their family's roots. The State of Israel, via the Ministry of Education, encourages young people to connect to their individual past, while simultaneously educating them in history class to deny the diaspora in favor of the more recent past of the founding of the state. These efforts, it must be emphasized, are not just limited to elementary schools or junior high schools. Even high schools deal with this issue and others like it through organized trips to Poland. The exposure of young students to the inhumane atrocities of the Holocaust, and the intimate encounter with the devastation that remained following the destruction of Polish Jewry, leads them to the inevitable conclusion that the possibility of a Jewish diaspora in Poland was abolished and encourages them to deduce the same for any [Jewish] diaspora in the world. The one and only conclusion of these trips is the necessity to preserve and strengthen the State of Israel (Feldman 2008).

The differences between trips to Poland which are organized by the Israeli educational system and private journeys to Morocco in search of one's roots are evident and obvious. However, there is a central and key player that is common to both; that is, the State of Israel. In both cases, the mechanisms that create the national political discourse are the ones that make the trips possible. Without Israel, and agreements of cooperation with Poland and Morocco, there would be no such trips. In other words, travelers, all kind of travelers, are first and foremost citizens.

Since the founding of the State of Israel there had been no diplomatic relations with Arab states. It is therefore not surprising that when King Hussein II publicly invited the sons and daughters of Morocco to visit their homeland, the response of Moroccan-born Israelis was one of unreserved enthusiasm. The Moroccan monarch explained that every Moroccan-born child was also his child. He invited his children to return whenever they wished; children never really left their home, their family. To all Moroccans in the diaspora this appeal marked a change in the overt Middle Eastern and global politics of Morocco, in the direction of active intervention toward resolving the conflict with Israel. It should be noted that this political direction was also part of the previous king's policy; for example, considerable influence is attributed to him toward resolving the conflict between Israel and Egypt and in the signing of a peace treaty in 1979.

The formal opening of the border to Moroccan-born Israelis was only the tip of the iceberg of the monarch's politics. Both his covert and overt involvement in resolving the conflict was based on the hope that the political relations between Israel and the United States would reflect onto Morocco's relations with the United States and would deepen the economic ties between the two. It is important to recall that already in May 1979 the king served in a very sensitive role in relation to the dispute; he was the president of the Al Quds (Jerusalem) Committee, which was founded on the recommendation of the Sixth Islamic Conference of Foreign Ministers of Member States of the Organization of the Islamic Conference (held in Jeddah, June 1975; Tessler 1988). He was awarded this role, partially due to his involvement of many years in the frequent Middle Eastern crises, despite the fact that his country was geographically removed (in the western region) from the conflict.

Acceptance of such a practical explanation makes the meaning of the king's invitation toward Moroccan-born Israelis somewhat less significant. Similarly, it minimizes the complexity of the implications of an invitation such as this. Also fused into the king's invitation to Moroccan-born Israelis was a unique national Moroccan discourse. As with certain other national discourses, this discourse used idioms of kinship to describe the relationship between Moroccan-born Israelis and their country, and even between Moroccan-born people and the monarch himself (compare: Herzfeld 1987). The connection between Morocco and its king is used often in the national Moroccan discourse. Clear evidence of this discourse is reflected in the many signs in Arabic, forged on the foot of mountains, stating, "God, the Country, and the

King," the last three words of the Moroccan hymn. An obvious conclusion to this discourse would be that the immigrants from Morocco never lost their national identity. However by using the discourse of kinship, the king was able to avoid explicitly stating whether the invitation was for permanent residence or for a temporary visit.

This deliberate ambiguity avoided public acknowledgment or recognition of Israel's right to serve as the homeland of the Jews. In fact, this purposefully indistinct approach rejected the Zionist discourse by arguing that the "natural" place for [Moroccan] Jews was in Morocco. It also afforded [the king] an opportunity to defend his decision to open the gates to Israelis, especially within the complex context of his serving as president of the Al Quds Committee.

From everything said until now it may be understood that what made the realization of the personal goals of the travelers to Morocco possible was the complicated and complex politics expressing unique political interests. Not only this, but another national discourse was involved in the process—the national Israeli approach. The interview in which the king invited his children to return home was broadcast on Channel One of Israeli television; at the time it was the only Israeli channel. Yisrael Segal, the influential newscaster that evening, was surprised by the show of joy among prominent Moroccan-born personalities who were invited to the studio for the dramatic broadcast. It was evident that he was unable to control his surprise or to hide his disappointment toward the unconditional loyalty to the king and the outburst of positive feelings toward Morocco. From his point of view, the revelation of these feelings implied a reduced sense of connection to Israel.

The relevance of higher politics that were involved in this seemingly private trip was not limited to granting permission to go to Morocco. It was also felt during the trip itself. For example, there was constant police supervision of the passengers, and it was clearly felt. Policeman appeared out of nowhere every time the bus stopped: in streets, tourist sites, Jewish cemeteries, and so on.

Even before we actually entered Morocco we felt the unusual involvement of state institutions. For example, the process of obtaining a visa to Morocco was particularly winding. On the trip in which I participated on the first time (and throughout the years since then), one could not fly directly to Morocco nor could an Israeli passport be stamped there. It was necessary for a third country to serve as a mediator and for the passengers to enter that country and go to the Moroccan consulate there in order to arrange entry permits. Our trip, like many others, stopped in Malaga, Spain. The consul himself, who signed the entry permits, came to greet the passengers in the hotel where we were staying. He made a short speech, where he reiterated the king's invitation. He gave us his blessings, "children of Maghreb," and mentioned the earlier good relations between Jews and Muslims. When the consul initially began speaking in French, there were interjections of enthusiastic cries: "Speak in our language!" The consul smiled with satisfaction and, switching to Darija, continued: "Anyone who wants to stay in Morocco is welcome to. Those who do not want to stay—may God lead them safely to their homes."

It was clear to the passengers that there were political tensions interlaced in the consul's short speech. These tensions were connected to the fact that he was providing entry permits to residents of a state that had no diplomatic relations with Morocco. Some of the participants expressed their reservations about this approach toward Israel and about the way the consul deliberately refrained from mentioning Israel by name. "We entered Morocco clandestinely, which personally bothered me a lot, the secret entry disturbed me the entire time and I said to myself: 'To hell with it! We are throwing them good money there,'" recalled Joe retrospectively. Joe's dissatisfaction expressed recognition in the hidden involvement of wider political considerations. He was not alone. The majority of the travelers felt that how things were going on behind the scenes had an impact on their trip. Joe's comments also gave insight to the future. Soon, travelers were requested not to reveal their Israeli citizenship in any documents, such as hotel registration. In the entry visa to Morocco, which was essentially a transit visa *(laissez-passer),* the box for "Country of Birth" was marked Morocco, while the space for current citizenship was left blank. In addition the Israeli tour guide asked all the travelers to avoid speaking Hebrew. There were those who took it so far as to replace their yarmulkes with a beret.

In the same way that the discussion of Israeli security surfaces on trips to Poland, so too on trips to Morocco. When, while still in Spain, I turned to one of the passengers with a question in Hebrew, he became alarmed and quietly blurted out: "They told us not to talk in Hebrew in Morocco and also in Spain!" In the airport in Barcelona one of the passengers reported seeing three Muslims in the terminal, a statement that quickly turned into a rumor and I was informed with frightened excitement by one of the passengers: "There are terrorists running around with guns!" And when we went to the central celebration, Laura said to the other travelers reproachfully, "In our great enthusiasm for this trip, we forget that they don't like us. There are some people who are pro-PLO."

Mari, Joe's wife, displayed similar concerns when upon her return to Israel she told me:

> Here in Israel, for example, I never worked with Arabs, I have no interest in Arabs, do you understand? I didn't grow up in Jaffa or in a neighborhood with Arabs, I lived with Jews all my life. From the moment I opened my eyes, I know only a Jewish home, a Jewish environment. For me all these stories . . . of Arabs in Morocco . . . some say it was good, others say they controlled us, so I was scared at first. Until Ahmed came (our Moroccan escort for the trip on behalf of the Moroccan Ministry of Tourism) and my husband Joe said to him: "Listen my wife doesn't feel comfortable here, she's scared. Do me a favor and please explain what it's like here." Ahmed took out my visa and said to me: "Mari! You have nothing to worry about. Do you know what it says on your visa? Woe to anyone that tries to lay a hand on you or who tries to harm you, or anyone . . ." I said to myself, "He's also an Arab. He can talk until tomorrow, I don't care! But when I walked along with him and Joe I was already less afraid. Because he (the escort) also looks like them with the Jellabiya and all.

There were those who took the whole security issue and flipped it around. Maxim said in an interview that "when we entered Morocco there were those who were afraid . . . of course . . . I remember. But I didn't think anything of it. I don't know. I went in feeling confident. Maybe in Israel it was put into my head that you shouldn't be afraid of Arabs." Implicitly, according to Maxim, "the fear of Arabs" is actually the result of past memories of the fear felt for the majority population in Morocco, and specifically in Israel he learned to overcome this fear. In contrast, Rivka, the daughter of Simi, our heroine from the opening episode of this chapter, relied on the rather precarious sense of security she remembered from her childhood and not on the Israeli experience. In that same conversation, she excitedly told me:

> As we entered Morocco I felt . . . suddenly that I am once again seeing the policeman's uniform I remembered so well from my childhood! And here we are once again! We entered and it was as if a gate was closing behind us, and who knows if we will leave again. . . . When I was a little girl I remember every time I wanted to leave this country I thought to myself: "When will we go, when will we go already? And I will certainly never come back here . . ." Do you understand? When we were little girls, we would say to each other, "When I leave, I will throw seven stones (gesturing: behind my back) and I will never return. I swear it!" I began remembering these words (when I made the decision to go on this trip in search of my roots). . . . Oh God! Only God should not hold me to my oath! (She laughs uncomfortably.) And here I am back again . . . and it's

as if you're going through an iron curtain. Do you know the feeling? It was then I began to feel tense: "When are we leaving?!"

Indeed, quite a few unique nationalistic components were recruited throughout the trip to the Jewish-Maghreb experience. The trip was also generally interpreted as a fulfillment of Jewish historiography: Exile from Israel to Spain, the exile from Spain to Morocco in 1492, and the extended stay in Morocco and back to Israel. It was a kind of meta-journey. The significance of the journey was bound and related to great historical national developments that were clearly articulated by the guide as we traveled down south from Malaga, through Costa del Sol, toward the Gibraltar Straits, and from there to north Africa. He said, "All these places have a continuous Jewish history and the trails of blood of many, many Jews, especially this path which we are traveling (through Costa del Sol). Surely, for one of our grandfathers, surely for many of our grandfathers this was their path of escape, and from here they went to Gibraltar and crossed the Strait and reached Morocco."

The connection between this journey and broad historical-mythological processes had surfaced earlier in an associative fashion. For example, when the plane was landing at dusk in Torremolinos, Spain, and as the runway lights were rapidly approaching, one of the passengers lost control and burst out: "Here's Haifa! Here's Haifa!" Her friend, who sat beside her, clarified matters and chimed in quickly after her: "When we moved to Israel and landed people clapped and cried: "Here's Haifa! Here's Haifa!" A third person added her own association in Darija, saying: "We do as our forefathers did when they came out of Egypt."

It seems as though the motif of exile and the return to the homeland were thoroughly interwoven into the trip and into the travelers' awareness. But interestingly enough, the theme of return came up associatively and specifically as we were arriving in Morocco. One may argue that the myth of return was stronger than the historical accuracy. But, it appeared to me that the travelers felt they were returning to their homeland. This may also explain the kissing of Morocco's land by some of the passengers.

The symbolic presence of the Moroccan State was everywhere: in Jewish cemeteries, holy sites, streets, and entrances to various cities. In all these places, huge pictures of Hassan II and red flags, decorated with a five-pointed green star, were on display. In addition to this symbolic presence, there was also concrete evidence of the presence of the state: For example, in the central Jewish celebration there were policeman and soldiers everywhere, symbolizing

FIGURE 10. Symbolic presence of the Moroccan state in a pilgrimage site

the state's patronage of the event. Government officials also came to greet the Jewish pilgrims, both as Moroccans and as Israelis.

In summary, the [present] national discourse and practices were implemented in the very heart of the trip, by various state agents bringing together "Morocco" and "Israel." Similarly, the travelers themselves recruited the national symbols and discourse. All these served to create borders and even prevented their ability to connect to the past in a direct way because they constructed a wall which divided them between past and present, here and there, homeland and diaspora.

THE FLUCTUATING PLACE OF DIASPORA AND HOMELAND

The encounter between the travelers from Israel and Jews in Morocco clearly inundated the dynamic relationships that exist between diaspora and homeland. This dynamic in turn re-created the split between the travelers and their past. While the unequivocal Muslims' rejection of the travelers' claims to a direct and authentic connection to Morocco was difficult, the encounter with the remaining Jews in Morocco was even more difficult. The expectation of "reuniting the family" was bound by the assumption that Jews in Morocco would form a sort of extension for them: an extension that chose a different historical path—to remain in Morocco. The rift that was created—I am tempted to say, the inevitable rift—between the Israeli travelers and their relatives in Morocco reached enormous proportions. These encounters were already intense in the central Lag Ba'omer celebration, but reached even more extreme proportions at the end of the organized part of the trip, during the free days in Casablanca before we returned home.

Alice, one of the younger passengers on the trip, invited me to join her when she went to visit her sister who lives in Casablanca. Her sister had chosen to stay in Morocco, while all the other family members, parents and children, migrated to Israel in the fifties. Alice asked me to join her because her French was poor and her Darija wasn't fluent. We arrived at her sister's house and almost immediately there was a quarrel between them. Alice was proudly boasting to her sister the many souvenirs she bought while showing indifference over the prices of these souvenirs. She also boasted about the seemingly expensive hotels we were staying at. Joëlle, her sister, tried repeatedly to explain to her sister that this merchandise could be found at much lower prices. Joëlle also pointed out that Alice should remember that in the past in Morocco the family did not have money readily available. "We were poor," she recalled. "We never acted like this!" she added with her tone rising. A similar event occurred to Sami. He strutted on the closed beach "Tahiti" like a peacock. Hanging onto his neck was a Moroccan escort. Sami declared loudly in Hebrew that he was "not like the Jews here who are afraid to go to a prostitute! I can spend a lot of money on her, but they cost nothing." One of the Jews who spoke Hebrew asked him to come toward him: "Why do you speak this way? I know you and your parents from a long time ago . . . they came from a poor, wretched village! I know your roots!" Sami did not react; he turned around and went on his way. Later I learned from one of the other travelers that "he left Morocco with nothing; he spent all his money on excessive entertainment with prostitutes."

Common elements found in these brief encounters between Israeli tourists and Moroccan Jews revealed a fascinating pattern; while the former emphasized their present situation (their ability to freely scatter their money, not being afraid of the Muslims), the Jews in Morocco recruited the past (or their parents' past) of these Israelis, to thus reduce their status. A different definition of the relevant reality of these encounters, or the bargaining over it (Rosen 1972a, 1972b), is connected to the different paradoxes that arise, whether explicitly or implicitly, in these interactions. For example, Moroccan Jews were given precedence in anything connected to authentic memory of the past. The symbolic authority of those that remained, seemingly planted in Moroccan soil, led the tourists to emphasize their improved present situation. In a tragically ironic way these efforts to emphasize the present damaged the tourists' ability to meet their Moroccan past. Specifically because of this, the attitude of the travelers toward the Jews living in Morocco was ambivalent. They adopted an accusing tone in their conversations with the Jews, especially concerning their reluctance to migrate to Israel. At the same time, the Jews who chose to remain in Morocco represented for the Israelis a type of hypothetical biography. The tourists saw in the Jews living in Morocco today representatives of their possible past and present had they or their parents not chosen "to become Israeli," to have migrated from Morocco. In their language there was an audible tone of jealousy for "the good life" of the Jews in Morocco, for the fact that their economic situation had improved (they had maids, spacious homes, beautiful clubs, etc.). Thus the basic assumption that it was necessary for them, or their parents, to have migrated from Morocco was undermined. The finality of their decision, or even more so, the irreversibility of the decision, became fractured. Because of this, for the tourists, the very existence of the Jews in Morocco was a provocation. To such an extent that many tried to find explanations that would strengthen their basic assumptions about those who remained: there were those who spoke in psychological terms ("mentally unstable," "mentally ill," "strange people," etc.) or in terms of their inability to see the present reality clearly ("money blinds them," "they don't see anything except the money," "the money is the only thing holding them," "they are irresponsible people," "they are not concerned about their children's future," etc.).

The motive for this approach was clearly nationalistic. The (Israeli) national discourse is what restructured for the tourists the validity of the decision to migrate to Israel. This discourse, which totally negates the diaspora, turned the Jews in Morocco into a group of unbalanced people; since there is now a feasible and simple solution to the longing for a homeland, the decision not to migrate to it, and certainly from exile in an Arab country, is irrational.

In and of itself, the Jews' decision not to migrate from Morocco to Israel casts doubts on the national Israeli discourse, and so is reinforced by the actions of these travelers to Morocco. They were disturbed by this throughout the entire trip, and especially in the first meetings with the Jews who remained in Morocco. Nevertheless, the intense longings for a place that was left accompanied the national discourse like a shadow. These longings were what motivated them in the first place to join the journey to discover their roots. Indeed, just by the fact that they participated in the trip, the tourists confirmed the sanctity of the land of Morocco; they confirmed its symbolic centrality, and thus they became, even if only momentarily, a model of the simple utopian relationship between homeland and diaspora. This reversal did not take place in its entirety because as the trip continued and as they met with the national Moroccan discourse that denied their connection to Morocco, the passengers strengthened their hold on the model of the national Israeli discourse. In this way, and with their own hands, they undermined their ability to fulfill their own dream of traveling to Morocco: their ability to return to their past, which changed from a homeland into a diaspora.

NOTES

1. For the sake of convenience and fluency, male gender is used and reflects no chauvinistic bias.

2. On the role of the Moroccan monarch as Muslim leader and his linkage to the Prophet, see Waterbury 1970.

3. I will elaborate on this political position in the following pages. For a partial explanation of this approach, see Tessler (1981b, 1988).

4. The street takes the name of the city of Longwy in the Lorraine region of France.

5. The exact phrasing says the following: *Le Consul de Royaume de Maroc à Malaga, prie les autorités civiles et militaries d'Espagne et des pays que doit traverse le titulaire du present titre, de bien vouloir permettre à . . . qui se rend au Maroc de regagner librement ce pays et de lui accorder aide et protection en cas de besoin.*

6. For obvious reasons I camouflage his/her identity.

7. In this article he notes that he changed his last name from Minkowitz to Shokeid, after the name of the *moshav* (a type of Israeli cooperative agricultural settlement) where he did fieldwork. Years later he disclosed the name of the *moshav:* Shokeida.

8. The edited book by Brettell (1993) exemplifies clearly the complex relationships formed between "the field" and "academia."

9. Even in states where academia is affluent in research resources anthropology is peripheral relative to other sciences. See, for instance, Herzfeld's (1987) analysis on the complex relationships between the peripheral positions of both anthropology and its fields of study.

10. My research in Morocco was a pioneering endeavor in this respect. As far as I can tell, I was the first Israeli student conducting fieldwork abroad. It took more than three decades for Israeli anthropology in general to conduct such research.

11. See: http://portal.unesco.org/en/ev.php-URL_ID=13132&URL_DO=DO_TOPIC&URL_SECTION=201.html

12. Maghreb (مغرب) in Arabic means "West." When Islam expanded from the Arab Peninsula toward the north African west, it seemed that Arabs reached the most western edge of earth. Hence, Morocco's formal name is Western Kingdom(المملكة المغربية) .

13. One might claim that it makes sense that "sociology" appears first, as it was they who established the departments. However, even at Ben Gurion University, where the department was established about a half a decade ago (beforehand it was the Behavioral Sciences Department), its members chose to put "sociology" first. Most conspicuous is Hebrew University, where during several decades its name was "Sociology and Social Anthropology." Only some two decades ago the name was altered to "Sociology and Anthropology." In informal parlance these departments carry the name of Sociology only.

14. During one of my compulsory undergraduate courses at the Hebrew University a distinguished sociologist claimed that anthropology was established in the United Kingdom, since they had "far too many Negros" who had nothing to do with them.

15. See an example of such articulation in Bar Yossef's paper. Goldberg and Bram (2008) indicate that in spite of the influence of American sociology, Israeli sociologists did not deal much with notions like "stereotypes" or "prejudice." It seems to me that such disinterest has affinity with the Zionist perspective that underplayed the role of cultural differences amongst migrants as part as the project of "exiles blend" (or "assimilation," in sociological terms).

16. See, for example, the elementary analytical distinction between the transformative capacities of "society" and "culture." For an analysis that presents the influence of the past, see Eitan Cohen (2002). For a critical perspective on such an essentialistic approach, see Levy (2004).

17. Part of these publications express an explicit awareness of the linkage between the study of north African communities and questions related to "the ethnic problem." See, for instance, Tsur's Introduction (Tsur 2001).

18. Jews had a unique position under the stressful colonial regime. I do not introduce here the fine works done on this topic.

19. See, for instance, the fourth chapter in Bernard Lewis's book where he describes changes in Jewish lives as resulting from European penetration (Lewis 1984). The metaphor of penetration is deliberately employed by Stillman when he states: "Suddenly and rudely, the physical penetration of the Middle East by Europe had begun" (Stillman 1991:3).

20. In this theoretical context I would stress that I do not concur with the way Paul Rabinow (1989b) conceptualizes the French mode of colonial operation, which offers a micro-historical analysis that demonstrates how global historical forces, along with the actions of Louis Hubert G. Lyautey—the architect of French colonialism in Morocco—converged into one logic that was implemented in Morocco. Rabinow attributes to Lyautey's grand ruling plan the peaceful way in which colonialism was implemented in Morocco. It seems that by morally accepting the supreme importance of the nation-state, he was able to ignore the ways in which colonialism could serve the interests of different groups within Morocco.

21. I mainly lean on Schroeter's two short articles about Ben Yais Halevi (Schroeter 1987, 1993).

22. *Hatzfira* was published, at intervals, between 1862 and 1931. It started as a weekly and then was transformed into a daily newspaper. It was first edited by Chaim Zelig Slonimsky and, only at the turn of the century, by Nahum Sokolov. Although Ben Yais Halevi published articles in other Hebrew newspapers, I will confine myself to his publications in *Hatzfira.*

23. Schroeter (1993) assumes that his initiative was generated after meeting a European tourist.

24. Ben Yais Halevi's text is saturated by insinuations and allusions to a multitude of Hebrew sources: biblical, Talmudic, and the evolving Modern Hebrew literature. For considerations of fluency, I will ignore these allusions and insinuations.

25. On February 1864 the Moroccan monarch agreed to meet with Sir Moses Montefiore. The latter presented complaints regarding the hardships of Jewish communities in Morocco. Unlike Ben Yais Halevi's impressions, historians claim that the meeting was not fruitful. Stillman, for instance, informs us that following the meeting, the sultan "issued a dahir (royal decree) on February 5, 1864, which stated his intention to protect his Jewish subjects from injustice and oppression in accordance with Islamic law. No change was made in the civil status of the Jews. Even this token gesture was considered too much of a concession by most Moroccans. . . . Soon after Montefiore's departure, Muhammad IV issued a second decree that clarified his original dahir to the point of nullifying it" (Stillman 1991). (See also Hirschberg (1965:310), or Abitbol (1986:313.)

26. The prohibition to wear shoes within Muslim spaces, and especially in the vicinity of mosques, resulted from the Jews' status as dhimmis.

27. He refers here to the *tujar al-Sultan,* the sultan's merchants. In Essawira, most of them were Jews (Abitbol 1977; Miege 1961–63; Schroeter 1982).

28. See, for instance, Flamand (1959), Goldberg (1983), Hirschberg (1974), and Stillman (1991).

29. For the impact of colonialism on the demography of Casablanca, see, for example, Adam (1968) and Ossman (1994).

30. I will not elaborate further on the commitment to an Arab collective identity; I will only say that it is far from being conclusive or unequivocal due to the complex relationships between Arabs and Amazighs.

31. The last two chapters of this book deal in detail with the ambivalent relation Jews have with Israel as a nation-state and as a homeland. Here I will only exemplify it through a short anecdote. Toward the (first) Gulf War there were growing signs of a tension Jews felt in Morocco. A dramatic sign was when many Jews received anonymous threatening letters. The letter carried a picture of Saddam Hussein and a statement encouraging them to "go home." The irony was clear; the senders assumed that Israel was the Jewish homeland. The reactions to the letter, however, were quite surprising. Many agreed that the letters were sent by Israeli Mossad to encourage Jews to leave Morocco. This assumption leans on a common truth that Israel is not considered a favorable destination for migration.

32. Many historical documents, as well as personal memoirs, inform us about this period of Zionist activities. For a Jewish perspective on these activities, see Bensimon (1993) and Segev (1984). On a perspective that strives to be impartial, see Stillman (1991), while for a relatively multifocal perspective, see Tsur and Hillel (1995).

33. Unlike Moroccan Jews, almost all Algerian Jews and about half of Tunisian Jews migrated to France. Only a quarter of Moroccan Jews chose this possibility. On the different choices Maghrebi Jews faced during that period of time see Abitbul (1986).

34. In the last decade several publications dealt with the socioeconomic and political circumstances that drove Jews to emigrate from Islamic states to Israel (see Shenhav 2003; Tsur 2001).

35. See: Geertz (1979); Rosen (1972a, 1972b, 1984); Dwyer (1982); and Munson (1984).

36. See also Laskier (1990); Mittelman (1987); Stillman (1973); as well as Udovich and Valensi (1984).

37. Important to mention that during a conference that took place in Sefrou in 2002, Geertz said *en passant* that it would be interesting studying the void in Morocco's socio-cultural spaces following the departure (see Boum 2013).

38. This avoidance has to do with the political wish to overlook the Amazigh as a relevant social category.

39. The Jewish educational system is divided into several sections: the Ittihad, which orients toward a European, namely French, education; the orthodox Otsar Ha-Torah school; the Chabad-Lubavitch; and Ort—a vocational school. Only a few schools welcome Muslim pupils. Such is the Ort that had in the last several years between 60 percent and 70 percent Muslim pupils. Others are more modest, like Ittihad. Clearly, orthodox schools do not accept Muslim pupils. One headmaster jokingly said that due to the high pressure put on him to accept Muslim pupils he was thinking of establishing a new Jewish school for Muslims.

40. On this specific setting see the following chapter.

41. This specific generic naming was employed also by Muslims.

42. One could claim, as Rollins does, that the neglect is a subversive act taken by the housekeeper (Rollins 1985). This explanation seems improbable considering Moroccan chauvinistic and puritanical attitudes regarding women. But, more important to my purposes is that I focus on the Jewish perspective and the way Jews comprehend Muslim rhetoric.

43. Abed is yet another generic name for a Muslim.

44. By this I wish to underline that a materialistic paradigm will not do. It cannot offer a comprehensive explanation of Jewish conduct; it cannot explain the mobilization of the JCC to help its poor people and it cannot explain the dissatisfaction poor Jews demonstrate when Muslim housekeepers are not impressed by the ethno-religious differences.

45. It seems to me that without the ethnographic close and detailed gaze one could be misled by this criterion. Michael Laskier (1990), for instance, sees in AJDC documentation of football games a testimony of tranquil relationships between Jews and Muslims. These complex relationships that are manifested and enacted during card games or football games (Levy 2003) evade the inquisitive eyes of the historian who relies only on documents.

46. A jockey rides horses professionally in horse racing or steeplechase racing. The jockey usually is not involved in the "big money" like horse owners.

47. During one of my last visits to the club I realized that this rule was abandoned. Women played against men for large sums of money. However, this activity was kept behind closed doors.

48. Unlike card games among Tiwi women (Goodale 1987), or among the Daulo (Sexton 1987), no meaningful economic repercussions were involved. Games were among more or less equal and affluent participants.

49. The popular notion of the term "Shrif" among urban Moroccans does not necessarily carry a holy meaning. They may use it when addressing older or senior person, friends, and sometimes even a non-Muslim (Susan Miller, personal communication, June 1995). However, in this case Sa'id deliberately chose this term to indicate he was aware of David's "holy genealogy." He pronounced it in such a manner as accentuated the "holy" meaning of the term.

50. Sa'id probably did not know the rules prohibiting the use of money on Shabbat or those banning gamblers from serving as witnesses in a rabbinic court of law. On institutional sanctions levied on gamblers in the Jewish north African context, see Goldberg (1978, 1993).

51. In a visit in 2004 Michael reported that he finally moved his father's body to Israel.

52. The more the community contracts the less is the number of Jews who die and are buried in Morocco. For instance, in a time span of a decade (1980–90) the number dropped more than 25 percent.

53. This pattern of migration was not unique to Robert. In many occasions parents follow their sons who leave for France or Canada. Often the case is that the father leaves after other members of the family depart; he concludes the liquidation of their affairs.

54. Nowadays, the stream of Israeli tourists to Morocco fluctuates according to the rapidly changing geopolitical conditions.

BIBLIOGRAPHY

Abitbol, Michel. 1977. Témoins et acteurs: Les Corcos et l'historie du Maroc contemporain. Jerusalem: Ben-Zvi.

———. 1978. The Corcos Family and the Contemporary History of Morocco. Jerusalem: Ben Zvi Institute [in Hebrew].

———. 1985. The Encounter between French Jewry and the Jews of North Africa, Analysis of a Discourse 1830–1914. *In* The Jews in Modern France. F. Malino and B. Wasserstein, eds., pp. 31–53. Hanover, MA: Published for Brandeis University Press by University Press of New England.

———. 1985–86. Introduction. *In* Jewish History in Islamic Countries. S. Etinger, ed., pp.

———. 1986. The Jews in North Africa and Egypt. *In* History of the Jews in the Islamic Countries: From the Middle of the Nineteenth to the Middle of the Twentieth Century [Part Two]. S. Ettinger, ed., pp. 363–468. Jerusalem: Zalman Shazar Center [in Hebrew].

Adam, André. 1950. Le bidonville de Ben Msik à Casablanca. Annales de l'institut d'Etudes Orientales d'Alger, vol. 8, 104–5.

———. 1968. Casablanca. Paris: Editions CNRS.

Almog, Oz. 2000. The Sabra: The Creation of the New Jew. Trans. Haim Watzman. Berkeley: University of California Press.

Anderson, Benedict. 1983. Imagined Communities: Reflections on the Origin and Spread of Nationalism. London: Verso.

Appadurai, Arjun. 1990. Disjuncture and Difference in the Global Cultural Economy. Public Culture 2(2):1–24.

———. 1991. Global Ethnospaces: Notes and Queries for a Transnational Anthropology. *In* Recapturing Anthropology. R. Fox, ed., pp. 191–210. Santa Fe: School of American Research Press.

Appadurai, Arjun, and Carol Breckenbridge. 1989. On Moving Targets. Public Culture 2:i–v.

Asad, Talal. 1973. Introduction. *In* Anthropology and the Colonial Encounter. T. Asad, ed., pp. 9–19. Atlantic Highlands, NJ: Humanities Press.

Attal, Robert. 1963. The Statistics of North-African Jewry. Jewish Journal of Sociology 5(1):27–34.

Auge, Marc. 1998. A Sense of the Other: The Timelessness and Relevance of Anthropology. Stanford, CA: Stanford University Press.

Ayache, Germain. 1987. La minorité juive dans le Maroc précolonial. Hesperis Tamuda XXV:147–68.

Bahloul, Joëlle. 1992. La maison de mémoire: ethnologie d'une demeure judéo-arabe en Algérie (1937–1961). Paris: Edition Anne-Marie Métailié.

———. 1996. The Architecture of Memory: A Jewish-Muslim Household in Colonial Algeria 1937–1962. M. C. Du Peloux, transl. Cambridge: Cambridge University Press.

Bashan, Eliezer. 2000. The Jews of Morocco: Their Past and Culture. Tel-Aviv: Hakibbutz Hameuchad [in Hebrew].

Bateson, Gregory. 1956. The Message "This is a Play." *In* Group Processes. B. Scheffner, ed., pp. 145–241. New York: Josiah Macy Foundation.

———. 1972. A Theory of Play and Fantasy. *In* Steps to an Ecology of Mind. G. Bateson, ed., pp. 177–193. New York: Ballantine.

Bat-Yeor (pseud.). 1985. The dhimmi: Jews and Christians under Islam. Rutherford, NJ: Fairleigh Dickinson University Press.

Baudrillard, Jean. 1975. The Mirror of Production. St. Louis: Telos Press.

———. 1994. Simulacra and Simulation. Ann Arbor: University of Michigan Press.

Ben-Ami, Issachar. 1998. Saint Veneration among the Jews in Morocco. Detroit: Wayne State University Press.

Ben-Ari, Eyal, and Yoram Bilu. 1987. Saints' Sanctuaries in Israeli Development Towns: On a Mechanism of Urban Transformation. Urban Anthropology 16(2):243–72.

Bensimon, Agnés. 1993. Hassan II et les juifs. Tel-Aviv: Yediot Ahronot Books and Chemed Books [in Hebrew].

Bilu, Yoram. 1984. Saint Veneration among Moroccan Jews in Israel: Contents and Meanings. *In* New Directions in the Study of Ethnic Problems. Vol. 8. N. Cohen and O. Ahimeir, eds., pp. 44–50. Jerusalem: Jerusalem Institute for Israel Studies,

———. 1987. Dreams and Wishes of the Saint. *In* Judaism Viewed from Within and from Without: Anthropological Studies. H. E. Goldberg, ed., pp. 285–313. Albany: State University of New York Press.

———. 1988. Rabbi Yaacov Wazana: A Jewish Healer in the Atlas Mountains. Culture, Medicine, and Psychiatry 12(1):113–35.

———. 1998. The Sanctification of Place in Israel's Civil and Traditional Religion. Jerusalem Studies in Jewish Folklore XIX–XX (Special Issue for Dan Ben-Amos):65–84.

———. 2000. Without Bonds: The Life and Death of Rabbi Ya'aqov Wazana. Detroit: Wayne State University Press.

———. 2010. The Saints' Impresarios. Brighton, MA: Academic Studies Press.

Bilu, Yoram, and André Levy. 1996. Nostalgia and Ambivalence: The Reconstruction of Jewish-Muslim Relations in Oulad-Mans our. *In* Modern Sephardi and Middle Eastern Jewries: History and Culture. H. E. Goldberg, ed., pp. 288–311. Bloomington: Indiana University Press.

Bottemley, Gillian. 1992. From Another Place: Migration and the Politics of Culture. Cambridge: Cambridge University Press.

Boum, Aomar. 2013. Memories of Absence: How Muslims Remember Jews in Morocco. Stanford, CA: Stanford University Press.

Bourdieu, Pierre. 1986. The Forms of Capital. *In* Handbook of Theory and Research for the Society of Education. J. G. Richardson, ed., pp. 241–58. New York: Greenwood.

———. 1999. Rethinking the State: Genesis and Structure of the Bureaucratic Field. *In* State/Culture: State-Formation after the Cultural Turn. G. Steinmetz, ed., pp. 53–75. Ithaca, NY: Cornell University Press.

Bourqia, Rahma. 1987. State and Tribes in Morocco: Continuity and Change. PhD thesis. Manchester University, UK.

———. 1999. The Cultural Legacy of Power in Morocco. *In* In the Shadow of the Sultan: Culture, Power, and Politics in Morocco. R. Bourqia and S. G. Miller, eds., pp. 243–58. Cambridge, MA: Harvard University Press.

Boyarin, Daniel, and Jonathan Boyarin. 1993. Diaspora: Generation and Ground of Jewish Identity. Critical Inquiry 19(3–4):693–725.

Boyarin, Jonathan, and Daniel Boyarin. 2002. Powers of Diaspora: Two Essays on the Relevance of Jewish culture. Minneapolis: University of Minnesota Press.

Brettell, Caroline B. 1993. When They Read What We Write: The Politics of Ethnography. Westport, CT: Bergin & Garvey.

Bunzl, Matti. 1996. The City and the Self: Narratives of Spatial Belonging among Austrian Jews. City and Society 1996:50–81.

Chouraqui, André N. 1968. Between East and West: A History of the Jews of North Africa. M. M. Bernet, transl. Philadelphia: Jewish Publication Society of America.

Clifford, James. 1997. Diasporas. *In* Routes: Travel and Translation in the Late Twentieth Century. J. Clifford, ed., pp. 244–77. Cambridge, MA: Harvard University Press.

Cohen, Anthony P. 1985. The Symbolic Construction of Community. London: Tavistock.

Cohen, Eitan. 2002. The Moroccans: The Negative of Ashkenazim. Tel Aviv: Resling [in Hebrew].

Cohen, Erik. 1977. Expatriate Communities. Current Sociology 24(3):5–133.

———. 1979. Phenomenology of Tourist Experiences. Sociology 13(2):179–201.

Cohen, Robin. 1997. Global Diasporas: An Introduction. Seattle: University of Washington Press.

Comaroff, Jean, and John L. Comaroff. 1991. Of Revelation and Revolution: Christianity, Colonialism, and Consciousness in South Africa. Chicago: University of Chicago Press.

Combs-Schilling, M Elaine. 1989. Sacred Performances: Islam, Sexuality, and Sacrifice. Columbia University Press: New York, New York.

Crapanzano, Vincent. 1985. Waiting: The Whites of South Africa. New York: Random House.

De Nesry, Carlos. 1958. Les Israélites marocains a l'heure du choix. Tangier: Editions Internationales.

Deshen, Shlomo. 1984. Urban Jews in Sherifian Morocco. Middle Eastern Studies 20(4):212–23.

———. 1989. The Mellah Society: Jewish Community Life in Sherifian Morocco. Chicago: University of Chicago Press.

Douglas, Mary. 1966. Purity and Danger: An Analysis of Concepts of Pollution and Taboo. London: Routledge & Kegan Paul.

Durkheim, Emile. 1964. The Division of Labor in Society. G. Simpson, transl. Glencoe, IL: Free Press.

Dwyer, Kevin. 1982. Moroccan Dialogues: Anthropology in Question. Baltimore: Johns Hopkins University Press.

Engle, Sally M. 1981. Urban Danger: Life in a Neighborhood of Strangers. Philadelphia: Temple University Press.

Entelis, John P. 1989. Culture and Counterculture in Moroccan Politics. Boulder, CO: Westview Press.

Feldman, Jackie. 2008. Above the Death Pits, Beneath the Flag: Youth Voyages to Poland and the Performance of Israeli National Identity. New York: Berghahn.

Ferguson, James, and Gupta, Akhil. 2002. Spatializing States: Toward an Ethnography of Neoliberal Governmentality. American Ethnologist 29 (4): 281–1002.

Flamand, Pierre. 1959. Diaspora en terre d'Islam: Les Communauté Israélites du sud-marocain. Casablanca: Presses des Imprimeries Réunis.

———. 1960. Diaspora en terre d'Islam: l'esprit populaire dans les juivries du sud-marocain. Casablanca: Presses des Imprimeries Réunis.

Foucault, Michel. 1978. The History of Sexuality. R. Hurley, transl. New York: Vintage Books.

Geertz, Clifford. 1968. Islam Observed: Religious Development in Morocco and Indonesia. New Haven, CT: Yale University Press.

———. 1973a. The Interpretation of Cultures; Selected Essays. New York: Basic Books.

———. 1973b. Notes on the Balinese Cockfight. *In* The Interpretation of Cultures. C. Geertz, ed., pp. 412–453. New York: Basic Books.

———. 1973c. Thick Description: Towards an Interpretive Theory of Culture. *In* The Interpretation of Cultures. C. Geertz, ed., pp. 3–30. New York: Basic Books.

———. 1988. Works and Lives: The Anthropologist as Author. Stanford, CA: Stanford University Press.

Gilman, Sander L. 1999. Introduction: The Frontier as a Model for Jewish History. *In* Jewries at the Frontier: Accommodation, Identity, Conflict. S. L. Gilman and M. Shain, eds., pp. 1–25. Urbana: University of Illinois Press.

Gilmore, David D. 1987. Honor and Shame and the Unity of the Mediterranean. Washington, DC: American Anthropological Association (Special Issue).

Goffman, Erving. 1970. Strategic Interaction. Oxford: B. Blackwell.

———. 1971. Relations in Public. New York: Harper & Row.

Goldberg, Harvey E. 1978. The Mimuna and the Minority Status of Moroccan Jews. Ethnology 17(1):75–87.

———. 1983. The Mellahs of Southern Morocco: A Report of a Survey. Maghreb Review 8(3):61–69.

———. 1985. Historical and Cultural Dimensions of Ethnic Phenomena in Israel. *In* Studies in Israeli Ethnicity. A. Weingrod, ed., pp. 179–200. New York: Gordon & Breach.

———. 1990. Jewish Life in Muslim Libya: Rivals and Relatives. Chicago: University of Chicago Press.

———. 1993. The Book of Mordechai: A Study of the Jews of Libya. London: Darf Publishers.

———. 2000. Jewish Life in Muslim Libya: Rivals and Relatives. Chicago: Chicago University Press.

Goldberg, Harvey E., and Chen Bram. 2008. Sephardic/Mizrahi/Arab-Jews: Reflections on Critical Sociology and the Study of Middle Eastern Jewries within the Context of Israeli Society. Studies in Contemporary Jewry XXII:227–56.

Goodale, Jane C. 1987. Gambling Is Hard Work: Card Playing in Tiwi Society. Oceania 58(1):6–21.

Gouvernement, Cherifien. 1953. Recensement général de la population en 1951–1952. Vol. 4, Population marocaine israélite. Rabat: Service Central des Statistiques.

Gurevitch, Zali, and Gideon Aran. 1994. The Land of Israel: Myth and Phenomenon. Studies in Contemporary Jewry X:191–210.

Handelman, Don. 1977. Play and Ritual: Complementary Frames of Meta-Communication. *In* It's a Funny Thing, Humor. A. J. Champman and H.C. Foot, eds., pp. 185–192. Cardiff, Wales: Pergamon Press.

Herr, Moshe D. 1982. Intermediate Days. Encyclopaedia Judaica 4:1178–1179.

Herzfeld, Michael. 1985. The Poetics of Manhood: Contest and Identity in a Cretan Mountain Village. Princeton, NJ: Princeton University Press.

———. 1987. Anthropology through the Looking-Glass: Critical Ethnography in the Margins of Europe. Cambridge [Cambridgeshire]: Cambridge University Press.

———. 1992. The Social Production of Indifference: Exploring the Symbolic Roots of Western Bureaucracy. New York: Berg.

———. 1997. Cultural Intimacy: Social Poetics in the Nation-State. New York: Routledge.

Hever, Hannan, Yehouda Shenhav, and Pnina Mutzafi-Haller. 2002. Mizrahim in Israel: A Critical Observation into Israel's Ethnicity. Jerusalem: Van Leer Jerusalem Institute and Hakibbutz Hameuchad.

Hirschberg, Haïm Z. 1965. A History of the Jews in North Africa: From Antiquity to Our Time. Two vols. Jerusalem: Bialik Institute [in Hebrew].

———. 1968. The Jewish Quarter in Muslim Cities and Berber Arabs. Judaism 17(4):405–21.

———. 1974. A History of the Jews in North Africa. Leiden: Brill.

Hobsbawm, Eric, and Terence O. Ranger. 1983. The Invention of Tradition. Cambridge: Cambridge University Press.

Jamous, Raymond. 1981. Honneur et Baraka: les structures sociales traditionelles dans le Rif. Cambridge, Paris: Cambridge University Press and Editions de la Maison des Sciences de l'Homme.

Kasinsky, Renee G. 1978. East Indians in British Columbia: Ethnic-Class Conflict and Cohision. Logan: Utah State University.

Kenbib, Mohammed. 1987. Juifs et Musulmans au Maroc à l'époque du Front Populaire, 1936–1938. Hesperis Tamuda 25:169–89.

———. 1994. Juifs et Musulmans au Maroc, 1859–1948. Contribution a l'histoire des relation inter-communautaires en terre d'Islam. Rabat: Faculté des lettres at des sciences humaines.

Laskier, Michael M. 1983. The Alliance Israélite Universelle and the Jewish Communities of Morocco, 1862–1962. Albany: State University of New York Press.

———. 1990. Developments in the Jewish Communities of Morocco: 1956–76. Middle Eastern Studies 26(4):465–505.

Lavie, Smadar, and Ted Swedenburg. 1996a. Displacement, Diaspora, and Geographies of Identity. Durham, NC: Duke University Press.

Lavie, Smadar, and Ted Swidenburg. 1996b. Between and Among the Boundaries of Culture: Bridging Text and Lived Experience in the Third Timespace. Cultural Studies 10(1):154–79.

Levi-Strauss, Claude. 1962. La pensée sauvage. Paris: Plon.

Levy, André. 1991. Une grande Hillulah et une 'Atzeret Tshuvah': étude d'un cas. *In* Recherches sur la Culture des Juifs d'Afrique du Nord. I. Ben-Ami, ed., pp. 167–79. Jerusalem: Communaute Israelite Nord-Africaine [in Hebrew].

———. 1994. The Structured Ambiguity of Minorities towards Decolonisation: The Case of the Moroccan Jews. Maghreb Review 19(1–2):133–46.

———. 2000. Diasporas through Anthropological Lenses: Contexts of Postmodernity. Diaspora 8(3): 137–57.

———. 2001. Center and Diaspora: Jews in Late Twentieth-Century Morocco. City and Society XIII(2): 245–70.

———. 2003. Notes on Jewish-Muslim Relationships: Revisiting the Vanishing Moroccan Jewish Community. Cultural Anthropology 18(4):365–97.

———. 2004. Book Review: The Moroccans—The Negative of the Ashkenazim. Sosciologya Israelit 6(1):195–97 [Hebrew].

———. 2005. The Diaspora That Turned into a Center: Contemporary Jews in Morocco. *In* Homelands and Diasporas: Holy Lands and Other Places. André Levy and Alex Weingrod, eds., pp. 68–96. Stanford, CA: Stanford University Press.

Lewis, Bernard. 1984. The Jews of Islam. Princeton, NJ: Princeton University Press.

Lissak, Moshe. 1989. The Great Immigration of the Fifties: The Failure of the Melting Pot. Jerusalem: Bialik Institute.

Malinowski, Bronislaw. 1961 (1922). Introduction: The Subject, Methods and Scope of This Inquiry. *In* Argonauts of the Western Pacific. Pp. 1–25. New York: E. P. Dutton.

Malkki, Liisa. 1995. Purity and Exile: Violence, Memory, and National Cosmology among Hutu Refugees in Tanzania. Chicago: University of Chicago Press.

McMurray, David A. 2001. In and Out of Morocco: Smuggling and Migration in a Frontier Boomtown. Minneapolis: University of Minnesota Press.

Memmi, Albert. 2003. The Colonizer and the Colonized. London: Earthscan.

Mernissi, Fatima. 1975. Beyond the Veil: Male-Female Dynamics in a Modern Muslim Society. New York: Schenkman.

———. 1995. Dreams of Trespass: Tales of a Harem Girlhood. New York: Perseus Books.

Miege, Jean L. 1961–63. Le Maroc et l'Europe (1930–1984). Paris: Presses Universitaires de France.

Mittelman, Roy. 1987. The Meknes Mellah and Casablancan Ville Nouvelle: A Comparative Study of Two Jewish Communities in Transformation. PhD thesis. Temple University, Philadelphia.

Munson, Henry, Jr. 1984. The House of Si Abd Allah: The Oral History of a Moroccan Family. New Haven, CT: Yale University Press.
———. 1988. Islam and Revolution in the Middle East. New Haven, CT: Yale University Press.
———. 1993. Religion and Power in Morocco. New Haven, CT: Yale University Press.
Narayan, Kirin. 1993. How Native Is a "Native" Anthropologist? American Anthropologist 95:671–86.
Nora, Pierre. 1989. Between Memory and History. Representations 26:7–25.
Ossman, Susan. 1994. Picturing Casablanca: Portraits of Power in a Moroccan City. Berkeley: University of California Press.
Pascon, Paul, and Daniel Schroeter. 1982. Le cimetière juif d'Iligh (1751–1955): étude des épitaphes comme documents d'histoire sociale (Tazerwalt, Sud-Ouest Marocain). Revue de l'Occident Musulman et de la Méditerané 34:34–67.
Pattie, Susan P. 1994. At Home in Diaspora: Armenians in America. Diaspora 3(2):185–98.
———. 1997. Faith in History: Armenians Rebuilding Community. Washington, DC: Smithsonian Institution Press.
Rabinow, Paul. 1977. Reflections on Fieldwork in Morocco. Berkeley: University of California Press.
———. 1989a. French Modern: Norms and Forms of the Social Environment. Chicago: University of Chicago Press.
———. 1989b. Techno-Cosmopolitanism: Governing Morocco. *In* French Modern: Norms and Forms of the Social Environment. P. Rabinow, ed., pp. 277–319. Chicago: University of Chicago Press.
Ram, Uri. 1993. The Israeli Society: Critical Perspectives. Tel Aviv: Breirot [in Hebrew].
Raz-Krakotzkin, Amnon. 1993. Exile from Sovereignty: On a Criticism of the "Negation of Exile" in Israeli Culture (Part One). Theory and Culture 4:23–55 [in Hebrew].
———. 1994. Exile from Sovereignty: On a Criticism of the "Negation of Exile" in Israeli Culture (Part Two). Theory and Culture 5:113–32 [in Hebrew].
Rodrigue, Aron. 1990. French Jews, Turkish Jews: The Alliance Israélite Universelle and the Politics of Jewish Schooling in Turkey, 1860–1925. Bloomington: Indiana University Press.
Rollins, Judith. 1985. Between Women: Domestics and Their Employers. Philadelphia: Temple University Press.
Rosaldo, Renato. 1980. Ilongot Headhunting, 1883–1974: A Study in Society and History. Stanford, CA: Stanford University Press.
———. 1989. Culture and Truth: The Remaking of Social Analysis. London: Routledge.
Rosen, Lawrence. 1968a. A Moroccan Jewish Community during a Middle Eastern Crisis. American Scholar 37(3):435–51.
———. 1968b. North African Jewish Studies. Judaism 17(4):422–29.
———. 1972a. The Social and Conceptual Framework of Arab-Berber Relations in Morocco. *In* Arabs and Berbers. E. Gellner and C. Micand, eds., pp. 155–73. Lexington, KY: Lexington Books.
———. 1972b. Muslim-Jewish Relations in a Moroccan City. International Journal of Middle East Studies 3:435–49.

———. 1984. Bargaining for Reality: The Construction of Social Relations in a Muslim Community. Chicago: University of Chicago Press.

———. 2002. The Culture of Islam: Changing Aspects of Contemporary Muslim Life. Chicago: University of Chicago Press.

Rotenberg, Robert. 1996. Metropolitan Spaces: A Panel of Essays on the Production of Histories and Identities in East-Central Europe. City and Society 1996:5–14.

Rubchak, Marian J. 1993. Dancing with the Bones: A Comparative Study of Two Ukrainian Exilic Societies. Valparaiso, IN: Valparaiso University.

Safrai, Shmuel. 1965. Pilgrimage to Jerusalem during Second Temple Times. Tel Aviv: Am Ha-Sefer.

Safran, William. 1991. Diasporas in Modern Societies: Myths of Homeland and Return. Diaspora 1(1):83–99.

Schroeter, Daniel. 1982. The Jews of Essaouira (Mogador) and the Trade of Southern Morocco. *In* Communautes juives des marges sahariennes du Maghreb. M. Abitbol, ed., pp. 365–390. Jerusalem: Ben-Zvi.

———. 1987. The Politics of Reform in Morocco: The Writings of Yishaq Ben Yaish Halewi in *Hasfirah*. *In* Misgav Yerushalayim Studies in Jewish Literature. E. Hazan, ed., pp. lxxiii–lxxxiv. Jerusalem: Misgav Yerushalayim.

———. 1988. Merchants of Essaouira: Urban Society and Imperialism in Southwestern Morocco, 1844–1886. Cambridge [Cambridgeshire]: Cambridge University Press.

———. 1993. Yishaq Ben Yaish Halewi: A Moroccan Reformer. *In* Struggle and Survival in the Modern Middle East. E. I. Burke, ed., pp. 44–58. Berkeley: University of California Press.

Schroeter, Daniel J., and Josef Chetrit. 1996. The Transformation of the Jewish Community of Essawira (Mogador) in the Nineteenth and Twentieth Centuries. *In* Modern Sephardi and Middle Eastern Jewries: History and Culture. H. E. Goldberg, ed., pp. 99–116. Bloomington: Indiana University Press.

Schuetz, Alfred. 1944. The Stranger. American Journal of Sociology 49(6):499–507.

———. 1945. The Homecomer. American Journal of Sociology 50 (5): 369–76.

Segev, Shmuel. 1984. Operation "Yakhin": The Secret Immigration of Moroccan Jews to Israel. Tel Aviv: Misrad Ha-Bitakhon [in Hebrew].

Sexton, Lorraine. 1987. The Social Construction of Card Playing among the Daulo. Oceania 58(1):38–46.

Shenhav, Yehouda. 2003. The Arab-Jews: Nationalism, Religion, and Ethnicity. Tel Aviv: Am Oved [in Hebrew].

Shields, Rob. 1991. Places on the Margin: Alternative Geographies of Modernity. London: Routledge.

Sibley, David. 1995. Geographies of Exclusion: Society and Difference in the West. London: Routledge.

Stillman, Norman A. 1973. The Sefrou Remnant. Jewish Social Studies 35(3–4):225–69.

———. 1974. Muslims and Jews in Morocco: Perceptions, Images, Stereotypes. Jewish Muslim Relations in North-Africa, May, 19, 1974, Princeton, NJ, pp. 13–27.

———. 1976. Muslims and Jews in Morocco. Jerusalem Quarterly 5:76–83.

———. 1978. The Moroccan Jewish Experience: A Revisionist View. Jerusalem Quarterly 8.9:111–23.
———. 1979. The Jews of Arab Lands: A History and Source Book. Philadelphia: Jewish Publication Society of America.
———. 1991. The Jews of Arab Lands in Modern Times. Philadelphia: Jewish Publication Society of America.
Suleiman, Michael W. 1989. Morocco in the Arab and Muslim World: Attitudes of Moroccan Youth. Maghreb Review 14(1–2):16–27.
Tessler, Mark A. 1978. The Identity of Religious Minorities in Non-Secular States: Jews in Tunisia and Morocco and Arabs in Israel. Comparative Studies in Society and History 20(3):359–73.
———. 1981a. Ethnic Change and Nonassimilating Minority Status: Jews in Tunisia and Morocco and Arabs in Israel. *In* Ethnic Change. C. F. Keyes, ed., pp. 154–97. Seattle: University of Washington Press.
———. 1981b. Politics in Morocco. Hanover, NH: American Universities Field Staff.
———. 1988. Moroccan-Israeli Relations and the Reasons for Moroccan Receptivity to Contact with Israel. Jerusalem Journal of International Relations 10(Spring):76–108.
Tessler, Mark A., Linda L. Hawkins, and J. Parsons. 1979. Minorities in Retreat: The Jews of the Maghreb. *In* The Political Role of Minority Groups in the Middle East. R. D. McLaurin, ed., pp. 188–220. New York: Praeger.
Tessler, Mark A., and Universities Field Staff International. 1984. Continuity and Change in Moroccan Politics. Hanover, NH: Universities Field Staff International.
Toledano, Moshe Y. 1910. The Western Candle. Jerusalem: A. M. Kuntz [in Hebrew].
Tölölyan, Khachig. 1996. Rethinking Diaspora(s): Stateless Power in the Transnational Moment. Diaspora 5(1):3–36.
Tsur, Yaron. 2001. A Torn Community: The Jews of Morocco and Nationalism, 1943–1954. Tel Aviv: Am Oved [in Hebrew].
Tsur, Yaron, and Hagar Hillel. 1995. Les Juifs de Casablanca: études sur la modernisation de l'élite politique juive en diaspora coloniale. Tel-Aviv: L'Université Ouverte [in Hebrew].
Turner, Victor W. 1967. Betwixt and Between: The Liminal Period in Rites de Passage. *In* The Forest of Symbols. V. W. Turner, ed., pp. 93–111. Ithaca, NY: Cornell University Press.
Udovich, Abraham L., and Lucette Valensi. 1984. The Last Arab Jews: The Communities of Jerba, Tunisia. London: Harwood Academic Publishers.
Waterbury, John. 1970. The Commander of the Faithful: The Moroccan Political Elite—A Study of Segmented Politics. London and New York: Weidenfeld & Nicolson and Columbia University Press.
Weingrod, Alex. 1966. Reluctant Pioneers Village Development in Israel. Ithaca, NY: Cornell University Press.
———. 1990. The Saint of Beersheba. Albany: State University of New York Press.
Zafrani, Haïm. 1983. Mille ans de vie au Maroc: histoire et culture, religion et magie. Paris: Maisonneuve et Larose.

INDEX

Page numbers in italics indicate illustrations.